Generations Lost

Generations Lost

✦

Pop Culture and Youth in Crisis

by Timothy Quinnan, Ph.D.

Writers Club Press
San Jose New York Lincoln Shanghai

Generations Lost
Pop Culture and Youth in Crisis

Writers Club Press
an imprint of iUniverse, Inc.

For information address:
iUniverse, Inc.
5220 S. 16th St., Suite 200
Lincoln, NE 68512
www.iuniverse.com

ISBN: 0-595-21770-2

Printed in the United States of America

To L.T.Q. who sees the signs and understands them too

Contents

Introduction

Adults in the United States are worried and with reason. Anyone who has teenagers or works with youth understands there is just cause for this anxiety. The kids aren't all right. They're letting us know it in increasingly destructive ways.

American society faces a grave health problem. Like patients receiving bad news, we've tried to conceal, then deny it. When those strategies didn't work, we attempted to explain away our illness as passing, with only random, isolated outbreaks. Unfortunately, the malady has metastasized into a cancer. The affliction of which I speak does not spare any age group but adolescents appear the most susceptible to its ravages. It is a epidemic rooted in our culture. Worse still, we're exporting it to the world.

In consequence, today's youth exist in a precarious state. Not toddlers, not adults, the interval of time—especially the teens—in between these mileposts is crucial in providing the experiences that mold personalities, impart values, allow for mistakes and teach the lessons that decide what kind of adults they end up becoming. Taken as a whole, these years no longer afford our offspring the time to simply enjoy childhood. Institutions traditionally responsible for the social grooming of youth such as the family, churches, and schools are a vanishing breed. Contributing to this dismal situation, prevailing cultural conditions further impair normal growth and development, regardless of how liberally one construes "normal" to be. They have distorted this critically important process into something unnatural.

From a delicate age, youth are barraged by messages and imagery beyond their experience to sift through. If ours is the Media age and adults have already been inured to or contaminated by this vulgar assault, that doesn't mean the same misfortune should befall posterity.

Insofar as it is possible, we ought to accept responsibility for these dire circumstances and rally to protect them from a popular culture that in almost every expression reflects a society in decline. With mass communication technologies invading our homes, public spaces, and schools, unprepared minds and immature personalities are being subjected to a parade of the grotesque. Regardless of the medium, inappropriate content saturates the airwaves, dominates the radio, and fills both the big and small screens young eyes are glued to. Unbridled wish fulfillment, family life as a dysfunctional prison, rampant, illicit sex, confrontation prompting hair–trigger violence as the best way to solve conflict—these represent some of its sordid but ubiquitous themes. Yet children are exposed to and imprinted by them from a tender age when mothers or fathers draft television (or other media) to fill in as a babysitter. With each passing year of life, the indoctrination continues.

This mad dance begins the instant that a child's senses first tunes into and incorporates input from his or her surroundings other than that provided by parents. Sadly, that defining moment is coming ever earlier thanks to our penchant of navigating without any maps, directions, or rules apart from those supplied by popular culture. Through lifelong encounters with a culture promoting values often at odds with those once taught at home, the confusion becomes internalized and damage is done. By the time they reach their teens, brains are buckling under the contradictions. For lack of a better alternative from adults, however, and conforming to the need for acceptance by peers, young people choose sides in this unequal contest and adopt a particular point of view. It is a socially–imposed worldview attuned to these times, full of omissions, oversights and obfuscations yet wrapped in shimmering, state–of–the–art electronic packaging. It's a postmodern perspective that rejects centuries of wisdom, experience, and struggle. It exists for the here and now, only in this moment, and beyond that its usefulness cannot be guaranteed. Yet it's the only legend available to them that makes sense of the chaotic world they have inherited.

In most instances, this cultural template overwhelms the knowledge instilled by parents, relatives and teachers. For, after all, what solitary voice or chorus of voices—parent or significant adults—dare challenges the primacy of the television or computer as the true source of everything a kid needs to know? Sons and daughters may sit still long enough to listen to our remonstrations and then, at the first possible moment, consult with the real oracles of knowledge—mass media. By mid–to–later teenage years, the gulf widens. As they come to rely more on cultural norms and expectations as their key to reality and less on the elders they once trusted, the relationship between adults and youth ultimately deteriorates to the point of no return.

It is here at this forlorn crossroads, when adolescents finally make that permanent break from their parents or significant other adults, heeding instead the compelling whispers of a popular culture telling them everything they want to hear, that they join hosts of waiting peers. In making this decision, they bid farewell to whatever chance they had of carving out their own destinies and tie their fate with those other unfortunates of the lost generations.

So we arrive at the thesis of this book. While at this stage the evidence is primarily intuitive, systematic efforts will be made to gather and arrange the facts in a manner way that supports a simple premise: Through a vast media machine that warps reality, increasingly distant and ineffectual adult presences in their lives, a weakened educational system, and self–serving social trends, popular culture impairs the normal, desirable development of American youth. The extent of this impairment will soon be made clear. In the essays and illustrations in the pages ahead, each dealing with different aspects of the harm done, we will return to this premise many times.

Surveying the environment, it is not difficult to imagine how things have degenerated into this dire state of affairs. Reality, here and now, may not be what we imagine. For mature individuals, the childhood we knew and fondly recall has passed into oblivion. Exploring the discontinuities between adolescence as it was for us versus *postmodern* life, that is, reality as experienced by those under 30, will supply us with valuable contrast. Striking and fundamental differences in the way this postmodern youth perceive and interact with the world versus the way we adults once did will be addressed. They will also explain the estrangement that exists between many parents and their kids.

A starting point in understanding the tension between younger and older emerges in youth's remorseless embrace of embrace contemporary culture. In these times, culture doesn't translate into what it formerly did—the accumulated knowledge, values, and traditions of the past transmitted across eras. Discard any dictionary that reduces it to such a definition because it would be an anachronism. To youth, culture is not an abstraction. Today's 'popular' incarnation actually dictates the nature of reality. This is especially true for younger persons, who, minus strong adult influences or firm alternatives, have been seduced by its titillating motifs, mythology, and heroes. That the pop culture universe and its architecture may not at all resemble the world presented to them at home or in school, sites where tradition might yet prevail, troubles them not in the least. With myriad outlets available to find reinforcement, pop culture's power over childish minds far exceeds what a mother, father, or teacher can do in a few hours each day to negate it.

In this sense, culture transcends its limitations as a static body of knowledge. Instead, it has become an epistemology, or way of knowing. Younger persons literally use it to make meaning out of what they see, feel, hear, and believe. Culture imparts to them a body of referents from which they collectively process information and find that all important common ground for interaction with peers. It equips them with a map for social survival. With popular culture, this map is continually being redrawn in deference to technology and changing social interests. These fluctuations render it hard for adults working from an anchored belief system to comprehend. Those that make the adjustment, unless very careful, are soon swept away into the same convoluted experience as their younger counterparts. In either case, the implications of this process are alarming. *Popular culture defines reality now.* Until very recently in social history, the reverse had always been axiomatic.

As a result, life as we know it is dominated by it. It sets the parameters for all social questions and considerations. In its all–encompassing reach, greatly aided by technology and entertainment, it has pre–empted the need for any consensus on truth, knowledge or ethics and tossed them up into the prevailing winds. Since youth comprise a sizable segment of the population in the United States, and their influence over pop culture becomes increasingly pronounced, we should take a keen interest in the interplay between the two and the ramifications of this relationship on the present and future.

Solutions, however, are not necessarily provided here, although many are inferred. This is not a how–to manual. In this age of quick–fix, self–help mania, still another sign of intellectual atrophy, we often look for, even expect the "Five Steps to…" answers. False elixirs won't work with a problem of this magnitude. If the reader anticipates a tidy set of recommendations that will make the problem go away, he or she will be disappointed. Answers can emerge only after a detailed appraisal of the situation. Thus, several suggestions for future action are outlined in the final chapter. However, before we can even talk about them, a starkly honest assessment of the crisis being faced must occur. That is the mission this book assigned itself in studying the consequences of the relationship between youth and popular culture. If the Columbine carnage was perhaps its worst manifestation thus far, there can be little doubt more of the same may be massing on the horizon. A phenomenon that first appeared relatively benign is only now starting to let its wrath be felt. What may yet be in store for us as the seeds it planted begin to flower consume much of the narrative ahead. At this point, it should be predicted that there may be types who deride this undertaking for its lack of mooring in a specific branch of social science. I admit that this work is neither a formal psychological or sociological study, nor does it claim to be. Declining any such label, instead it cuts across these fields and others to address a range of overlapping concerns. As the author, my wish is to develop the broadest possible perspective for dealing with a syndrome whose power appears to growing and whose hold over youth deepening. The wider my scope, the more information that can be collected and analyzed and, ideally, the more supportable the conclusions.

Still, this book has modest aims. I do not pretend to tackle the gamut of social problems youth currently face. Issues of neglect, substance abuse, teen pregnancy, physical health and wellness, clinical mental illness, et.al., may be touched on in discussions but peripherally as they support other arguments rather than becoming focal points themselves. These crucial matters I leave to other researchers. For while they are legitimate ills that impact adversely on adolescents, our emphasis here must not stray from *cultural* considerations. By that, I mean this narrative prefers to concentrate on what children and adolescents are *learning* from their environment. Culture begs for attention, assimilation and perpetuation from its creators. It needs new blood to endure. Youth are its guarantors of survival. Thus, what they are exposed to in using assorted media, are being told by peers, hear or see in school, gain or miss from parents—each of these serving as a source of cultural transmission, will be stressed in the pages ahead.

Because this book focuses on postmodern life, it will draw heavily on contemporary sources for information and insight. It is the media of popular culture which propounds the seminal ideas and moods of the period, after all. I will use data downloaded from cyberspace, articles published in high-circulation newspapers and magazines, and the messages readily detectable in mass entertainment. Utilizing these sources is essential if I am to accurately capture the spirit of this era. In building a compelling case, the voices and matter engendered by pop culture rather than pedantic research studies done in isolated think-tanks clearly do the job more effectively.

The reader will note that for the most part the tone of this narrative is understated. Facts are stated, connections between them suggested, and inferences made. Do not mistake this objectivity for indifference on my part. Like many of you, I am terribly concerned about the world our children are growing up in. But injecting personal prejudices into this discussion, no matter how passionate, will not advance my cause. It isn't even necessary, as the reader will soon see. The truth of the matter is that on its own, the insidiousness of pop culture will become so painfully obvious that pontificating about the abject state of the society which enabled it is unnecessary. Facts speak for themselves. I merely collected and arranged them.

Regarding the book, it has been organized into discrete chapters concentrating on different dimensions of the interplay between youth and popular culture. Each essay stands alone, although there is enough overlap to keep the reader mindful of the 'bigger picture' being constructed. However, they are best read in the sequence they appear, for the discussions often build on the arguments and illustrations of those preceding it.

Typically, at this juncture, most authors bid their readers a good journey and implore them to enjoy the coming narrative. Given our somber subject, I hesitate to offer the same advice. I do hope that the pages ahead make a difference to my reader. For it is only after they are adequately informed of the situation that Americans, young and old, will realize the odds they are up against. Once enlightened, perhaps the first steps will be taken in outlining a strategy to curb the power of a popular culture that robs youth of of both its innocence and future.

1

Columbine Awakens a Nation

o o o o o o o o o o o o o o o o o o o o o o o o o o o o o o o o

"The Lord of the Flies is '…an attempt to trace the defects of society back to defects in human nature. The moral is that the shape of a society must depend on the ethical nature of the individual…"

—_William Golding, author_

If Golding's 1962 novel is an allegory for all ages, its cast of characters and plot could not have been conceived in any time more appropriate than the present. This classic work follows the psychological and moral degeneration of proper English schoolboys stranded on a Pacific island. Their decline culminates in ritualistic murder carried out by the "tribe" that now forms the basis of their primitive society. Without the steadying presence of grown–ups to remind them of the rules and tell them what to do, these boys gradually lose touch with society's norms, succumb to their baser instincts, and awaken that dormant brutality buried deep within the human species. Resonant in Golding's theme is the idea that even good children will revert to savagery under the wrong set of circumstances, particularly when adults and the order they embody have been removed from the environment.

If anything, that 'society depends on the ethical nature of the individual' _does not exclude or excuse youth_. Golding's masterpiece makes this point abundantly clear. Now think about today's social landscape, what has happened, and the uneasiness we feel when considering the crises befalling our children. Is his premise any less valid in our reality as on his fictional island? Actual events serve as sufficient reply.

The Darkest Day

As fate would have it, on April 20, 1999, I was visiting my sister in Colorado. My wife and I had just returned this Tuesday from a few days of vacationing at Keystone ski resort.

Unpacking in the guest bedroom of my sister's home in a Denver suburb, the program airing on the television was interrupted by an excited anchorman. Less than three miles away from our room, an unknown number of gunmen had unleashed their rage and a flurry of bullets on unsuspecting students at Columbine High School. Live aerial pictures broadcast from the scene showed an armada of police cars, ambulances, and SWAT vans camped outside the cafeteria of the school. Body–armored peace officers carrying rifles moved cautiously between these vehicles and inched toward the building. The anchorman claimed that unknown assailants, terrorists maybe, had gone on a bloody rampage inside. For me, stunned and horrified, this scene forever swept away the idyll that schools were the last sanctuaries where children remained safe from the evils of society. As these images were relayed to living rooms across America, evoking sorrow and regret similar to mine, they marked the end of a nation's innocence.

Hours later, sketchy reports of the gruesome toll started to filter out. Twelve students shot in cold blood along with one heroic teacher. Perhaps fittingly, two gunmen, themselves Columbine students it turned out, died in a macabre murder–suicide pact. Over twenty wounded survivors had been evacuated to area hospitals. At eight o'clock that evening, my wife, family and I debated going to a bluff overlooking Columbine High where flowers and wreaths were already being arranged by grieving residents in a shrine to the fallen. In the end we decided not to go since the sheriff had asked people to keep the roads clear for police investigators and other emergency personnel. But the pictures and the words of that terrible day burned an indelible mark on our collective consciousness.

By the next morning, the first bits of reliable information on the killers and their motives began to emerge (*Denver Post,* 4/21/99, 1–24a). Branded as social outcasts and singled out for persecution by the "jocks" and other school celebrities they so loathed, the tandem originally formed a friendship more for protection than revenge. Self–described members of the Trench Coat Mafia, they were part of an oddball clique of students who often dressed in black Goth clothing, supposedly relished the misery–loves–company music of Marilyn Manson, and swore eventual retribution on those who made their daily experience at school a 'living hell.'

These murderers, Eric Harris, 18, and Dylan Klebold, 17, came from apparently stable homes in Littleton, an affluent community primarily composed of professional people. Both had cars—Harris a BMW—money, and sadly enough, access to weapons. From other accounts, we learned that they enjoyed playing violent video games such as *Doom*, so much so that Harris customized his version to include a realistic killing zone modeled on the layout of his own neighborhood. Another interest of Harris' involved maintaining his own homepage on the World Wide Web. Among the frightful and foreboding items posted on it were references to Nazism and Hitler, on whose birthday the Columbine slayings would take place. Apocalyptically, he foretold a day of reckoning where all those who hurt him and his friends would be subject to swift and merciless vengeance. Based on stories told by fellow students who knew him, this electronic link permitted Harris to communicate with other pariahs in Internet chat rooms where they regaled each other with their psychotic fantasies.

Even as I wrote this, several months later, the information trickling in from the ongoing investigation struck hard in its madness. A diary kept by Harris showed that he hoped to kill "at least 500 people" and then blow up the entire school. After escaping, he planned to hijack a jet and crash it and himself into New York City (Whitcomb, 1999) in a doomsday scenario sounding more like the far–fetched plot of a *Die Hard* movie than real life. Horrible as it is to say, fortunately neither Harris or Klebold lived long enough to achieve this monumentally maniacal ambition.

As is the case with any tragedy, with a little time comes clarity of perception. Surely in this monstrous event, there were countless lessons to be learned, which, if obscure at the time, emerged clearer with the benefit of hindsight. The wisdom of these lessons can best be gleaned using the Socratic method—posing a series of questions which lead the inquirer closer to a meaningful understanding of the object under scrutiny. Because this process elicits important insights, let us apply it here.

Where did these juvenile sociopaths acquire such colossal ideas of mayhem and murder and how could they conceal their dastardly plot so well for so long? Where were their parents and how could they miss detecting the signs which, in retrospect, certainly seemed noticeable if not abundant? Did their teachers or counselors note any early symptoms of danger in their attitudes and actions during school or in private meetings with the two? On a broader level, what kind of society must we live in when a calamity such as this can be engineered by two adolescents and put in motion on school premises? More egregious still, are current cultural conditions ripe for future school–age killers? If possible, what are the causes and how can concerned adults take steps to prevent like–minded catastrophes in the days and months ahead?

Answers to these questions will surely consume the analytical energies of the finest minds among us for years to come. Yet there are some things that can fairly be stated in relation to this event. Harris and Klebold did not live in a vacuum. Socially, intellectually, domestically, and technologically they were functional. A fellow Columbine student who knew them personally testified that they "…had many friends and were liked by many students." (Marquez, 1999). She adds that they were "raised with strong morals" and came from visibly stable families. Both held part–time jobs at a pizza parlor. Neither was flunking out of school although neither won accolades from their teachers. They entertained themselves with the recreational outlets of "popular" culture. Movies, music, the 'Net and other electronic media fascinated them. Throw casually indifferent parents into the mix, persecution complexes, access to weapons, and a network of adults—teachers, social workers, and police officers—who failed to get involved in their young lives and a formula for disaster emerged.

Ultimately, however, the answer to one overriding issue gnaws away at our brains. What was it that pushed them over the edge? Although we will never know for certain, enough anecdotal evidence survived the carnage for us to formulate a hypothesis. Difficult as it once would have been to believe, there is a distinct possibility that the accumulated, nefarious influences prominent in popular culture played a crucial role in propelling these otherwise unremarkable boys to commit the worst mass murder in American educational history. Although the event was far too complex in its premeditation to accuse a thing as amorphous as pop culture as the solitary culprit, it is evident from what we have learned about the interests and habits of Harris and Klebold that a square measure of blame can be apportioned here. At minimum, the themes promoted by and messages contained in popular culture did nothing to inhibit and indirectly facilitated their diabolical scheme.

Peruse the introduction to the December 20, 1999, *Time* magazine cover story which detailed the contents of five secret videos they recorded ahead of the massacre:

> "Dylan Klebold sits in the tan La–Z–Boy chewing a toothpick. Eric Harris adjusts the video camera a few feet away, then settles into his chair with a bottle of Jack Daniels and a sawed off shotgun in his lap. He calls it Arlene, after a favorite character in the gory Doom video and books that he like so much…These videos, they predict, will be shown all around the world one day—once they have produced their masterpiece and everyone wants to know how, and why." (Gibbs & Roche, 40–41)

After Klebold announces that he hopes the pair will kill "250 of you", Harris gleefully adds, "It's going to be f___ing *DOOM!*" Thinking like make–believe characters from a cartoon or movie, the two talk later on about the Hollywood film that will surely be made about their lurid story. Steven Spielberg or Questin Tarantino are their choices of directors who could do it cinematic justice. Jokingly using a personal code, they called the chosen time and place of their slaughter 'Judgement Day', a thinly veiled reference to *Terminator 2: Judgement Day* which cast Arnold Schwarzenneger as a half–human, half–robot killing machine. Among the personal effects Harris bequeaths to a girlfriend during taping was a compact disk called *Bombthreat Before She Blows*. Showing his facility with electronic media, the venomous Web site Harris maintained before America OnLine shut it down, carried apocalyptic warnings of what lay ahead. "I'm coming for EVERYONE soon and I WILL be armed to the f___ing teeth and I WILL shoot to kill."

Regarding their relationships with parents, these same videotapes reveal the boys had confused feelings. "It f___ing sucks to do this to them," Harris laments. "They're going to be put through hell once we do this…There's nothing you guys could have done to prevent this." A few moments later, however, his tone abruptly changes to insulting. "I don't want to spend any more time with them…I wish they were out of town so I didn't have to look at them and bond more." Although he is the more taciturn of the pair, Klebold projects a similar disdain. He talks about how clueless his parents were when recounting the time he was trying on his trench coat with a sawed–off shotgun bulging underneath. "They didn't even know it was there." Concerning the other adults in his life, namely teachers, Klebold boasts "I could convince them I'm going to climb Mt. Everest or that I have a twin brother growing out of my back…I can make you believe anything. "

These tapes and the boy's statements are steeped in ideas and images predominant in mass media and this media, as we all know, exists as the voice of popular culture. More than that, it is obvious that these cultural interactions made a profoundly negative impact on their minds, however unstable they might have already been. In two personalities as amenable to homicide as theirs, its prolific anti–social messages and perverted ethics were far from wasted.

For Harris and Klebold, pop culture's shadowy recesses—Web hate sites, violent video games, teen slasher films, fratricidal music—provided a gateway to an alternate world of existence. In it, they were persecutors instead of victims and this power proved intoxicating. Mentally, if not physically, dwelling in this realm of fantasy enabled them to first nurture and later give free reign to their destructive impulses. Emotionally stranded in a matrix of simulations, they exerted ultimate control over their environment and became accustomed to eliminating any obstacles in godlike fashion, behavior which survivors of the shooting said they displayed in selecting and chiding those they ended up killing. In time, the divide between reality and this netherworld of simulation where law and morality never applied grew thinner and thinner. Unfettered by troublesome social convention or pangs of conscience, their disturbed minds yielded to the omnipotence they wielded here and tragically, along with other innocents, they died importing it into our world.

Symptoms of Cultural Sickness

Madness and murder is nothing new in human communities, nor is its appeal. All one needs to do is recall the bloodthirsty mob of the Roman colosseum howling before the grisly gladiatorial combats or sepia photographs of crowds gathered in their Sunday–best to watch the hanging of an outlaw in the old American West.

Organized sports touches the same human nerve here in the present. From peewee to professional levels, it is merely violent spectacle transported to modern arenas where contestants are cloaked in protective gear. How many rabid fans go to hockey games hoping for fisticuffs between the players and don't stop screaming for it until blood splatters on the ice? Ditto for auto racing and those packing the stands waiting for collisions among the cars and fatalities among the drivers participating. Even the fake drama of wrestling with its steroid–inflated combatants scored a hit with Americans in appealing to our primitive instincts to throw, body slam, and humiliate our enemies. It alleviates the stresses we are feeling in our own lives but unable to constructively release. We rationalize our interest as a healthy outlet for competition, downplaying the aggression that underlies all athletic events. And our fascination with it never subsides.

In his book *Why We Watch*, Jeffrey Goldstein examined how ingrained aggression and the impulse toward violence are in all human cultures, from tribal to technological. He intelligently argues how our taste for it even now cuts across almost every situation or setting—in religious creeds (see any of the books of the Old Testament), our work environments (unscrupulously beating out the competition for promotion), at school (establishing student pecking orders and cliques), our literature (even the darker episodes/characters in children's fairy tales), family life (the Oedipus and Electra elements) and recreationally (from athletic contests to shoot–em–up video games or 'action' movies). Progress and technical advancement hasn't eliminated this hankering but only instead made it easier to gratify. Rather than having to wait for mass public spectacles like in days of yore, we can view and even participate in barbaric reenactments through television, video games, and organized sports. Dolf Zillman, a contributing essayist cuts to the heart of it: "In light of such powerful universal appeal, could it be that there is something archaic in all of us that attracts us to these exhibitions of brutality and terror, and that even lets us enjoy what we witness? Could it be that we are all attracted to, and, in awe of, heroes that display basal fighting skills—rather than ingenuity, say, in engineering, which much of modern civilization is built upon?" (1998, 180). A culture built and gorged on violent archetypes is one condemned to periodic outbreaks of it, and Western civilization, an oxymoron in this light, sits atop a savage historical foundation. From the farthest corners of the globe to the nearest street corner of the towns we reside in, world wars, regional conflicts and ethnic cleansings, and now school shootings are manifestations of these tendencies humanity still cannot control.

Renowned psychoanalyst Erich Fromm may have been the first to suggest that a whole culture, rather than a few demented individuals, may be beset by mental pathology. In a landmark text, *The Sane Society*, he explored this idea in the unexpected link between our visible material comfort and our hidden emotional emptiness. "Nothing is more common than the idea that we, the people living in the Western World of the twentieth century, are eminently sane…Can we be so sure that we are not deceiving ourselves?" Fromm then identified the signs of mental illness in the organism of our culture. Over the last hundred years, millions were needlessly sacrificed in world and regional wars, although every one of them died convinced of the righteousness of their cause. Capitalism, the world's predominant economic system perpetuated gross disparities in standards of living and social classes but has never been employed to assure human equality. Greatly increased industrial efficiency reduced the amount of time we work yet introduced boredom into our lives along with a novel desire to 'kill the time' we ended up saving. And, despite having a literacy rate above ninety percent, we don't use it for self–improvement but to devour a media goulash of "the cheapest trash, lacking in any sense of reality, with sadistic phantasies which a halfway cultured person would be embarrassed to entertain even once in a while." (pp. 4–5) If fellow psychiatrists wanted to ignore the facts, Fromm did not. He rebuked them for refusing to concede that the problem of the mental health of a society cannot only be counted by cases of disturbed individuals but by the "possible unadjustment of the culture itself." Perhaps the most fascinating aspect of Fromm's argument was that he published *The Sane Society* back in 1955, correctly anticipating the worsening of this cultural ailment. As lonely as his thesis might have been then, it certainly resonates with us here at the dawn of a new millennium.

The incident at Columbine provided a demented dramatization of the interplay between troubled adolescents and their environment when the disordered personality finds an accomplice in the larger culture that spawned it and breaks loose from the rusted and weakened chains of moral restraint. It demonstrated, in excruciating fashion, what can happen when conditions are ripe for disaster but no one close to the powder keg sees or bothers to notice the smoldering matches tossed only a few inches away.

Aggravating an already nervous public were the background characteristics of the perpetrators. Harris and Klebold didn't belong to any organized groups nor was theirs an act of gang warfare. Their so–called membership in a Trench Coat Mafia that roamed Columbine's corridors and of which both were originally tabbed as members, has since been discredited by later investigations (as a crutch for school officials and law enforcement officers groping for scapegoats at the scene). No reports have surfaced of their abusing drugs or alcohol excessively, so we cannot rationalize away their heinous crime as done in a drug–induced haze. Their lucidity, however diabolical, in planning the event shines through in the videotaped testimony left behind. Apart from being busted for petty theft, neither showed felonious potential. Their social worker described them in soft and fuzzy terms and felt that with a bit of guidance and structure, both would end up being well–adjusted, successful adults someday. Bottom line: these killers were middle–class, suburban white kids who on the surface, at least, enjoyed all the amenities of modern life. Truth be told, they simply did not fit society's profile of mass murderers. Not gang–bangers, not poor, not driven to desperation by hunger or want, not able to use the excuse that innocent bystanders were killed only because they 'got in the way,' the story of the these boys stunned us for its proximity to home. Either could have been the kid next door. Worse still, they might have been our own. It is this very profile which haunts us.

Since that April day, stories have appeared almost daily in newspapers, network news programs and the Internet considering the impact of entertainment on our children. The leisure–time pursuits of young people have fallen under the microscope as a nation's anxiety peaked. Politicians, ministers, educators, and parents have closed ranks in articulating this concern. Still in the shadow of Columbine, President Clinton called on his friends among Hollywood studio chiefs to act more responsibly in deciding what films to make and in producing more family–friendly pictures. From May through July of 1999, the United States Senate summoned various entertainment industry heads before its committee hearings as they debated passing legislation requiring guidelines for heightened media responsibility. Child and parent advocacy organizations like the National Coalition on Television Violence (**www.nctvv.org**), enlisting the aid of several Senators and former Presidents ratcheted up public pressure campaigns such as their "National Appeal to Hollywood", an electronic petition calling for stricter rules on media content and additional control mechanisms such as the V–chip for television. As before, this appeal met with a thunderous silence in the entertainment community like most every grassroots effort to protest the products they market. By January of 2000, when the furor had receded, president of the Motion Picture Association of America, Jack Valenti, would go on record saying that Clinton's proposal for higher standards was "barren of any chance of survival." (Stern, 2000). In the interim, nothing changed.

In an interesting twist, even one of the purported sources of inspiration for the Columbine massacre, rock star Marilyn Manson, spoke out about the causes of youth disaffection. Don't make me or my music the scapegoat for a much wider and severe social crisis, Manson argued in his own inimitable style. Over the course of a young life, it is the day to day culture the child absorbs—dark, duplicitous, and disheartening, that worked it's unholy magic. In his own words:

> Marilyn Manson has never celebrated the sad fact that America puts killers on the cover of *Time* magazine, giving them as much notoriety as our favorite movie stars. From Jesse James to Charles Manson, the media, since their inception, have turned criminals

into folk heroes. They just created two new ones when they plas-tered those dipshits Dylan Klebold and Eric Harris' picture on the front of every newspaper.

We applaud the creation of a bomb whose sole purpose is to destroy all of mankind, and we grow up watching our president's (Kennedy's) brains splattered all over Texas. Times have not become more violent. They have just become more televised...Dis-gusting vultures (the media) looking for corpses, exploiting, fuck-ing, filming and serving it up for our hungry appetites in a gluttonous display of endless human stupidity

It's no wonder that kids are growing up more cynical; they have a lot of information in front of them. They can see that they are liv-ing in a world made of bullshit...

source: a May 28, 1999 statement published on the Rolling Stone magazine web site (**www.rollingstone.com**)

In spite of his crude tone and wish to dodge all responsibility, what Manson says is basically sound. There are those who still wish to deny it and in their desperate search to mete blame, heap it largely upon Manson along with other pop icons. Yet while it is true that these anti–heroes of youth bear some responsibility, individually they amount to no more than a few brushstrokes on the broader cultural canvas.

Adolescents may not be rich in experience but neither are they obtuse. To them, the irony between the Truth according to Parents or the Truth according to Media is obvious. Parents warn them about smoking pot but sip down those three martinis every night after work or tell them to refrain from premarital sex when statistics indicate they are engaging in extramarital liaisons in record numbers. Civic leaders decry school violence and kids killing kids but cannot stop bickering long enough to pass gun control legislation because the NRA keeps stuffing money into their campaign coffers. Teachers insist that educa-tion is the surest way to life success, but television shows teens that mixing rap records, becoming a sports star, or winning the grand prize on an instant millionaire game show is surer still. As Manson observed, irony is a concept that American kids learn to grasp early.

In an environment such as this, deciding which side to ally oneself with is a no–brainer. Popular culture speaks eloquently to adolescent psychology. Striking all the right chords, it points the way to endless amusements, shows them the socially–acceptable shortcuts to success, and at the same time, mocks the old–school and outdated values of the adult world.

Demise of Character and Ascending Amorality

Because this issue will be debated at length in subsequent sections of this book, we will not dwell too long on it here. Still, some mention of the moral climate of the United States ought to be made in any discussion connecting Columbine and popular culture. For though it might be ephemeral and as an intuition undeserving of scientific consideration, a lot of Americans hold a sneaking suspicion that a tragedy like Columbine would have been inconceivable in any time other than the present. Until recently, family structures, for all intents and purposes, were still intact and parents put a premium on instilling values. Teachers reinforced this important work done at home by extending it to social settings. From a tender age, children were taught to be honest, fair, and responsible. Living a virtuous life was the ideal adults held up to their children and many fathers and mothers tried to model it in their own behavior.

Then a funny thing happened on our way through this century. A loosening of social norms and accompanying ethics whose origins roughly coincide with the anti–establishment 1960's gathered momentum until climaxing in its final decade. Two national events, one a public spectacle in the form of a trial and the other a political scandal, epitomized this trend in vivid detail.

The criminal case of football star O.J. Simpson didn't just put the defendant or our judicial system on trial. In effect, it put American morality on trial where it failed abysmally. The integrity of so–called witnesses, attorneys, public officials, even the system itself, none emerged untainted. Mismanagement of the crime scene by shady detectives like Mark Fuhrman, Kato Kaelin's shaggy–maned buffoon-ery, the theatric grandstanding of lead defense counsel Johnny Cochran, the weak handling of the case by a press–conscious prosecution team (Marcia Clark and Christopher Darden) eyeing lucrative book contracts, and the maddening impotence of Judge Ito to regain control and see that justice rather than dramatics determined the outcome, all these reflected a travesty in ethics. If adults were disillusioned, so were their kids. The lessons of this sensational episode weren't lost on them. Every day the trial dragged on, I overheard students not only discussing the latest developments, but mainly debating the right and wrong of the case as I crossed campus on route to my office.

Between 1998–99, a fresh scandal erupted that rocked America in reaching to the highest elected office of the country. President Clinton was accused by independent counsel Kenneth Starr of violating his oath of office by concealing an illicit affair with unlikely *femme fatale* Monica Lewinsky. Through exquisitely worded evasions and legal gymnastics, Clinton dodged Starr's bullets and survived a Congressional attempt to impeach him. Once again, however, Americans witnessed how accountability for one's actions took a back seat to legal vindication. The President of the Unites States skillfully demonstrated how porous our standards had become. In *The Death of Outrage* (1999), arch–conservative William Bennett claimed that people's refusal to condemn Clinton's behavior masked their own corruption and wish to keep it secret. Whether one agrees with his politics, Bennett landed upon a widening trend in the general public toward overlooking serious ethical transgressions in those who ought to serve as exemplars. If the masses have suffered moral atrophying, historians, at least, have retained their perspective. In a survey conducted by public affairs channel C-SPAN, Clinton won the dubious honor of placing last of all forty–one U.S. presidents in moral authority (*Netscape Netcenter News*, 2/21/00). Still, if the majority of citizens are not troubled at conduct unfit or unbecoming of their leaders, can it be long before we extend the same latitude toward our own behavior? Or our children's? Have we already? It appears so.

At first glance, neither of these events appears to have any bearing on what happened at Columbine. Or do they? Neither Simpson or Clinton assumed responsibility for their actions. They were simply the victims of unscrupulous foes motivated purely by racism and political ideology, respectively. Viewed in an ethical context, we can intuit that, however fine, a common thread winds its way through them and the spate of crimes perpetrated by American youth. If prominent adults, one a celebrity, the other, the President of the United States, cannot be held accountable, how can a mere teenager? Adolescents are the biggest users of media and both of the above cases garnered prolonged television, radio, and Internet coverage. Is it a stretch to think that through this media saturation youth have grown wise to and seen through the hypocritical atmosphere that prevails in important cultural questions?

Instances of this duplicity abound. Tobacco companies like R.J. Reynolds or Phillip Morris spent millions plying cigarettes to teenage consumers. After a number of costly court cases, they agreed to settlements requiring them to launch national anti–smoking campaigns geared toward teenagers, the same clientele they have been trying to hook on nicotine for years using billboards strategically placed within eyesight of school yards. The notorious Joe Camel advertising campaign using a hip cartoon character to attract young, potential smokers' attention revealed the lies behind proclamations of innocence. Character, both on a corporate or individual scale, has disappeared from the American scene. Like morality, its fabric has become moth–eaten and full of holes even where it purportedly exists. Sadder still, the venerable institutions expected to cultivate character also continue to let us down.

Thanks to a powerful, well–funded lobby of church–state separatists, public schools have seen their right to teach traditional morality gradually erode. In Rabbi Menachem Schneerson's book, *Toward a Meaningful Life*, he argues forcefully for the restoration of character cultivation in schools, public moreso than private institutions. Education for character, he believes, should even supersede education for the intellect. All learning programs we create will fail at a fundamental level when student character development is neglected. In his estimation, ignoring moral training in schools led to the grave situation in which our society finds itself. Without a moral compass, young people are groping for direction and, unfortunately, making countless wrong choices that hurt them and others.

Has the transparency of adult caveats such as 'do as I say, not as I do,' at last registered in young minds? Kids have observed firsthand how individual responsibility for one's actions is at a low ebb and that with the proper defense team, dodge–then–counter tactics, and media spin doctors, adults routinely evade crimes and misdemeanors. No one is held accountable for their wrongdoing. Invariably, children see, malfeasance is the result of outside forces or factors. How could parents, relatives, teachers or clergy dare instruct them about right and wrong when they created this hypocrisy? If grown–ups can plead, bargain or bluff their way out of trouble by sidestepping personal fault and blaming their misdeeds on phantom attackers (Simpson), partisan politics (Clinton), or in the case of Harris and Klebold, assorted social factors (a lifetime of cruel peers, detached parents, and destructive media messages), youth can too.

The wrenching case of Sherrice Iverson demonstrated that this same mental disassociation from dark deeds committed is already occurring. She was the 7 year–old girl molested then murdered by University of California, Berkeley, freshman, Jeremy Strohmeyer in a Las Vegas casino bathroom in 1997. Returning from the crime scene, Strohmeyer casually told his waiting friend, David Cash, that he had killed the girl. Cash took no action to inform the authorities and the two allegedly went back to Berkeley and classes as if nothing had happened. It wasn't until after police arrested and charged Strohmeyer that word of his friend's silent complicity hit newspaper headlines, provoking a firestorm of outrage. Since that time, Cash, still enrolled as a Berkeley student, has been hounded by merciless protesting from fellow students intent on seeing him prosecuted for abetting this homicide. The university finds itself in the awkward position of being hamstrung by an obsolete code of conduct that never envisioned acts so heinous, effectively countenancing Cash's continued enrollment by announcing it has no mechanism for dealing with off–campus crimes. As for Strohmeyer, his legal defense hinged on blaming "…his best friend (Cash), his ex–girlfriend, his psychologists, American Online, the Nevada gaming commission, Los Angeles county adoption officials…and everyone but Ken Starr and the one–armed man." (Jacobs, 1998, 2). Seeing the pattern so successfully executed by other public personas, Strohmeyer learned his lessons well. He understood that "every American has an inalienable right to be a victim." Sentenced to life in prison without the possibility of parole, he will have plenty of time to contemplate how society let him down.

Of course, it would be a terrible mistake to stereotype all teens as unfettered by conscience in matters of character. Surely, the Strohmeyers and Cashes must be exceptions to the rule. Ambar Martinez, then a 15–year old high school student, wrote an article defending her generation called "Teen Morality Lives!!!" (Los Angeles Youth Notebook, *Los Angeles Times*, March/April Issue, 1999). Irked by a *Times* cartoon showing two gravestones, one of which bore the inscription "Teen Morality" next to the other reading "Sherrice Iverson", Martinez felt a duty to reply. Commenting on Strohmeyer's crime, she wrote, "…I can't dwell on it or it will eat me up. Am I being cold when I say this? Am I another immoral teen who doesn't care? I don't think I am but there's nothing I can do about it." Reading between the lines of her apology, we can detect signs of nihilism creeping in. Consistent with the new morality of America, we see another instance of the me–first variety. Ethical considerations are fine as long as they don't put one in an uncomfortable position or require becoming involved in a dilemma. Her view of the incident is skewed toward its effect *on her*. Its impact on the victim and American society are regrettable, but secondary.

Martinez is also wrong about taking action. There is something she and her peers can do. They could put the victims first, take a hard line and speak out against classmates who would hurt or have injured others in strong, unambiguous terms. When teens become involved in the madness of a Harris, Klebold, or Strohmeyer they should talk about it to everyone who will listen, not run or hide from it and in doing so, relieve themselves of culpability when things take a tragic turn. Instead, Martinez takes refuge in that all–too–common stance that what's done is done, no need to dwell on it for fear of becoming "depressed" and "paranoid" (her words). Apart from poor Sherrice Iverson and her immediate family, it's time to move on.

Let us hope that hers is a minority opinion and that other adolescents have not yet been so acculturated to violence and callous to suffering that hearing of it provokes unnecessary stress they needn't be inconvenienced with . I fear, however, that the sentiments Martinez expresses are shared by many. Youth morality, like that espoused by adults has weathered poorly over recent years. Issues covered in the chapters ahead will show how hard it has become for young persons to find a center from which to absorb values, order priorities, and guide the decisions they must make to survive as caring and principled members of society.

An alternative explanation, unsupportable by any means, exists for both the sociopathic behavior we have been witnessing as well as the ruthless indifference of the perpetrators. Forces far darker and more sinister could be at work. Could it be that sprinkled among the innocent, fresh–faces of youth are soulless beings bent solely on harm and destruction? Jeremy Strohmeyer qualifies. His defense smacked entirely of excuses and devoid of any regret. Survivors of the Columbine massacre talked about the mechanical movements and steely 'dead eyes' of Harris and Klebold as victims mounted and their stalking continued. The existence of evil incarnate in our children is simply to much to fathom. Mere mention of it is unsettling. Logically, it cannot be supported by anything more than individual imagination. Therefore, pursuing this line of thought any longer is something better left to theologians. As a social scientist, I deal only in facts and possible links between them. Anything above that falls outside my realm of knowledge. At times, however, given the sheer horror of these acts, there is cause to wonder about the sources that seem to be whispering inspiration to our children.

Summary

The Columbine massacre showed a nation that the time for wondering had passed. American youth stood at the edge of a precipice. As concerned adults, our next move, regardless of how supple or slight, could either push them over or bring them back to safety. As a society, this tragedy compelled us to take notice. What have we done in responding? To most observers, myself included, once the finger-pointing stopped and the public debate receded it was business as usual. Our outrage seems to have had a short if emotional existence.

In hoping to gain a deeper understanding of how Columbine happened, our gaze gradually moved beyond two deranged teenage boys and the media to other American institutions; the family, education and society. While the entertainment industry has rightly borne the brunt of our indignation, Columbine forced us to take a critical look at the roles of families and schools in preventing anti-social behavior among adolescents. If the media is outside our control, perhaps family life and schools can yet reverse the detrimental influences of popular culture. Of course, to accomplish this, they must both do far more than they are currently doing to properly raise and teach our children. For, truth be told, if films, television, and music have been excoriated for eroding morality, we must also acknowledge that a declining parental presence in kids' lives has contributed to the injuries done. As the American family has suffered, so has the foundation of society. A commensurate rise in child pathology has paralleled this familial fragmentation. Still others complain about how education has failed in curbing any anti-social tendencies. Rocked by its own internal identity crises, education, by itself, is not up to the challenge. Schools cannot make up for the early teaching of values students no longer receive at home. What youth see daily in their exposure to the media add to their confusion. Can adults dare tell them about right and wrong when they have taken to unprecedented levels the art of evading responsibility for their own words and deeds? In such a world, even the harshest remonstrations ring hollow.

So many of us are wondering if it's too late. Can things still be righted? Or have we already sacrificed this and future generations of youth to a popular culture that demeans former social verities and replaces them with an ulterior, incompatible, and perhaps sinister agenda of its own?

These issues will be attended to in the coming chapters. Before we get to them, however, let us consider how recent events brought us to the doorstep of these troubled times.

2

The Road Recently Travelled

"Toward the end of the twentieth century America's economic power was preeminent, and the competitive strength of the countries of Europe and the Pacific Rim was itself an American accomplishment...No design has been nobler in conception or more brilliant in execution than the complex of international organizations for economic health, welfare, health, education, collective security and human rights that America has nurtured in the second half of the century." (xv.)

------_Harold Evans, The American Century_

In his homage, is Evans accidentally identifying a dilemma which faces the United States? For if indeed Americans can pride themselves on these notable achievements and others while shaking congratulatory hands atop the summit of the free world, what does the moment after bring? Perhaps, for all of these accomplishments, we are, at heart, an unassuming people, proud of but slightly embarrassed by this renown. It is possible that wary of our contributions to human dignity and freedom over the last hundred years, we face an inevitable yearning to step back from the international stage, catch our breath, and retire into domestic tranquility.

It has always been a distinctly American tendency to retreat into the vast physical and psychological spaces of this continent once we fulfilled our obligations to the world order. Isolationism pulses through our veins. Noticing this, Evans alluded to our peculiar nature of alternating moods between 'private interest and public purpose'. For example, following World War II, the United States went beyond the call of duty in both Germany and Japan, propping up these defeated, ravaged nations with generous economic aid. With the conflict ended, it didn't take long for returning soldiers to forget about the war and focus on important matters like family, education, and work. Investing as much effort into their jobs as they did fighting, the biggest industrial boom in the history of the United States occurred, doubling the national output between 1946–1960, and escorting in an unheard of standard of living that promised every family a home, a pantry full of food, electric appliances and an automobile, creating our first, full–fledged middle class. As before, however, with several exceptions—Korea, Vietnam, and other Cold War proxy conflicts, the years since World War II have been filled with social prosperity, economic enrichment, and in an initially healthy way, absorption with one's own affairs.

If the pendulum swung toward and stuck fast on one's self, we gradually went from minding our own affairs to lapsing into self–indulgence. Unfortunately, problems have a habit of cropping up when Americans go too long without some dire domestic or world crisis to unite them. During these respites, history shows we, especially the young, have a habit of living wantonly—the roaring 20's after the Great War, the "rebels without a cause" 50's after WWII and Korea, the drug–hazed 70's and rapacious 80's in the aftermath of Vietnam. Yet war need not be the only catalyst arousing our philanthropic instincts either. The Civil Rights movements, the Apollo space program, or the crashing down of the Berlin Wall, a victory, from any angle, of U.S.–championed democracy over totalitarian regimes, each of these events made us forget about our own wants and brought a surge of pride in the ultimate triumph of the American way. Yet during quieter times, sans a worthy crusade, we regress into that self–centered side of human psychology preoccupied mainly with satisfying individual desires. Oddly, it is during these interludes that our society faces imminent danger. Presently in the midst of one unusually lengthy stretch, this lack of purpose paved the road for a surge of excess whose reach now pervades all areas of modern existence.

Average men and women sense it, too. Under the surface, anxiety simmers. According to *USA Weekend's* 1999 Third Annual "America's Poll" published on July 4th, people expressed conflicting emotions about the state of their nation. This ambivalence is interesting for the irony it implies. While we reap clear benefits from existing in a time of political stability, economic growth and technological achievement, there remains a nagging feeling that something is amiss in the soul of our society.

Several telling examples emerged from the survey. The majority of Americans expressed their unbounded faith in the Constitution as a timeless protector of liberties and admired its fundamental freedoms of speech, press, assembly. However, their appreciation of the freedoms provided for in this document aren't unqualified. Fifty–two percent said the Constitution's guarantee of an individual's "right to bear arms" should either be modified or eliminated. A consistent wariness among those surveyed extended to cultural questions. Fifty–nine percent would restrict violence in movies and music. An even larger share, 64%, favored regulating violent content in music videos and the Internet, while 67% wanted to limit violent content on television and in video games. Children through adolescents, they feared, are being woefully desensitized by these entertainment options. Evidence of this learned disregard for human life is mounting around us in the rising teen–on–teen incidences of violence. Adults worry but feel powerless to stop the trend.

What accounts for these at best contradictory, at worst, pessimistic, opinions? Gregg Easterbrook, a contributing editor to both *The Atlantic Monthly* and *The New Republic*, who wrote the *USA* article around the survey data, offered his impressions. "The poll (done three months after Columbine) suggests that Columbine may have been a defining moment in public opinion...Indeed, Columbine may have changed sensibilities in many areas. Poll respondents indicate surprising willingness to impose new restrictions...even amend the Constitution—in return for greater safety for themselves and their children." If Easterbrook's guess is right and this terrible event turns out to be a an epiphany in mass consciousness, it might explain the apprehension suffusing these responses. People aren't just worried, they feel a certainty that things cannot go on as they have been. As a society, we stand at a crossroads and wonder in which direction our destination lies. Public awareness continues peaks toward a particular conclusion—that in spite of improving material comforts and technological conveniences, something is desperately wrong in our society. 'Things need to change.' Like a mantra for deliverance, we hear it from family and friends and repeat it to others almost every day.

For those who prefer empirical data over journalistic, let us refer to another national survey collecting Americans thoughts on contemporary life. This study, undertaken by The Pew Research Center for The People and The Press in conjunction with Princeton University, imparts a similar sense of foreboding, reinforcing the marked uneasiness that hovered over the United States at the close of the 20th century. The title of the report, *Public Perspectives on the American century: TECHNOLOGY TRIUMPHS, MORALITY FALTERS* leaves little doubt as to how participants feel.

In brief, people saw the 20th Century as a time of unrivalled material, cultural and technical progress. Two–thirds said they have improved their circumstances since the 1950's. Above all things, Americans think that science and technology have been the engines of our prosperity and pointed to advancements in these fields as contributing to their own family's well–being. Although less enthusiastic about selected research discoveries such as Viagra or cloning, Americans opined that scientific advancement, specifically, landing a man on the moon, was the single greatest achievement of this century. Pleased with the positive difference technical innovation has made in their lives, it comes as no surprise that in the area of communications, majorities in the 60%+ range thought e–mail, the Internet, cellular phones, and cable television all meant changes for the better. A full 87% agreed that computers were a good thing. Technology, however, wasn't the only area which drew favorable responses in the Pew study. Those polled overwhelmingly credited the governmental and economic *system* of the United States—the Constitution, meritocracy, and free enterprise as crucially important in fostering our collective success.

"Yet beneath this picture of economic well–being and national accomplishment, there is a parallel story not nearly so triumphant," the Pew research team concluded. Especially troubling to people 'from all walks of life' was the declining moral climate of the country. While some social changes were clearly seen as constructive, such as civil rights and women's movements, other trends like legalized abortion and acceptance of divorce bothered 42% and 53% of respondents, respectively. The breakdown of family structures, decrease of civility, rise in crime, and the casual use of drugs also factored into people's perception of this moral decay. Intriguingly, despite a strong vote of confidence in 'the system,' doubt about the integrity of our leaders and governmental agencies revealed a widening cynicism toward authority.

Other findings of importance were:

> when asked if 'Life in the United State since the 1950's has got-ten…', 30% replied 'worse' and 26% 'don't know', indicating that at least 56% of all those contacted displayed pessimism about the quality of life in the U.S.

> when asked the question 'Life has gotten worse for…', 56% said 'teenagers' and 44% mentioned 'children', an admission fraught with frightful repercussions for youth

Thus, the polls have spoken. Truthfully, they only tell us what any informed citizen of this country already senses. Democracy, in princi-ple, exceeded the founding fathers' dreams and even now gives each of us a chance to grow and prosper without interference. Significant strides have been made in technology and its applications to everyday life. In our homes, offices, and schools, we are wired to a world of information and recreation. The economy keeps buzzing along. People are earning more than ever. Yet within those seemingly prosperous conditions that comprise our daily existence, we still cling to a gut feeling that deep down the domestic picture is not nearly so rosy.

Before we delve further into what the present offers American youth, let us take time to consider where we have come from, concentrating on the last hundred years. To supply us with context for the coming discussion, a review of social history during this period is the appropriate place to begin. Mindful of our mission, however, this has to be a selective analysis, focusing on a handful of watershed developments unique to the United States while, for the sake of space, omitting many others. In this chronicling, special attention will be paid to events that prompted *cultural changes.* In reviewing this centenary's cultural streams and currents, we will obtain a wider understanding of how America arrived at its present place and what that may mean to our children.

The Last Hundred Years: Remaking U.S. Society

Twentieth century American history should be reasonably familiar to anyone born and educated in the United States. Reiterating this record from scratch, as already rendered by trained historians, would prove a fruitless and unnecessary undertaking here. Doing so would replicate the work already done by those better qualified to assemble such chronicles. Instead, this narrative prefers to take a snapshot approach of American history, inspecting a handful of momentous events that molded society into its present shape. A handful of these events were either *orchestrated or guided by youth.* They merit special consideration since adolescents and the social realities they brought about serve as the subjects of this text.

The 20th century saw unprecedented shifts in human social organization, economies, and living standards. In 1960, the world's population hit 3 billion people, ballooned to 5 billion in 1987 and attained the incredible mark of 6 billion on October 12, 1999, effectively doubling in thirty–nine years, according to a United Nations Population Fund report (Zabarenko, 1999). The population count taken by the U.S. Census Bureau shows that there were over 281,000,000 people in the country as of the 2000 survey. Estimates by the Bureau safely project the population near the 300 million mark by 2010. If these figures astound, the repercussions of this growth and what it means in terms of resources needed to support this human mass should evoke a more profound impression. Apart from the very real problems this poses for world ecology, a peculiar situation related to resource consumption arose in the United States.

As Christopher Lasch observed in *The Minimal Self*, the U.S. gave birth to the unmanageable twins of mass production and mass consumption. Starting in the 1920's, a *consumer culture* began to emerge which paralleled the advent of mass production in industry. To feed this industrial machine, combing and culling the land for coal, oil, and mineral ores to fuel it proceeded unquestioned, a corollary to the doctrine of manifest destiny. That was only the first step. Lasch accurately pointed out that mass production and the consumerist mentality it bred provoked a "far reaching series of cultural changes." Rather rapidly, Americans gave up the self–reliant spirit of their pioneering forefathers and providing for their own wants. Within a generation, they submitted to the immediate satisfaction of factory–made staples available in general and later department stores springing up all around them. Today, neither old or young can conceive of a time when things were any different.

Unfortunately, the rise of consumerism portended a plethora of problems which haunts us to this day. Once hooked, consumers rather quickly displayed a curious, insatiable hunger for newer and better products. Whether or not the one they owned still filled its function became irrelevant. An unstoppable cycle started. As we've learned, consumerism rests on a psychology of fleeting gratification. The high derived from the experience of the purchase and, once home, unwrapping the box and removing our shiny new shoes is every bit as important as how well they wear or long they last. Durable goods, appliances, amenities, even entertainment—none can maintain our interest or compete with the flow of new items and services forever flooding the marketplace. Born and indoctrinated into such a society, children certainly learned this lesson early. They constitute a formidable segment of America's consumers, as obvious from the advertisements and products we see oriented toward, in corporate lexicon, that barely tapped younger demographic. This phenomenon of swift disenchantment and endlessly roaming tastes extends beyond the shopping mall and governs the approach many of us, old but especially young, raised as consumers in a material society, bring to living. It also precipitated a graver problem.

Lasch, for one, believed that as people were *re-socialized into consumers*, they lost their capacity for independent thinking and judgement. Automation and its surplus of goods discouraged cottage industry innovation. In its wake, it imbued a dependence on products and industries outside one's own house or holdings. Why create with our own hands the materials needed to support a household when they waited, factory–fresh, at the corner grocery or newfangled department stores sprouting up in every city, or so argued the new conventional wisdom. Even if Lasch is implying that Americans became stupider and lazier, our concerns lay elsewhere. With this switch to a consumer psychology, self–reliance forever vanished under an avalanche of mass–produced items. As individual ingenuity declined, so did restraints on consumption. Within a couple of generations, making, taking, using, or buying only what was required to maintain the household yielded to a trend of reckless indulgence. The massive credit debt our nation has amassed, personal savings at record lows, and a collective taste for luxury in the goods and services purchased—all these illustrate the trend.

Another important change occurred on the American scene during this period. Along with the rise in consumerism came the need for a large labor force to mind the machinery of industry. As manufacturing centers multiplied, so did the communities around them. Unlike farms with seasonally intensive work during as planting and harvesting, factory work demanded a labor force available to put in consistent, regular, and even overtime hours. Workers had to live near their employer. With the chance for high–paying, steady employment that dwarfed income earned from agriculture, the population permanently moved toward cities. This shift proved highly significant in cultural terms.

In 1900, The U.S was primarily an agrarian nation, with over 60% of its people residing in rural areas (see U.S. Census Bureau web page). By 1930, a dozen years after World War I, a more cosmopolitan populace, swelled by veterans returning from Europe as well as an expanding working–class, exhibited a preference for urban living, with 56% settling in urban areas. This exodus to centers of commerce continued through the war–driven economy of the 1940's and in the decades that followed as strides in agriculture and animal husbandry reduced the number of privately–owned farms while managing to raise output. By 1990, 75% of Americans lived in places designated as urban and by then our cultural axis tilted toward an urban orientation. Youth, in particular, would ride this wave to new heights as urban cultural expressions (e.g. hip–hop) blossomed.

Human migration on a scale of this magnitude meant more than just people relocating to find jobs. Accompanying it were radical changes in the way Americans lived. Urban and suburban existence translated into varied opportunities for employment, instant access to media, multiple modes of transportation, and maybe most significantly, the *luxury of time for leisurely pursuits.* All of these came to be seen as indispensable features of the modern American landscape. Materially, the standard of living rose considerably for most citizens. Electricity, indoor plumbing, and waste disposal systems were introduced in all but the most remote locations. For the first time, affordable housing became widely available. Bedroom communities and housing tracts dotted the landscape outside every major city and were glowingly viewed as proof of attainment of the American dream. (This belief would persist until these separate enclaves ended up merging into that scourge of the modern landscape—suburban sprawl). Cheap public transit, expanding air travel, and, by the last quarter of the century, and over two automobiles per household made rendered us the most mobile group of people the world has ever known.

These century–long demographic shifts paralleled a corresponding increase in educational opportunities. Where before education beyond the sixth grade had been restricted to the privileged children of the wealthy, quality public school systems flourished and opened their doors to students from all strata of society. The doors of many former ivory towers were also opened. Conceived by Congress as debt of gratitude for serving in the armed forces and preventing massive unemployment while industry scrambled to find trades for millions of returning men, the GI Bill following World War II brought an influx of ex–servicemen to college campuses. Many of them, from humble socio–economic origins, would never have dreamt of a college education nor been afforded such an opportunity. In hindsight, this single piece of legislation may have unwittingly led to the formation of the middle-class (Quinnan, 1995) and kindled a desire in them for their children to receive a higher education as well.

Socially, two movements of the 1960's and early 70's ushered in sweeping changes in how we viewed each other and authority. First, the Civil Rights movement began inauspiciously enough with Rosa Parks sitting fast on an Alabama bus in 1955 and slowly gained momentum. Through the restaurant sit–ins, boycotts, and March on Washington under the moral stewardship of Martin Luther King, African–Americans and, in time, other people of color finally received not only equal protection under the law but the chance to publicly raise their voices and celebrate a rich cultural heritage. The racial and ethnic diversification of our society continued under a renewed surge of immigration and loosened residency laws. Tens of thousands of came to America in search of a better life, a trend that roughly coincided with the end of the Vietnam war in 1975. Some immigrants were indeed fleeing political persecution in Asia, others civil wars and revolutions in Central and South America, and after the fall of the Berlin Wall in 1989, throngs sought to escape economic hardship in Eastern Europe and the former Soviet Union. This tide of refugees quietly altered the complexion of the United States just as surely as the preceding Irish, Italian and Slavic waves processed through Ellis Island in the early 1900's. By 2005, Latinos will easily constitute the largest minority group in the nation and their influence over popular culture, from politics to cuisine is already being felt on the American scene (*Newsweek*, 7/12/99). The vociferous protests of Cuban–Americans in Miami in 2000 over the return of changeling Elian Gonzalez to Castro's Cuba showcased their clout on the political scene. During the course of the twentieth century, despite pockets of resistance, the United States morphed into a *multicultural society*.

A second temblor that shook American society to its core took place in the student protests flaring up across campuses during the 60's. Iconoclasm, the attacking of established institutions and ideals, reached a fever pitch as college students challenged the morality of a proxy war in Vietnam and a government that insisted it was necessary. Cherished beliefs that democracy always took the higher moral road and the leaders we elected were inherently honest fell headlong into disfavor and were excoriated by students as the lies of long 'dead white men' in a patent damning of Western culture. Although there were some self–serving elements in these protests, the general impact, though years in the telling, was clear. Caught off guard by the scope of these protests and conceding the legitimacy of at least some of the items on the student's agenda, the authorities were compelled to give ground. Confronting this youthful rebellion, government, from this point on, would appear more responsive to the popular mood. By extension, parents too, suddenly fell under suspicion. Mesmerized by the chants of anti–establishment gurus, students rallied around the pro–youth euphemism that no one over thirty could be trusted.

Destroyed faith in the traditional cells of power, parents, civic and religious leaders, created a void that has never been wholly filled since. These young crusaders, in a further slap at the strictures of the establishment, experimented widely with drugs and enjoyed previously unheard of sexual freedom.

Something else not immediately discernible took place during these tumultuous times. A fundamental shift in the focus of American culture occurred. On the whole, young people had demonstrated that their judgement on complex matters of state and society could be trusted. Richard Nixon's resignation after news of Watergate assured his impeachment, seemed vindication to the crowds of students who had disparagingly dubbed him Tricky Dick for his machinations. In the wake of the student movement, ours shifted to a *culture oriented toward and manipulated by youth.* If, on the surface, government, education, and family outwardly seemed to be controlled by adults, social realities were increasingly determined by the whims of the young. Fashion, music, entertainment, relations between the sexes, behavioral norms and mores, came and went at the pleasure of the 18–30 year old cohort statisticians classify as 'adolescent to young adult.'

By the 1980's, things calmed down socially and the United States lapsed into a kind of post–climactic contentment after the heady Sixties and vacuous Seventies. The Reagan presidency dominated the decade and with this sweet, grandfatherly, and inert presence in the White House, a nostalgic wave of neo–conservatism washed over the country. Trickle–down economics, the Preppy Handbook, and a return to family values characterized this era, lulling people into a politically numbing, socially torporous mode of existence. Compared to prior decades, not much happened on the domestic scene except for the frightening onset of HIV/AIDS which soon altered the sexual habits of the young and single. Racism, sexism and economic discrimination persisted, of course, but they were effectively ignored by all those who avoided their sting in the unbridled Yuppie rush to make money and stake a piece of the high life.

A new era dawned in the nineties. Americans shook off the conservative lethargy of the prior decade, perhaps thought twice about how little had been accomplished, and headed down a much different road. Most everything that ruled in the eighties was eventually reviled as narcissistic and irredeemable. A new type of President, Bill Clinton, the first baby boomer, was elected and stressed public service instead of personal gain as a policy push. A revitalized urban life introduced Main Street to hip–hop culture, a savvy blend of multiculturalism, commercial street smarts, and gathering political muscle, as it rose from and catered to a cadre of post–baby boomers unkindly dubbed Generation X.

Lambasted for their alleged aversion to education and work, Gen X'ers spurned conventional wisdom, developed their own mythology and injected it into popular culture. Among their heroes were celebrities—musicians, television and film stars, professional athletes, and their own breed of unorthodox wunderkind entrepreneurs who started technology ventures in their basements or garages, made millions on an idea, and managed to finally kill formal business attire. Because they were often raised in homes that didn't resemble the nuclear family of old or offer its tapestry of loving and supporting relationships, Generation X befriended technology in a way that none before them did. Televisions, walkmans and computers served as babysitters for working parents, escapes when the jocks–and–faces crowd at school rejected them, and later, passports to their own economic futures in that vast and still largely unexplored realm known as cyberspace which they, along with their successors, "Generation Y", followed by the "Millenials", would conquer.

Compared side by side, American social institutions and culture as they stood at the end of the 20th century would seem totally foreign to a person of 1900. The changes these last 100 years introduced gave rise to the unusual reality in which we currently reside. If our perspective has been sharpened by recounting this originally American saga, then the time has come to consider a companion set of changes that stealthily but effectively altered that body of knowledge, aesthetics, morality, and collective memory typically referred to as culture.

MODERN VS. POSTMODERN PERSPECTIVES

Overarching recent history is a template dictating the dominant cultural motifs of the times. If society evolved, so did the cultural axis—wisdom, beliefs and conventions—it embraced. Notions once taken for granted lost currency in this emerging milieu. The grip of venerable institutions—churches, government, schools—over the masses gradually weakened during these turbulent years. With this weakening came a reevaluation of beliefs and values once abided by as sacrosanct. Public perception, jaded by catastrophic wars and domestic unrest, began to detect the hypocrisy of Western cultural traditions. What we had been taught to believe were the cornerstones of civilization; universal moral truths, science and technology as beneficial, and humanity's natural goodness didn't hold up in the harsh light of recent experience. Aware of this, people slowly shrugged off the culture that perpetuated these half–truths and searched for an alternative. This marked a turning point. Over the last fifty years, as modern thought died a protracted death, a postmodern consciousness arose in the masses.

Table–1 highlights the key themes and conditions of each period. It compares and contrasts differences between modernism and postmodernism. An earlier version of this chart appeared in my first book. The ideas presented in Table–1 , however, have been revised and expanded. Postmodern thought is complex enough that scholars like Henry Giroux, William Tierney, and David Kellner have devoted hundreds of books, including an earlier work of my own, to plumbing its depths. What I present here is merely an introduction to its primary themes and concepts. For even though academics, artists and the literati have used the term to explain trends in their fields of endeavor, many men and women beyond the academic community still lack a general sense of what postmodernism entails. Table–1 is for them.

Simplified, modernism and postmodernism capture distinctive periods in cultural history. They are mainly differentiated by the points of reference people use to construct meaning out of the world around them. Because one preceded the other in time, they cannot help but be linked. However, the fact that modernism unwittingly sired postmodernism is as far as the resemblance goes. Each as a *cultural frame of reference*, for that is really what they are, possesses its own original character. Our private experiences as well as those interactions with other people and our environment, are tinged by the distinct lens each places over our eyes. Respectively, each of these filters brings along with it a mindset enabling one to understand his or her environment.

Appreciating the differences in these perceptual prisms is critical. Most people over thirty–five today grew up with a modernist worldview. On the other end, anyone of student age (approx. age 5 to 22) today approaches the world and processes matter from a postmodern perspective. On its own, this can explain the discrepancies of views between parents and children, not to mention teachers and students. In the past, we often shrugged off this rift as a 'generation gap'. Problems in communication between generations, however, are actually prompted by opposing orientations to culture as well as age.

Postmodernism's rising star also explains much of the unbridgeable difference between classic models of culture and youth culture. Psychological and ideological gulfs between parents and teens on the verge of adulthood have always existed. Adolescence perennially serves as a time of severing filial ties, exploring the world, rejecting the creeds of teachers and parents, and developing one's own values, however naïve and untested, rather than those imparted. Usually this rebellious period culminates with a wistful understanding on the young adult's part that the collective views, ideas, and ethics of mainstream society do indeed possess value. Oats are sown, barriers broken, but eventually the wayward son or daughter returns to the fold, newly aware that social and cultural expectations serve a purpose. Until now, such was the pattern. On becoming an adult and gaining entry to that world, certain attitudes and behaviors had to be adopted for a person to be functional in society as well as literate culturally. Postmodernism altered that.

Absolutes and truths parents once taught their children have been deconstructed, dismembered, despoiled. Promoted by a media bent on exploiting them commercially, youth revel in today's chaotic for–entertainment–purposes–only variety of culture. Libraries or the Web, piano lessons or MTV, church doctrines or self–help fads, out–of–touch parents or hip–to–the scene peers—it isn't much of a contest. The old order was razed and with it the bedrock of existing culture. Ethics, philosophy, and history held in common—these cornerstones of Western civilization culture ossified rapidly during the information age. Intellectual cultivation, spiritual quests, and higher artistic endeavors are utterly alien to the postmodern reality youth live in. Dexterity with a computer mouse, staying tuned into and knowledgeable about the latest television shows or movie blockbusters, fluency in the language, fashions, and word of the street as conveyed by media representations—these are the real coins of the realm in contemporary society. So divergent are these orientations to culture; modern versus postmodern, or traditional versus youthful, reconciling them appears almost a hopeless task. With the media and its corporate sponsors now purveying culture, and them squarely in the corner of youth, there is slight reason to think adolescents will ever return to modernist, mainstream, adult models of culture.

In addition to the data shown in Table–1, disparities among modern and postmodern philosophies also account for the basic problems facing education today. At its unchallenged peak, modernism endorsed a curriculum of reading, writing, and arithmetic, making the task of academicians simple. As long as they adhered to this fundamental formula, students acquired the knowledge necessary to become productive members of society. Postmodernism, on the other hand, as a new scheme of thought that gradually rooted itself in America's social psychology, inspired deviation from these "three R's". To a large degree, it pushed the focus of education toward those politically correct, previously esoteric regions of multicultural studies, gender relations, and racial and ethnic empowerment. In the process, it undermined

Table-1
MODERN VS. POST MODERN MOTIFS

	Modernism	Post Modernism
Organization	Top–down, herarchical, power–centralized	Leveled, relationship/systems based power–decentralized
Culture	Universal truths, elevation of reason metanarratives (Great Books) speaking for all	Cultural relativism, elevation of desire, disparate texts; interpretations, speaking for individuals/groups
Society	Assimilation, mainstreaming of difference, nuclear family, marriage	Fragmentation, multicultural expression, single–parent family, cohabitation
Psychology	Authentic "Self," personality as biologically disposed	De–centered ego, personality as social construction
Education	Goals of social reproduction, cultural transmission	Goals of individual/group empowerment, cognitive differentiation
Reality	Known, fixed, ordered	Uncertain, fluctuating, chaotic
Art	Classical forms, styles, "schools", (Renaissance, Baroque, Impressionist)	Arbitrary, formless, (Abstract, Expressionist, "Performance Art")
Economy	Mass production, manual labor, factories	Service/information, mental indention, "business without walls(e–commence)"

curricular rigor and teacher authority. As movement dedicated to reclaiming the voices of minorities and other oppressed groups, including students, (Awkward, 1995), it realigned school politics away from administrators and teachers and leveraged the balance of power in favor of youth. Along with education, other social institutions, primarily the family, were irrevocably changed with the transition from modern to postmodern eras. The consequences set in motion by this cultural adaptation deserve a closer look.

If social reality as we've known it has been recreated, so too have the borders of individual identity. Determining how much of personality is inherently ours versus how much is incorporated from our surroundings becomes increasingly hard given the "technologies of social saturation" that rule over contemporary life. Kenneth Gergen, author of perhaps the most insightful work on identity formation in postmodern times, *The Saturated Self* (1991), argues that social saturation decides who we are and what we become these days. As he explains, "…we are now bombarded with ever–increasing intensity by the images and actions of others; our range of social participation is expanding exponentially. As we absorb the views, values, and visions of others, and live out the multiple plots in which we are enmeshed, we enter a postmodern consciousness." (p. 15) Individuality, then, as social scientists once predicted it developed and differentiated, has metamorphosed into something altogether unfamiliar. If this phenomenon of 'social saturation' hampers the normal development of a personal awareness, Gergen believes that that over time, it literally "erases" individualized personality, substituting in its stead a multiphrenic self—or amalgamation of partial identities a person absorbs through this a lifetime of exposure to social saturation.

For youth, whose adolescent years are consumed by the search for identity, this bodes an especially prickly rite of passage and one bound to increase inner confusion as they seek to establish an individuality purely their own.

THE MEANING OF CULTURE: PAST AND PRESENT

Now equipped with a sense of where we have come from, let us move on to cultural concerns in contemporary America. Since this book raises issues of culture on virtually every page, there is a need to clarify this concept and how it applies to this narrative. On its own, volumes have been penned by history's most lucid thinkers on its origins, permutations, and purposes. This book has no intention of competing with those epic works. Here, we have more limited aims. Our attention must be directed toward what is commonly known as popular culture. Building on the previous history and the perspective it enabled, the time is right to narrow our field of vision and take a closer look at United States culture at the advent of the 21st century.

Like language, the currency of all societies, the meaning of culture evolved considerably over time, varying widely across peoples, places, and periods. A time–traveller assigned to investigate this issue for us, for instance, would collect some very different interpretations of the term if he stopped at random intervals and questioned an adolesecent, say, a high school or university–level student of that specific period.

Suspending our disbelief for the next few moments for the sake of this illustration, assume he went back to Italy of the late Middle ages and stopped a blue–robed seminarian (student) on his way to lecture at the church–sanctioned University of Milan. Queried about culture, this thirty–something man, seminarians were often in their late 20's or 30's, would likely extol the moral dicta of the Bible, the primacy of Catholicism and the philosophy contained in Aquinas' *Summa Theologica*. If pressed on these other matters, he would undoubtedly wish his province'divinely–appointed monarch and feudal lords long lives, and as concerned aesthetics, praise the beauty of Greco–Roman art and architecture. These, our seminarian, might conclude, comprised the basis of medieval culture.

Satisfied, our wayfarer hopped back into his time capsule and hurtled forward through the ages to Weimar Republic Germany of the 1920's. There, a vastly different conception of culture prevailed. The reply given to him by a *realschule* student who narrowly missed conscription in the Great War, would be original in its substance and nuance. Cynical, at first, once this student consented to talk to our interviewer, he might mention several axes of modern culture: in literature, Goethe; in music, Wagner; and in art, the Flemish school of

Rembrandt and Reubens as opposed to those untutored schools of impressionism or come–lately cubism. Religion, dialectically proven to be the opiate of the masses, would have had lost much of its social relevance. But, he would inform our traveller, those who still practiced it enjoyed a more refined and earthly dogma thanks to Luther and other Reformation leaders. This student might see politics instead of faith as the anchor of culture and speak about the inevitability of Marxist revolution or liberal national socialism. Another part of modern culture, according to this student, revolved around scientific research (in sociology and genetics) and technical progress (in transportation and factory automation). If asked, this gymnasium lad would likely voice skepticism about any cultural pursuit not originating in Germany which he and others his age felt led the world in this area.

Intrigued by the contrast in these statements during his two stops, our voyager returns to his vehicle and whizzes forward to 2000. Alighting in New York and seeking one last interview, he disembarks his incredible machine and stops a girl of seven–or–eighteen walking across Times Square. What description might she offer? After shooting the traveller a suspicious look and resisting her initial impulse to flee from the stranger daring to speak to her, this girl surprises the interviewer by saying that she couldn't really define culture. It changed too quickly and what was 'in' one day might be 'out' the next. Scratching her head, she might ask for clarification and after getting it, reformulate his inquiry in a manner different from her predecessors in the past. Thinking it over for a few moments, she assumes the traveller's interrogative must be about *popular culture.* High cultural forms may not even be familiar to her apart from those buildings called the Guggenheim and the Metropolitan Museum of Art she visited on grade–school field trips. Social institutions? Well, yes, they still existed but schools, churches, and even family life didn't exercise a whole lot of influence over pop culture. With this resolved, she would mention the media as the arbiter of culture and speak emphatically about its power to shape ideas, attitudes, and values, and point a finger at the Panasonic mega–

screen raining images down upon fellow passersby in Times Square. The traveller might notice her temperament swing as she first talks excitedly about the hip–hop scene but then turn sullen as decries the violence in America as well as the out–of–touch bureaucrats in Washington. Of course, this student would be quick to add that she liked to forget about it all in a dozen forms of diversion, from the game arcade, to satellite TV, to cruising the Web to calling friends on her cellular phone. Yes, that about sums up culture these days, the girl tells our researcher as her beeper buzzes, she checks the message, and bids him a hasty goodbye.

If nothing else, it would become crystal clear to the traveller (and us) that not only did this final opinion differ completely from the others but that prior understandings of culture had no utility in the present. The young denizen of New York didn't view culture as intellectual, political, social, or religious legacies. She *imagined* culture to be movies and television shows, changing fashions, music and computers, snippets and soundbytes, icons and images. In her mind, she perceived culture to be entertainment rather than education. If the above illustration holds even a grain of truth, culture, as reckoned by youth today, has virtually no connection to its lineage. This represents a significant split from the past, one that should alarm us. It also reflects an irreconcilable schism between modernism, when knowledge, art and tradition were preserved as valued inheritances versus postmodernism, where such things have been brushed aside as relics and culture reduced to a choice of entertainment options.

On the other hand, the one constant among all three definitions given to our investigator, was a common belief that culture serves as a platform on which social unity can be built. Therein lies both the promise and peril of culture. In ideal circumstances, it joins individuals together under the aegis of a common reality. Personal differences, views, and agendas are sacrificed in the quest for solidarity. Improperly manipulated by pernicious people or circumstances, however, which there is ample historical evidence of, culture can serve as a instrument of widespread escapism, delusion, at its extreme, social pathology and even genocide.

Changing Characteristics of Culture

Webster's II New College Dictionary 1995 defined *culture* as "1. The totality of socially transmitted behavior patterns, arts, beliefs, institutions, and all other products of human thought typical of a population or community at a given time. 2. A style of social and artistic expression peculiar to a class or society. 3. Intellectual and artistic creativity. 4. The act of developing the social, moral, and intellectual faculties through education." These segmentations cover those areas we have already associated with traditional notions of culture. It's also worth noting that Webster's denotation clearly displays a *modernist* bent. It fairly drips with erudition. Reading it, one can almost picture a periwigged Jefferson drafting the Constitution, Mozart with baton in hand conducting the Salzburg symphony, or Monet blending pigments on a palette in his garden as he paints *Water Lilies*.

For something suited to present times, let us consider a more contemporary interpretation of culture, one originally articulated in my first book. It was derived from the work of renowned thinkers such as Peter McLaren, and Jurgen Habermas. As I proposed then, "'Culture' denotes the representation of a specific social experience and *epistemology*, or way of making meaning, in time." (1997, p. 34). Excerpting further, culture can be understood through a "preferred set" of behaviors, attitudes, points of reference, and shared language that permits a population to develop a shared sense of self–awareness. At the same time it galvanizes a group of people under a common standard, it displays an "opaqueness" that those outside its reach have difficulty breaching (e.g. the generation gap between kids and parents). Therefore, "culture may be summarized as the realization of a collective identity and communality of expression that binds persons together."

Apply the parts of this definition to the United States and you can see how neatly they fit. Beginning with culture's most important code, language, we adapted the King's English into a dozen or more regional dialects laden with slang and idiom, any one of which could well be impenetrable to a British, Irish, or Scottish national even though English happens to be their mother tongue as well. Along with language, perspective is another essence of culture addressed in my earlier definition. Our view of the world is perhaps skewed more heavily any other people by what we are able to visualize, i.e., images, film footage, and pictographs, as opposed to what we read, discuss or debate. This is a byproduct of living in an age where television and computer screens dominate every room and ongoing intellectual self–improvement has become a hopelessly archaic practice. Our tastes in food, fashion and entertainment arise from New York, Miami or Los Angeles and supply us with common ground for recreation and socializing. Behaviorally, we developed an unusual set of social graces that would elude non–Americans—it may be rude to stare in public but if a man leers at our wife or girlfriend it's okay to challenge his behavior or, if forced, even brawl to protect her honor. Nonverbal gestures like a palms–up sweep of the hand invites the person coming after you to go first through a door, while others, such as the extending of a middle finger while driving on the highway, can get you killed. In another country, these identical gestures may be interpreted exactly the opposite, yet here they are widely used and understood in a specific approach to living called American culture.

All these items speak to the knowledge required to get along personally and socially. Culture, as it now stands, transcends its traditional definition and former borders. It has been transformed from an abstraction into a practical instrument which lets us appraise, organize, and comprehend our surroundings and each other. Going one step further, popular culture, as it traverses individual differences, translates into a guidebook for social acceptance and survival

A last word on the reinvention of culture into its popular forte is provided by Neil Postman in his *Amusing Ourselves to Death: Public Discourse in the Age of Show Business*. Postman believes that culture is nothing more than the collection of public discussions or 'conversations' common to a society at any given time as they speak to issues of politics, art, education, religion, etc. For him, the term 'conversation' is metaphoric. Postman uses it to "…refer not only to speech but to all techniques and technologies that permit people of a particular culture to exchange messages. In this sense, all culture is a conversation, or more precisely, a corporation of conversations." (1985, 6). Communication surfaces in his telling as indispensable to the exchange of ideas upon which culture is built, but only insofar as the 'techniques and technologies' that enable it to occur. This is a point worth remembering and one which will be revisited ahead.

In a world where yesterday's maxims are today's falsehoods, where social boundaries are constantly being re–drawn, and the earth continually shifts beneath our feet, it goes without saying that culture has become a chameleon, altering its colors to match the moods of the time. If adults have trouble keeping up with these changes, youth don't suffer from the same deficiency and seem to thrive on its unpredictability.

A New Anatomy of Knowledge and Rise of Popular Culture

Whether clinging to past or adhering to present interpretations, culture rests on foundation of knowledge. When this body of knowledge is challenged, as happened with postmodernism's attack on tradition, the cultural scaffolding towering over it cannot help but sway in different directions too. In *The Roar of the Crowd*, Michael O'Neill says pioneering technology brought with it a 'new anatomy of knowledge':

> "Rapidly advancing technology has extended the range of public knowledge across the barriers of space, illiteracy, and national sovereignty to reach virtually all of the inhabited earth. The sheer volume of information now crashing down on the human mind is staggering. Equally significant, much of the information is being delivered in an *oral–visual* form that breaks the monopoly of the world's literate classes. Thanks to television, the daily experiences

of mankind are brought down from the skies to city and village alike, to peasant and mandarin and with an emotional intensity words cannot match. The eyes of countless millions are opened to an outside world they have never seen, and their emotional responses are merged by rapid communication into networks of collective opinion." (p.23)

Precisely who these 'widening rings of informed and active publics' happen to be leaves little guesswork. Versed and skilled in the variety of communications media, youth are embracing this new schematic of knowledge far faster than adults. Information made available through the mass communications media has, for all practical purposes, put education out of business. Formal schooling, teaching and academic pursuits have rapidly become anachronisms on the verge of extinction. All an individual has to do now is flip on their television or log on to a racing information superhighway to find out what they need to know. *Cultural literacy* now depends on access to and familiarity with this planetary matrix of information, which is unstructured, undisciplined, and unlimited. And, if older Americans remain reticent, youth excel in navigating their way through this exponentially expanding universe of data.

This same revolution in interlinking systems of communication also hastened the *standardization* of culture. As technology extends its reach even farther, indications are that popular culture American–style soon go global. Again, citing O'Neill,

> "Mass societies, dense and highly interactive human conglomerates made possible by mass media, are spreading rapidly from the advanced Industrial nations to other countries around the world…As the speed of communication rises, social distance shrinks and ever larger numbers of people, widely separated by space, are drawn into common experiences. Human interactions increase exponentially in a whirl of mass media, mass marketing, mass consumerism and mass culture." (24)

O' Neill is not alone among scholars in predicting the eventual glo-balization of culture. In fact, it's already underway. What really begs our interest is the issue of whose culture it is that will bring us to the doorstep of a world society. Since the United States leads the world in developing cutting–edge technologies, and it is our know–how being exported throughout the world, it follows that our culture will be car-ried over these billions of fiber optic threads. Furthermore, since Amer-ican culture has become synonomous with popular culture, and pop culture responds to the whims of youth, it will likely be our children who indirectly preside over this coming global community. Signs of its progress are everywhere.

Stand on a street corner in downtown Athens, like I recently did, Singapore, or Rio de Janeiro, and within eyesight crowd signs advertis-ing Coca Cola, shops promoting Hollywood's latest blockbuster on a score of television screens in their windows, and teenagers strolling by wearing the baggy pants, FUBU jackets, Yankees baseball caps, and bronze studs glistening in their lobes and lips. This vista, which for-merly characterized the urban landscape of the United States, has dis-persed throughout the rest of the world. Forget about the complaints you hear from France about Eurodisney, China about politically sub-versive chat rooms, or Iran about Western cultural pollution. Those doing the groaning are the authorities; middle–aged adults fearful of losing control as their own progeny hasten to join this international community.

The August 1999 issue of *National Geographic* dealt with this world–wide movement in its feature article on "Global Culture". Its authors, Joel Swerdlow and Erla Zwingle opened with an observation on the lightning–fast diffusion of media technology that started this trend. "Human societies have always mixed and changed, but goods, people, and ideas move farther and faster today, spreading an urban–oriented, technology–based culture around the globe in just a few gen-erations. Thanks to radio, television, and videos, this budding world culture reaches virtually everyone, even the world's nearly one billion illiterate people." Astonishingly, they add, while it "took television 13 years to acquire 50 million users; the Internet took only five." (p. 12).

The force propelling this fusion of cultures is youth. "The critical mass of teenagers—800 million in the world, the most there have ever been—with time and money to spend is one of the powerful engines of merging global cultures." If parents in foreign lands still consider it making a pact with the devil, their kids have embraced American pop culture without so much as a backward glance. Adolescents in these countries have made it clear that the future they envision includes malls, McDonalds, and MTV. Will posterity end up living in what some have bemoaned as the future "McWorld"? Doubtful things will get that far, but it's safe to say that an American accent on this global culture will be discernible for decades to come. And the children shall lead it.

The implications of this last statement resonate. As the world imports our chaotic creed of culture, it unwittingly accepts our morality with all its flaws and inconsistencies. Assuming American pop culture eventually pervades the planet, will other peoples, bushmen to technological, be any better prepared to handle its noxious side effects? Only time will tell. But just as we could no longer deny a problem existed in society after the Columbine massacre, those seeds at which technology has scattered to remote reaches of the earth may not bear the fruit expected.

Implications

Commencing with social changes of the sixties and early seventies, America permanently inclined toward being a culture of the young. Interestingly, this unrest was much more serious and issue–oriented at the start. Terminating a war costing thousands of young lives as well as gaining equality for women and minorities lay at heart of the student cries for social reform. In subsequent years, however, it's utopian edge gradually dulled by the disco–drug craze and yuppie materialism, then faded altogether as its original leaders succumbed to middle age. Nonetheless, though its ideology changed, pop culture remained a powerful vehicle for adolescent expression as its current incarnation beautifully demonstrates. Today youth act out their rebellious impulses in current forms; with rap music, 'homeboy' talk and dress, and a rehearsed apathy that drive adults crazy.

Yet what renders popular culture more influential than ever before is its inescapability. The technologies of social saturation noted by Gergen have seen to it that nary a nook or cranny survived where the sounds of a radio, the pictures of a television, the interactive experience of a computer, do not beckon to us. Practically speaking, there are few sanctuaries from its long arms. If these media once informed us, now they rule us. Whether at work, school, or home, Americans undertake very few activities that don't require engaging these contraptions. Once we flip the "on" switch of any of these devices, we establish a link to a media carnival that keeps us mesmerized. Remove them from our lives, and we're groping in the darkness for instruction, guidance, and entertainment. Sitting together around the table talking with each other instead of retiring to individual rooms where each family member indulges in their preference—Sega games, home theaters with Dolby surround–sound, or on–line chatting, these are tableaus that should shame us. Our dependence on technological overload to get us through the day effectively destroyed family life at a time when parents and children alike could benefit from its support.

Darkening an already bleak outlook, adolescents possess far more expertise manipulating these electronic tools than any adult trying to limit their access. A study released in November 1999 by the Kaiser Family Foundation, a California–based philanthropy, showed the average American child spends an average of 38 hours per week using 'several forms of media outside of school.' This translates into nearly *5.5 hours daily*, the majority of which is unsupervised.

In terms of education, the vulnerability of young minds to the pounding cadence of pop culture poses serious problems. It does more than drown students in a sea of discordant and paradoxical messages.

For all intents and purposes, pop culture is anti–intellectual. Not so subtly, it whispers to youth that it is uncool to study or be smart. Spun from a postmodern fiber that deprecates learning, pop culture actively undermines a student's natural curiosity. Through recurrent media reinforcement, it dampens any desire to learn through inquiring, examining, and reflecting. Instead, popular culture implores kids not to burden their minds with the unnecessary work of thinking when all they'll ever really need to know can be vicariously absorbed from television or other informational technologies.

<u>Summary</u>

In sum, our history and culture coalesce to configure the world we know. They are inseparable and cannot be understood apart from the other. A ripple in one provokes a wave in the other. As we have seen, historical events of the 20th century brought about the transformation of American culture. In the United States, social and technological developments took on an unprecedented character and brought about a set of peculiar cultural conditions academics call postmodernism. It is in this postmodern experience that Americans living today are situated.

The interplay between these things are important to understand as they shaped the individual. As society and culture changed, so did the psychology of the person. Younger persons living today see the world in very different terms than preceding generations. Accepted views, social mores and treasured traditions, may not have relevance to their current existence. They comprehend only that which they experienced early on and continued to believe in as they matured. From what we have seen, adults aren't the primary source of their inspiration any more.

We are now ready to begin dealing with concrete facts and hard truths rather than historical analyses. Knowledgeable about how we arrived at our present place in history, we have been prepared to begin our investigation of the current realities exerting pressure on American youth.

3

Social Realities and Youth

○ ○
"As a 'social being, the individual is little more than a…particular embodiment of collective life and consciousness; his ideas, desires, interests and experiences are never properly or exclusively his own, but always held in common with others."

——_Elizabeth Bannet_

Human beings are a product of socialization. Experiences, events and expectations, personal and social, converge to shape the person we become. If the genes we inherit provide the foundation for intelligence and personality, environment still exerts a measurable impact on individual growth. In her best–selling if pedestrian book, _It Takes A Village_, Hillary Clinton underscored the role of outside influences on child development, borrowing ancedotes from her own youth.

> "Parents bear the first and primary responsibility for their sons and daughters…But I was also blessed with caring neighbors, attentive doctors, challenging public schools, safe streets, and an economy that supported my father's job. Much of my family's good fortune was beyond my parent's control, but not beyond the control of other adults whose actions affected my life.
>
> Children exist in the world as well as in the family. From the moment they are born, they depend on a host of other "grown–

ups"—grandparents, neighbors, teachers, ministers, employers, political leaders, and untold others who touch their lives directly and indirectly." (p 11)

This citation stresses the premise of Clinton's book—entire communities have a stake in rearing a child. We can extend this to mean that while parents may be the dominant factor, other people and things in our surroundings clearly impact on forming minds. Although Clinton exhibits a knack for oversimplifying, her ideas are generally sound. One of the more luminous among them appears in a later passage. Although she extols the virtues of community, she recognizes the problem that accompanies it. "The horizons of the contemporary village extend well beyond the town line…we are exposed to vast numbers of other people and influences through radio, television, newspapers, books, movies, computers…Technology connects us to this impersonal global village it had created." (p.13) Unfortunately, "dehumanizing" and "inhospitable" as it may be, this emerging techno–village is all we have to work with.

If contacts with the environment help to define our personalities and the social beings we become, what forces assume the lead in this formative process? Traditionally, there have been three institutions charged with this critical task—family, churches, and schools. As we've seen, however, the lay of the modern landscape is different than it used to be and of those entities outside a person which make a lasting mark, churches have tumbled from this triumvirate. Dwindling attendance, only 34% of 13–17 year olds attend church services weekly (*New York Times/CBS News* Teen Survey, 1999, p.24), and a widening cultural aversion to the strictures of religious dogma confirm this fall. If conservative critics, the Christian Coalition, or even the lobbying arms of secular parenting groups are to be believed, the constant attacks on organized religion by the entertainment industry seem to have exacted a toll.

With churches largely removed from social scene, two remaining agencies that impinge upon child development are families and schools. Their role in the socialization process will be examined closely in the coming paragraphs. Added into this formula, however, is a new variable, one that must be taken into account in any current analysis. Rounding out the third spot in the triumvirate once held by churches, an alternative movement generating enthusiasm of quasi–religious proportions has surfaced. Nondenominational, it has many millions of adherents and inspires tremendous fervor among its youngest followers. Popular culture, in its glittering vestments, new, hip mythology, and surprising power to mesmerize, fills the spiritual void. In fact, a good portion of postmodern morality has risen out of its motifs, creeds, and icons. With digital arms extending 'virtually' everywhere, pop culture has surpassed home and school as the single most powerful influence on the socialization of American youth.

In this chapter, we will explore the impact of these three forces on adolescents. To begin, a glimpse of contemporary family life will take place to illuminate the injuries dysfunctional family structures inflict on many children. Next, we will consider the school experience in molding tender personalities. Special attention will be paid to how decaying social conditions foisted expectations on learning institutions they were never designed to handle. Last, we will open a discussion on the ascendance of popular culture and its predominance in the lives of American youth.

I. THE HOME FRONT

Raging Economies and Surplus Wealth

Like Japan's economy of the 1980's, working residents of the United States enjoyed a period of unparalleled prosperity over the last few years. On February 1, 2000, the Department of Commerce announced this present expansion, starting in March of 1991 and failing to pause and catch its breath since, has become the longest ever in American history. Our information/service–driven economy is responsible for creating hundreds of thousands of new jobs annually and providing employees, in salaries, bonuses and pensions, generous compensation packages. Increasingly interconnected with stock exchanges around the globe, the American equities market, after a few hiccups caused by bouts with the Asian financial flu during 1997–98, rocketed upward over the last few years and sparked a sizzling economy whose growth limits are still unknown.

During the last half of the 1990's, we witnessed a period of phenomenal mercantile expansion. The Gross Domestic Product (GDP), foolproof barometer of our nations's economic output, leapt nearly two trillion dollars during the last five years of the decade (1994–99) to a whopping figure of $9,072,700,000,000. This is ten times the amount it was in 1969 (Bureau of Economic Analysis, U.S. Dept. of Commerce home page) In concert, the stock market's Dow Jones Industrial Average hit record heights almost weekly from 1998–2000, as it roared past the 9–, 10–and 11,000 point plateaus. The technology–loaded NASDAQ fared better still, setting almost daily records over the last six weeks of 1999, generating unheard of wealth among people who invested even small sums. A report released in the fall of 1999 by the Census Bureau revealed that personal income, not unexpectedly, also rose to all–time highs. In the United States, the median income surged to $38,000 per household, eclipsing the previous record set in 1989. This same report indicated that a million fewer Americans were living below the federal poverty line and that the percentage of people living under this line dropped to its lowest since 1979. While noting a growing disparity between the richest and poorest citizens, the boom on Wall Street has been credited for fueling higher earnings *among all Americans*, with the top quintile seeing this rate jump by 15% between 1988 and 1998 (McCaffrey, 2000). Consider the implications.

Socially, wealth of this kind creates a spiritual vacuum. America's history contains marquee memories of it. Fading morality, decadent jazz music, and riotous underground speakeasies inspired by Prohibition in the 'Roaring 20's' before buying stock on the margins led to the

1929 crash offers a case in point. F. Scott Fitzgerald whimsically depicted the hedonism of this era in his classic, *The Great Gatsby*, and though fashions have changed lifestyles aren't really so different now. More recently, it's become common to look back with disdain on the 1980's as a decade of insatiable greed. Then, it was restricted to a handful of corporate raiders or junk bond kings and their avaricious disciples who ruled the financial world until insider trading and other illegal dealings prosecuted by the authorities ended their reign. Unlike both these past periods, however, wealth is spread much more evenly today. The meteoric rise of technology stocks Microsoft, Yahoo! or Amazon.Com also made overnight "dot.com" millionaires out of many first–time and even twenty–something investors.

Eventually, this U.S. bubble economy, reminiscent of Japan's before it imploded under the collapse of several prominent banks, will burst. The first cracks appeared at the time of this writing in the winter of 2001. Be it after the stock market falls back to reality or because sustaining economic expansion at the pace seen in the last half of the 1990's is simply impossible as Federal Reserve Chairman Alan Greenspan repeatedly warned in Congressional hearings. Yet, in itself, the continuing health of the economy does not really concern us here. Instead, its what these heady financial times bred that begs consideration.

First, with labor demand outpacing supply, unemployment is at its lowest levels in a generation, making it easy for fathers and mothers to find and keep good–paying positions. According to the U.S. government, the jobless rate has plummeted to its lowest point since 1970. If they're working in record numbers, that means the proportion of adults away from home for long hours during the day is also at an all–time peak. So who is providing supervision for their children?

Secondly, teens who choose to work also have their pick of part–time jobs as the Help Wanted signs peppering the windows of almost every fast–food restaurant or strip mall store show us, with hourly pay often starting at $10 or more. If they don't want to hold down a job to earn spending money, it doesn't really matter. Households are wealthier today than ever before as the Census data showed. In spite of rising interest rates, new home constructions are still somehow outpacing those of 1999. If families find themselves with greater disposable income, so too, do their younger members. Kids have the cash to purchase items that prior generations couldn't. Computers, compact disc players, clothing, jewelry, even cars, are not beyond their reach with the backing of parents.

Unfortunately, while younger individuals get to share in its rewards, they seldom put in the labor or discipline it took to earn this surplus. This presages a dangerous pattern. Minus the hours of exertion it took to earn it, teenagers will struggle to understand the value of money. Failing to appreciate this, spending becomes wanton. A false illusion is created. With their parents spending more time away from home, their children are free to enjoy significant purchasing power and indulge their assorted tastes with little interference. This freedom can have troubling repercussions.

Relatively rich, adolescents have been given no reason to think responsibly. They have begun to behave recklessly because the prospect of social and financial restitution for any misdeeds has been eliminated. Enough cash can buy you out of a world of legal trouble as several high profile political investigations or celebrity trials have regularly shown the public. Aware that household wealth empowers them, today's youth feel few restraints on personal liberty. Flush with cash from parents *in absentia*, overwhelmed by media messages encouraging them to instantly gratify their assorted wants, and with too much unsupervised time on their hands, their ability to resist the overtures of a popular culture that equates happiness with materialism has suffered a serious setback.

Intergenerational Alienation and Disintegrating Families

Two integral components of human development are biological inheritance (nature) and early environmental experiences (nurture). In theory, genes determine native intelligence but the rich assortment of stimuli available throughout childhood as it is mediated by parents and others make a major contribution to the formation of the individual. Just as parents are responsible for supplying the necessary biological material, they also assume a pivotal part in the emotional, social, and cultural education of their progeny. If Locke's notion of the mind is accurate, *tabula rasa*—an empty tablet in need of imprinting—this influence begins at birth and lasts throughout adolescence, diminishing gradually with each passing year. Among the many roles parents juggle during these intervening fifteen to twenty years are provider and pro-tector and, as the child matures, the repertoire widens to include teacher, mentor, and at one time, disciplinarian.

The constant during these years, whether influence is waxing or waning, is parental engagement. As countless studies indicate, if it occurred, a child will grow up happier, healthier and better–adjusted. If it isn't, the likelihood of behavioral problems occurring as the child ages increases. Few would quarrel with this logic. But what happens when we try to export these conventional views of the family to post-modern society? Do they still apply? Conditions today are a far cry from what they were twenty or thirty years ago.

Experts tell us over and over that kids and parents are "emotionally disconnected." In his book *Real Boys: Rescuing our Sons from the Myths of Boyhood*, Harvard psychologist William Pollack studied this estrangement in its impact on males. Although he identifies several causes; career–consumed adults too tired to parent, pre–and teen boys responding to this apathy with emotional detachment and resorting to desperate measures (substance abuse, sex, violence) in seeking peer acceptance and companionship, even our sons' desire to find greater meaning in their lives, all these sources spring from the same cultural fountain. When a society places greater emphasis on occupational and material success than on the welfare of human beings, consequences are sure to arise. Never shown how to deal appropriately with intense feel-ings nor having experienced them towards other, young males borrowed a page from pop culture mythology and adopted anti–social methods of channeling the rage collecting inside them. Hence Pollock's hypothesis on youth violence: when boys don't cry tears, they cry bullets. Of course, parents don't need the 'experts' to tell us that which we already know. Even those who try to exert a guiding presence in their kid's lives wonder about their success. Paul Daugherty, an award–winning columnist for *The Cincinnati Enquirer,* and father, provides a poignant glimpse into this fragile relationship.

"The Kid Down the Hall will be 13 in a week. We've already fought the clothes war (please pull up your pants over your butt), the movie war (no Saving Private Ryan) and the music war. We've put the parental controls on the computer.

We've done all that and yet I know there's a part of him we'll never reach. I used to think that was OK, that everyone was entitled to a private life, even a teenager. But since Colorado (Columbine), I'm not so sure.

Teenagers are the same as always. They live to defy.

The boy whose hand you held at the school bus stop now regards you as an alien."

Regret rises to the surface in this passage. Sons and daughters may live with us in the same house but have become strangers somewhere along the way. The dynamics of families today are not what they once were. Many feel it. A handful have the courage to admit it. Few are those who know how to remedy it. Lifelong commitments to each other and children have come under siege as marriages end and families routinely break apart. The survival of marriage as a viable institution cannot be taken for granted. Whether anchoring a family or symbolizing the emotional bond between two loving adults, marriage as the cornerstone of family structure has suffered the slings and arrows of a troubling age.

A comprehensive report issued by the Rutgers University National Marriage Project in 1999 sketched a stark profile of marriage and the domicile. Researchers found the nation's marriage rate fell by 43% since 1960, its "lowest point in recorded history." This unprecedented rate, in tandem with exploding divorce figures, has resulted in what the study authors called a "dramatically altered attitude toward one of society's most fundamental institutions." Proof of this arises in the growing numbers of young adults, especially females, who express doubt about finding a lasting marriage partner and are therefore "more accepting of alternatives to marriage, including single parenthood and living together outside of marriage." Reported in a *USA Today* commentary, the National Center for Health Statistics revealed that "...births to unwed mothers are at an all time high. The mothers of almost a third of the 3.94 million babies born in 1998 were single women." (Holmes, 2000).

This revisionist attitude toward marriage and traditional family is not restricted to young, unmarried adults, if the data can be trusted. These 'alternatives' are already being practiced today in record–high numbers. "In the post–World War II generation, 80 percent of children grew up in a family with two biological parents. That number since has dropped to 60 percent." If current trends hold, one could safely hypothesize that this figure will continue to decline. A related news brief running in *USA Today* said by the early 1990's, *more than half* of the first children born to young women were conceived outside of marriage, a rate nearly three times that of the 1930's. Moving ahead to the next stop on this unfortunate slide, a study coordinated by the National Opinion Research Center at the University of Chicago reported in late 1999 that the percentage of U.S. households made up of married couples with children dipped from 45% in 1970 to 26% in 1998, confirming the results of the preceding studies.

In spite of our better judgement, fatherhood and the role of adult men in American families rests atop especially shaky ground. The Washington, D.C.–based National Fatherhood Initiative (www.fatherhood.org) reports that nearly *23 million children* do not live with their natural fathers for various reasons. With the growing preference for cohabitation instead of marriage, male partners in such arrangements, on the whole, feel less reluctance to leave when their female partners get pregnant. Turn on any news program and within a matter of minutes you're likely to hear yet another tragic tale from the 'deadbeat dad' wars.

Area papers have been running stories about James Brooks, a former professional football player who made millions during the years he played for the Cincinnati Bengals. Claiming financial destitution with his playing career ended, he now faces charges of being $100,000 in arrears on child support between the two women he fathered children with, neither of whom were his wives. This provincial story of shame pales in comparison to those of various NBA stars whose impregnate–then–deny–and–flee escapades involving up to four separate children were the hair–raising subject of a recent American Broadcasting Company's *20/20* news program.

Not a fraction of deadbeat dad stories are as sensational, but what they lack in media coverage they make up for in the indignation they provoke. The grassroots appeal of organizations stressing atonement for child neglect and advocating fatherly accountability, from the Nation Islam's Million Man March in 1997, to the conservative Christian Promise Keepers, are male–oriented movements reacting to the progressive disintegration of family life among all races and creeds in America. The runaway success of the books of Armin Brott, author of *Throwaway Dads* and other pro–paternal literature, challenges the lingering bias that men are incapable of parenting as well as women. Despite the fact that appalling numbers of men shirk their obligations as family heads, the logic that fathers are key to the healthy development of children seems so obvious that it barely needs to be supported by informed testimony: "It is well documented in social and psychological literature that children who come from families with psychologically involved fathers are cognitively more competent, have higher degrees of compassion for others, manifested fewer sex–stereotyped beliefs, and have a more solid internal locus of control." (S. Moradi, M.D.) Still, a recent *New York Times/CBS News* nation–wide telephone poll of 13 to 17 year–olds supports the contention that many teens reside in homes without both parents. One fifth of respondents (20%) indicated they did not live with a mother and father. If one happens to believe that both parents instill a sense of right and wrong in their children, the absence of so may father is distressing. While approximately 52% of all teens surveyed said it was primarily their parents who taught them these distinctions, a mere 7% identified their father as the 'most important' person in teaching them these values.

Tragically, fathers appear to be an endangered species. The real and perceived benefits of their presence in families continues to diminish along with two–parent homes and the incidence of marriage as a stabilizing factor in domestic life. Perhaps on an unconscious level, adolescents may even resent the adults in their lives for being part of a society that condoned the ruin of the family. Although a stretch, that could explain their greater anger, higher levels of aggression, and increasingly maladjusted reactions to social pressures.

Dilemmas of Day–Care Youth: Seeds are Planted Early

Although our primary concern lay with teens, it's necessary to start even earlier to comprehend the circumstances that shaped them on their path to young adulthood. As the data suggests, a snapshot of today's domicile would look strange to people who raised children a generation ago. Today, mothers tend not to stay at home contenting themselves with housework and child–rearing while dutiful fathers earn enough at the office to support a household. According to *Working Mother* magazine, in 1999, 70% of mothers worked outside the home, as contrasted with 30% in 1970. While one might interpret this trend to be a good thing; stimulating the economy and bringing more discretionary income into American homes, it infers a disturbing corollary. Over five million school–age children spend time as latchkey kids during a normal week. Strangers, even if adequately trained to do so, are raising millions of our kids.

If this is a healthy trend depends on one's point of view. If so, certain assumptions are being made about the qualification of those providing care that should not automatically be taken for granted. Apart from center managers, many front–line day care workers typically have limited educational backgrounds or skills. Many receive on–the–job training, know little about child development, not to mention basic first aid. To be employed, they simply undergo a cursory police background check. Does this one formal precondition qualify them as surrogate parents? What about their attitudes and values—traits which really end up affecting impressionable minds? Can we presume they are compatible with ours as the parents?

The intent here isn't to denigrate those working in this field, nor is it to alarm mothers and fathers utilizing such services. My stance is philosophical. Children absorb much of their personalities from adults close to them. Parents now compete for the minds and hearts of their own children with the adult caregivers whom they know little about but who nonetheless spend forty–plus hours a week talking to and playing with their kids. A further complication develops in the wake of our reliance on child care. In order to keep their productivity high and jobs safe, mothers and fathers are working longer hours away from home. In search of the good life, they are torn between earning enough to provide their children with the amenities and the sacrifice it takes to make enough money to achieve it.

Sixty–five percent of mothers with children under 6 are in the labor force, while 78% of women with kids between ages 6–17 work (*National School Boards Association* data, 1999). An unrelated study done by the Employment and Careers Institute at Cornell University detailed the first data set. Researchers found that nearly three–quarters of middle–income, working couples scaled back work commitments for the sake of their family. Respondents did this to resist the omnivorous 'demands of a greedy workplace'. The result is what the study authors coined a 'neotraditional' arrangement with the husband's *career* being the primary one while the wife settled for a lesser *job*. Yet neither actually stopped working. (My 'radical' proposal: let one or the other of the parents *stop working* to provide primary child care. That might mean having to scale back the family's standard of living a bit, however, and the idea of life without a new house, a new minivan, or the annual pilgrimage to Disneyworld is unacceptable.) Interestingly, such findings imply that while parents understand their children are being neglected, they make only the smallest accommodations in trying to right a sinking ship—i.e., mom will work a few hours less. Earning the income necessary to attain the high life comes at a price. The cost is guilt.

Aware that they aren't spending enough time at home raising their kids, parents allay their guilt by showering their sons and daughters with luxuries they never had. Janey turns sixteen, gets her driver's license and immediately asks for a car. On the first weekend he's at home after another whirlwind business trip, Dad runs out and buys her a brand new Volkswagen Beetle. Janey might not even work yet the car she drives, due to her father's desire to overcome the regret the feel for not being as big a part in Janey's life as he should be, turns out to be nicer than many adults. A survey of the parking lot of almost any suburban high school, with its likely high proportion of imported sedans, might validate this hypothesis. This theoretical example along with thousands of actual ones hint at a crisis. Themselves victims of a popular culture that puts instant personal gratification above all else, parents have confused *giving love with giving things*. They prefer demonstrating their affection with gifts. Cars, credit cards, trips—these are visible proof of their love and, well, less time–consuming than giving their kids the attention they deserve

Compounding one misjudgment with still another, the application of discipline, a concept now considered downright primitive, also prompts strong objections from many adults who should be constructively employing it. Just as parents have been told never to tell their children no, so too have they abrogated their right to set reasonable boundaries. Afraid of widening the estrangement, they accede to the stupidest pleas on everything from vacations to diet. "The kids (ages 8 and 12) ask for McDonald's Happy meals on Monday, Taco Bell on Wednesday, and Pizza Hut on Friday," my neighbor confided to me with a shrug of resignation. Nutrition didn't enter into her mind. The kids *expect* these concessions, so naturally they get them. Her husband is an environmental engineer–consultant whose work takes him away for two to three weeks at a time. So she rises at 7 am, dresses the kids and gets them off to school, shuttles off to work 8–4 every day, and enrolls both of them in an after school latchkey program until she can collect them at 6pm. Feeling she is letting them down by being away so much, she seeks redemption in their eyes by allowing them to decide what's for dinner.

Ironically, as concessions and commodities mount, the farther the parent–child relationship strays from normalcy. This pattern persists throughout childhood, frequently climaxing during the late teenage years. Thus, an illusion is propagated. We have all seen it in friends or acquaintances. "I gave my daughter a (three–week) trip to Europe for her seventeenth birthday." "My kids have both VISA cards and cell phones in case of an emergency." "I paid for my son's college tuition for six years." Each of these parents punctuate their proud claims with the same unspoken refrain:...*therefore, I'm a good parent.* A dichotomy has arisen between the soul of parenting and society's superficial perception of it. Showering an son or a daughter with money or gifts does not substitute for personal investment in their lives. Accolades for parenthood can't be purchased but earned over years of patching scraped knees, going to soccer games, or offering them a shoulder to cry on when their first crush ends. Yet studies show many mothers and fathers still trying to buy the affection of their offspring. One led by researchers at Ohio State University and published in the December, 1999 issue of *American Demographics* found the median (i.e., midpoint of the range) allowance a teen gets is $50 per week, though some reported receiving up to $200 a week, an amount which surprised even the research team.

Regrettably, a functioning yet utterly warped relationship between generations now exists. Rather than being based on mutual affection and interest, the relationship rests on *barter*. Kids play by the ridiculously loose rules parents pretend to set as long as their material needs are met when and where they want. In turn, parents ignore all but the most grievous infractions of these rules and reward this minimal level of obedience not with emotional attention but with almost any item that money can buy. By mid–to–late teens, the bizarre tale below shows what can happen when this unholy alliance reaches its full potential.

The 'Lost Children of Rockdale'–Parable of Postmodern Families

In the autumn of 1999, the Public Broadcasting System aired a special installment of its *Frontline* series called "The Lost Children of Rockdale County." It painted a frightful portrait of family dysfunction in an affluent Georgia community not far from Atlanta. Graphic, gritty, and hard–hitting, this documentary gave shocking glimpses into the perverted relationships of the postmodern family. Still troubled the morning after I watched the program, a fact–finding mission to the PBS home page gave me access to the transcripts and research used in the making of this program. Quoting directly from the introduction to it:

"'The Lost Children of Rockdale County' explores how a 1996 syphilis outbreak in a well–off Atlanta suburb affected over 200 teenagers and revealed their hidden lives, unknown to parents: group sex, binge drinking, drugs and violence. Some were as young as twelve and thirteen years old."

The 'unknown to parents' qualifier doesn't quite ring true. As the Rockdale story unfolds, evidence indicates that these parents may not have been so blameless in this affair. A few might have been misled by their children and the excuses they offered. Others however, elected not to know about what was happening because they either weren't around to notice or simply closed their eyes to it. Preoccupied with making money, taking luxury vacations, and living their own version of the good life away from their children characterized the majority of Rockdale adults. A pediatric psychiatrist asked by PBS to study the case commented that they were either "clueless or blatantly unconcerned" so as not to have to deal with this outrageous conduct.

A divorced mother profiled during the program talks airily about her dismay over her daughter's actions. She acknowledges that her career demands regular trips away from home for up to a week at a time, whereupon her daughter, aged 16 years, set up in a spacious mansion, lives alone except for friends who are welcome to spend the night. Still other mothers and fathers plead ignorance only to be implicated later during on–camera sessions with the interviewers. Perhaps the most memorable item caught on film was the tired indifference seeping through repeated claims of outrage. Resignation rather than disappointment or anger flavored their remarks. Yes, their children misbehaved. Inexcusable incidents occurred. The attitudes and actions of these wild teens certainly needed to be corrected. Thank goodness the authorities—teachers, public health officials, police—found out and put a stop to it. But, wringing their hands in despair, there was nothing they could have done to prevent it. Nowhere did a single parent in Rockdale admit to neglect or vow that things around the house were going to change. Rules, discipline, and punishment were concepts as remote to these adults as cosmic string theory is to the rest of us.

Interspersed with these clips of ineffectual parents, the producers included extensive interviews with the teens at the center of this scandal. Hardened beyond their years, they spoke candidly about sexual experimentation and substance abuse gone to unimaginable extremes. Weekend parties degenerated into orgies with the consent of all present. The viewer soon surmised that pharmaceuticals like crack cocaine, Ecstasy, and (the "date–rape" drug) Rohypnol flowed freely along with torrents of alcohol. Regardless of the drug cocktail used, participation in the debauchery was strictly voluntary. Girls slept with boys because they drove Mercedes or BMWs or came from the richest families and toniest neighborhoods. Boys sharing their girlfriends sexually with male friends on the same night because it was the cool thing to do—none of these depravations embarrassed them. Some of the tales they told were so sordid, like the teenage girl who willingly had intercourse with every boy at a party until she staggered from the bedroom bleeding vaginally and…that they are unfit to print here. Emotionally and physically scarred, this mismatched band of acquaintances broke the taboos of decent society with pornographic abandon. Like their parents, they too, seemed psychologically arrested and morally adrift. There were few burdened consciences. In fact, nurses reported that there was high–fiving and congratulatory back–slapping among the group of boys awaiting treatment for venereal disease in the local hospital. It appears as though the only mistake the teens believe they made was catching syphilis and thereby the scrutiny of the authorities.

One mother questioned about the promiscuity of her daughter who had multiple sex partners by age 15 made a pathetic admission. When asked who runs her children's lives, she replied "I guess they do up to a point…I think what it is, is we've lost control over our children. You can't spank them now or they'll turn you into the police." Probing further, the interviewer got this mother to concede that the balance of power has shifted in favor of the children, and her "…kids know that." One father regretted that he didn't spend as much time as he should have with his adolescent daughter. He wanted to give her the leeway to 'make some mistakes and learn from them', though in retrospect, he saw the folly of being too permissive for too long in order not to have to confront his daughter's walk on the wild side. Now the consequences had come back to haunt him.

Discussions with the teens confirmed that if choices about their conduct were being made, they were the ones making them. Sitting in a bedroom whose walls were littered with obscene graffiti, smoking cigarettes, faces covered in pancake make–up, sporting pierced tongues, ear lobes, and tattoos, three fourteen–year old girls talked about how distant they had become from their parents. Between lurid tales about losing their virginity, drug abuse, and ongoing sexual activity, inklings of regret over this alienation peeked through their bravado. Yes, it probably would have been better if they had waited a while for their first sexual encounters and had them in the context of a loving relationship. But alas, there was no use in dwelling on what might have been. Even at this age, they seemed resigned to their fate and said that it was too late for their parents to step in now. Peers had replaced adults as a source of advice and support. Predictably, then, their decisions about right and wrong no longer had the benefit of grown–up wisdom but compounded bad judgment in the past with an unabashed pursuit of pleasure in the present.

PBS' Web site included analyses of the disturbing disconnect in these families observed by various doctors, psychologists, and counselors. One of them titled "Adrift in America", authored by Dr. Michael Resnick, Director of the National Teen Pregnancy Prevention Research Center, did a masterful job at cutting to a key issue. Shocked by the 'starkness' of the Rockdale story, Resnick wastes little time guessing at which group is 'more lost', the parents or the children. Had these parents taken a greater interest in their kid's lives, set some parameters, and imposed consequences if these boundaries were violated, they wouldn't be wringing their hands in despair now. "Bereft of external expectations, personal responsibilities, and constructive options for recreation and entertainment, not to mention a notable absence of involved parents, these kids gave vent to their basest desires with horrific results."

Topping a dismal list of concerns about Rockdale county is the probability that it is not an isolated case. Can anyone really guess at how many more Rockdale counties there might be across the United States? How many other adolescents whose parents have disappeared from their lives are walking around unhindered by scruples and with the slightest prodding would engage in the same bestial behavior? Perhaps the real tragedy is that situations such as this need not ever have happened. Preventing it could have been simple enough. As Resnick intoned, "…parents, families, and adults outside of the family are fundamentally important to the healthy development of youth." If the mothers and fathers in Rockdale had been a fraction more involved in the lives of their kids as the latter grew up, this is a tale of woe story that might never have happened.

Backlash to Indifference?

   In the wake of a Rockdale or Columbine shooting, a smattering of youth across the country are beginning to ask harder–edged questions themselves. How could the parents of these Littleton killers or the girls who willingly participated in multiple–partner sex acts not have known what was occurring? In this small cross–section , some are wondering, would my *own parents* have seen the signs of danger if it had been me hatching such a heinous plot or partaking in those sexual excesses? Teens see things more clearly than adults give them credit for, I've learned from my work with them. They realize that their parents are out of touch with the day to day doings of their lives. Although they prefer it that way much of the time, a few are pleading for a little more interest.

   Adults who are honest know it too. In an indignant essay published in *Time* (5/3/99, p.40), contributor Amy Dickinson wonders "…where in the hell where the parents?" of the Columbine killers. If you have children, she argued, pleading ignorance can be no defense. While most teens dread parental intrusions into their guarded lives, mothers and fathers cannot afford to be casual. "But surely a parent can risk his child's embarrassment, and his own discomfort to get in his or face a little bit. Surely we can manage to love them a little louder." Like Dickinson, Columbine produced sufficient anxiety to have almost everyone lamenting the shrinking role of parents in their kid's lives. Obviously, passive parenting, under the guide of respecting a son or daughter's privacy, failed miserably.

In an article published by the *Washington Post* two months after the massacre, Columbine High School survivors held a meeting to challenge the adults in their lives to show an interest and do more. Their message reverberated through a nation reeling with recriminations. That parents should spend more time with their children and do a better job of instilling values was the message sent loud and clear (Kenworthy, 1999). Determined to call it the way she saw it, a 17 year–old female student said it plainly: "We need to attack the roots…Our main problem is at home." Her sentiments were echoed by a classmate who added, "The reason I turned out good is I was blessed with a mother who still built me up regardless of what other people thought of me. That's what parents need to do."

One of the murdered students, Cassie Bernall, has even become a rallying point for a new surge of teen evangelism attracting young believers and sprouting assorted Web pages honoring her martyrdom. Although conflicting reports exist, Bernall was alleged by one eyewitness who survived Columbine to have proclaimed her faith with her last words. When asked at gunpoint by Klebold if she believed in God, Cassie apparently replied yes before he pulled the trigger. The veracity of this event is not as important as the reaction it prompted among adolescents struggling to find mooring in amoral times. Teenagers might pretend as though parents and teachers don't exert much influence over them, but research suggests the contrary. As Dr. Resnick points out;

"Granted, many adolescents are very skillful at telling us, as adults, that we have become irrelevant in their lives. And we make the mistake of believing that! What is clear from the national studies of adolescent health and resilience is that caring and competent adults who recognize, value, and reward pro–social behavior in young people can have a profound effect on what adolescents value and believe, about themselves and the world around them."

No matter how nonchalantly youth approach us, they still look to adults for support, direction and love. Take the time, ask us questions, and show you care, they seem to be saying through the sagging shoulders, averted glances, and grunted, monosyllabic replies. Dig a little deeper. Even if we don't seem to notice, this will show us you care, seems to be the distress signal they are sending. Millions of fathers and mothers ought to pay more heed to this implicit request.

II. SCHOOL INFLUENCES

If family life—a stable home and interested parents—isn't what it once was, a crucial ingredient in the recipe for success in life is missing. Perhaps, however, this deficit can be overcome. Maybe others can pick where families dropped the ball. Hillary Clinton stressed the responsibility of communities in producing healthy and happy youth in *It Takes a Village*. Building on the work of experts, Clinton rearranged the hierarchy to place an equal onus on social institutions, schools the salient one among them all. Indeed, schools fill a close support role to the family in human socialization, complementing and or reinforcing the early work done by parents in the home. If parents teach children to be individuals, education grooms them to be responsible members of society. Schools train children in constructive ways of relating to others, experiencing authority, assimilating culture, and conforming to social standards.

This said, we can see that the primary purpose of schooling is cultural reproduction. America's most renowned educator, John Dewey, expounded this premise in his *Democracy and Education* (1916) and few have argued successfully against it since. In brief, Dewey said that education has a duty to transmit the cream of existing culture and, in doing so, replicate the knowledge, values, ideals of past and present generations for posterity. In nations such as the United States, education becomes the friend of democracy by creating an enlightened citizenry who are able to think critically, behave appropriately and in deference to the common good, vote wisely in electing a leadership.

Complications arose, however, when a fresh set of expectations never conceived by Dewey or subsequent generations until ours were thrust upon schools. Parents, it seems, also want them to serve in their stead for eight to ten hours a day while they are away at work. Consequently, schools have been asked to take on the operations of comprehensive social service agencies. They perform a range of functions, starting with latchkey programs in elementary schools, to birth–control clinics in junior high, to day–care for the infants of students in high school and then credit/debt management counseling in colleges. Primary intellectual and social training formerly done by parents has been shifted first to child care facilities and, once children reach the proper age, schools. Our educational system, never designed to take on this menu of responsibilities, cannot help but fail at it. Add to it a pervasive climate that countenances anti–social and anti–intellectual behavior and the results are dismal, as we shall see ahead.

Ground Zero: The Fortressing of Schools

The most immediate crisis facing American public education today is school violence. No other country among the so–called technologically advanced nations approaches the level of violence committed by children in the United States. Few even come close. Gang fights, sexual assaults, attacks on teachers, weapons carrying, and now homicide, none of these are alien to primary or secondary school campuses. The actual damage incurred, psychological and physical, seldom makes itself felt in statistical data, however. Below are those incidents of school violence which made national headlines between 1997–2000. Others, such as a plot uncovered by horrified parents in Lake Station, Indiana, where three 7–year old girls put together a detailed plan with drawings for executing a classmate, are not. Cynical as it is, by the time this book goes to press there will inevitably be several additions to this gruesome list.

October 1, 1997—16 year–old in Pearl, MS, kills mother, then goes to his high school shoots nine students, killing two

December 1, 1997—A 14 year–old in West Paducah, KY, shoots eight students at his high school, three fatally.

March 24, 1998—Four students and a teacher are shot to death, ten more wounded, at a middle school when two boys, ages 11 and 13, open fire from nearby woods.

April 24, 1998—A science teacher is murdered in front of students at an 8th–grade school dance. A 14 year–old is charged.

May 19, 1998—An 18 year–old in Fayetteville, TN, kills a classmate who is dating His former girlfriend in the school parking lot.

May 21, 1998—A 15 year–old Oregon boy kills his parents at home, then proceeds to his high school where he mows down twenty, slaying two.

April 20, 1999—Columbine High School murders

May 20, 1999—One month after Columbine, a student in Conyers, GA, wounds six classmates before surrendering.

December 6, 1999—A 7th–grade boy in Fort Gibson, OK, opens fire in his middle School, wounding four students.

February 29, 2000—A 6–year old boy shoots and kills a 6–year old classmate in front of the first–grade class with a stolen gun brought from home a day after they quarreled in Mt. Morris, Michigan.

March 6, 2001—a 'belittled' 15–year old high freshman kills two and wounds thirteen at a suburban San Diego high school. Revenge appears to be his motive.

sources: *The New York Times*, "Student Violence in America's Schools; *Yahoo! News*.

In the aftermath of widespread shootings and slayings on school grounds, public institutions are being transformed into police precincts and military camps. Uniformed guards, often armed, patrol the hallways. Walk–through metal detectors stand at the ready at every building entrance. Hand–held metal detecting wands wave over thousands of students' backpacks each morning. The electronic eyes of surveillance cameras prowl common areas from the cafeteria to the courtyard. Zero–tolerance policies for the slightest infraction against codes barring students from carrying any object that might be used as a weapon have been put into effect. A student caught giving Tylenol to a peer can be suspended for breaking draconian rules against possession of drugs. A number of public schools have passed or are debating policies requiring students to wear uniforms in an effort to do away with gang–related 'colors' and other insignia which can heighten interpersonal tensions.

This reconfiguration into fortresses should unnerve all of us regardless of our age. Adults can recall how schools used to be among the sanest and safest of public places. Imaginary or not, it still burns in our collective memory that when we crossed the line over to school grounds, we felt an almost magical protection on the premises. Bad things simply couldn't happen here. Today, no parent, teacher, or administrator is pleased about the change but all concede the wisdom in exercising every possible precaution. Yet even with the steps that have been taken, there are no guarantees. An article picked up by Gannet News services titled "Schools fail at a Stopping Violence," (Mathis, 1999) draws a comparison between modern schools and Potemkin villages. To the eye, schools appear far better prepared than before Columbine—intricate security equipment has been installed, guards added, and stricter policies implemented. The public has convinced itself that the worst is over. However, experts who study the situation disagree. Turning schools into military compounds won't solve the crisis. The disaffection that prompts hostile outbursts comes from a student's home life. Until parents accept this responsibility, danger lingers. The Fort Gibson middle–school shootings coming eight months after Columbine in December, 1999, demonstrated how thin the line is between what Americans want to believe and reality. Schools and students still aren't immune to random violence.

It is a damning indictment of America's priorities that conditions have sunk to such an alarming and volatile state. Youth cannot help but notice and be affected in distressing psychological ways. Academically, how can they concentrate on learning when getting safely through each day has become their exclusive ambition?

Teachers and Administrators

Teachers fight against many misconceptions and adding to the criticisms of them, just or not, gives one reason to pause before proceeding. However, sufficient weakness in our educational system has been documented for us to also consider the role of the educators themselves.

Teachers face a daunting task. In the public's estimation, if they, as learning specialists, can't solve a student's behavioral problems acquired over his lifetime as well as simultaneously instruct him, they somehow aren't doing their job. 'Psychologist' and 'social worker' have been added by the general population to their job description. By way of illustration, among their students, attention deficit disorder has emerged as the *carte blanche du jour* for justifying disruptive behavior and learning deficiency in the classroom. It is a problem teachers are forced to contend with every day of the school year. Over one million students receive Ritalin every day in schools across the country (*US News & World Report*, 11/23/98). These are just the students whose condition has been diagnosed——probably three to four times as many suffer from the same condition without the benefit of diagnosis and treatment. Yet teachers are expected by parents to treat, counsel, and help ADD kids while at the same time serving as pedagogue to a room with twenty or thirty other easily distracted children. Never mind that classes overflowing with students coming from abusive or neglectful homes, some are high on crack or alcohol, or still others developmentally disabled from years of attending schools where they learned little but were 'socially promoted' as in the case of the Los Angeles City school district. (Sterngold, 1999). More scandalous are allegations of widespread cheating—orchestrated by teachers and principals—on standardized tests that determine district academic ratings, educator salaries, and additional government funding dot the map from California to Ohio to Maryland. If students can't cut it academically, it appears, pedagogues will ensure, dishonestly or not, they get to the next grade rather than risk losing "bonuses of as much as $25,000". (*Newsweek*, June 19, 2000, p. 48)

Unfortunately, counseling offices are understaffed and overworked everywhere. Counselor–to–student ratios in the range of 1 to a 100+ are not unusual and often times far worse. Buckling under such case loads, it's absurd to think that counseling staff have the opportunity to do what they were hired to do. Meeting each student, discussing academic goals, and closely observing individual behavior may occur within plush confines of a handful of elite private academies but these clearly don't represent the majority of public schools. Most of our kids tell us that id they meet with their counselor two or three times per year, and then, just to go over their class schedule, that is the extent of their contacts with the counselor assigned to them.

Principals and school administrators confront equally harsh realities. 'Do more with less' is a maxim so familiar to them they mutter it in their sleep. The struggle to obtain funding to keep pace with rising teacher salaries and benefits, the push for higher academic standards, and pressure from parents and students to offer athletic and other expensive extracurricular activities never ends. Tom Mooney, president of the state of Ohio's teacher's union, voiced this exasperation when he went on record saying, "The state is becoming more and more heavy–handed in governing education, what to teach and where to teach it, but they still won't belly up to the bar and guarantee equitable fund-

ing." (DiFilippo, 1999). State–based appropriations for K–12 education limps along in most sections of the United States, with the general
funding pattern hovering between 0 to 6% in annual increases. Despite
popular assumptions of educational waste, these monies invariably turn
out to be insufficient to meet the plethora of demands heaped on
schools and their staffs. Consequently, superintendents find themselves
in a vicious, annual cycle of paring district expenses even when bone is
already exposed, while simultaneously being roasted in the press for
declining student performance or limiting teacher training opportunities.

Understandably, the morale of educators in the K–12 school stands
at low ebb. Perhaps this apathy explains the bizarre turn of events in
New York City, where forty–three teachers and two principals in the
city school district have been charged with giving students the answers
on standardized tests used to gauge achievement and promote to the
next grade (Goodnough, 1999). Bleaker still are prospects for rescue
any time soon. Americans want access to the best education available
but, as shown by the issues that inspire the most passion in political
campaigns, both local levies and new formulas for funding at state and
federal levels are regularly defeated at the ballot box. By contrast, everyone complains about the rising costs of college education. However,
the tuition universities collect that supplement governmental appropriations explains how U.S. higher education remains the envy of the
world.

Decaying Facilities

In segue, it's the greatest of ironies that while the United States
offers the finest higher education in the world, it provides, paradoxi-
cally, the weakest kindergarten through high school (K–12) system.
Concerned parties typically attribute this to a chronic dearth of funding. For decades, many claim, colleges and universities reaped windfalls
from legislative bodies across the country while lower–profile elementary and secondary education got the scraps from the appropriations

table. In wooing commercial enterprises to their home environs, politicians are indeed quick to point out the partnerships available with in-state universities to business leaders considering expansion. Higher education, after all, is widely recognized as an engine of economic growth and no governor wants his or her state left behind for a lack of university–based research facilities. Objectively speaking, there is validity to the argument that colleges and universities, if not the darlings of state funding boards, are at least treated more generously than K–12 recipients.

Fueling this inequity is a stubborn reluctance among taxpayers to help. If the rejection rate among school referendums is any indication, they have shown an stern resistance to footing the bill for academic improvement. Across the nation, teachers' unions and school districts persist in asking for more money while at the same time, unfortunately, and by most standardized measures, the quality of education continues to decline. Furthermore, even when cash is poured into education, experience shows it is routinely mismanaged. Enough is enough typified the overburdened taxpayers' mood as they frequently vote down new funding initiatives on the ballot.

Take the situation of New York City. As covered in a July 27th, 1999 New York Times feature, a staggering price has been paid for efforts to revitalize one of the country's biggest school districts. Nine billion dollars have been spent over the last decade along with $7 billion more over the coming five years. What did it produce? Approximately 115,575 seats have been added to the city's school capacity. This is a great accomplishment, but of this total, less than half—46.4%—of these seats were actually added by new construction. Fifty–three percent were either "leased or converted" seating (space leased in buildings, subdivided classrooms, or building converted for classroom use or, "temporary seating" that means primarily in trailers). Obviously, both of these plug–a–leaking–dike measures merely postpone dealing with the long–term problem. One new school that opened in 1995 waited three years before repairs were completed on loose floor tiles and a broken elevator. Political infighting and pressures from organized labor caused much of these cost overruns and work delays. Factor in an academic computer system on the design board for ten years that still doesn't work, and monies consumed by graft, and this multibillion dollar allocation resulted in far less facilities improvement than what should have occurred. Although occurring on a grander scale, the quandary confronted by New Yorkers is not foreign to many cities across the United States.

The bottom line: students are being asked to attend schools that are literally crumbling around them. Noticing it, they cannot help but wonder where the priorities of adults—community and regional leaders, especially—lay, when they can spend millions on building new stadiums for professional sports teams (Cleveland, Seattle, Denver) yet cannot find the resources to properly maintain school buildings. Such a paradox provides a sterling example of the differences between modern (intellectually–oriented) and postmodern (entertainment–geared) social agendas. With facilities not up to the task, learning become a hit or miss endeavor. Except in the cases of the most gifted teachers, physical and psychological conditions are uncooperative to learning. When classrooms reek of cold and damp or swelter hot and stifling, when the corridors are clogged with metal detectors, guards, and gang graffiti, and when districts are unable to provide basic support services such as equipped libraries, functioning science labs, or extracurricular activities, opportunities for student development soon evaporate.

Hunting for Alternatives

Given the rather grim profile sketched, a crisis of confidence taints our opinions about public schools. In response, alternatives to public education schools continue to gather grassroots support. Two of them, the hotly–contested voucher program and rise of charter schools warrant a closer look.

The heated debate between opposing sides over government–sponsored vouchers offering parents a choice between dilapidated public schools and private institutions shows little sign of abatement. A week before school started in August, 1999, a federal judge in Cleveland halted Ohio's voucher program, deciding it violated the separation between church and state (*US News and World Report*, 9/6/99). On appeal, this case eventually reached the U.S. Supreme Court, which in December let stand an appellate court ruling that prohibited using vouchers for tuition at religious schools. (Vicini, 1999). The outcome of this case concerns many of us, but no more than the momentum behind it. Lower and middle income parents, tired of waiting for improvements in government–sponsored education and desperate to secure a better future for their children, see the voucher program as a passport to it. In Cleveland's public school district, for example, 17,000 applications vouchers were collected for 4,300 vouchers in 1999. Concurrently, it is impossible to reject the court–upheld logic of separatists who decry the use of public money in supporting church–affiliated schools which most institutions redeeming vouchers seem to be. As are many complex issues, this has become a battle pitting moral against legal rights. Parents simply want the best education for their children, regardless of whether their own tax dollars are being shifted away from public schools and allocated to private ones. Who can blame them?

Far less controversial and drawing many converts among parents are charter schools. These are public schools created and governed by concerned educators, parents or community leaders and which wield more freedom in establishing entrance standards, curricula and administrative polices than mainstream institutions. They must be non–sectarian and meet specific criteria set forth in their missions, or *charters*, hence the name. While some elected officials endure withering criticism for supporting voucher programs, the public has welcomed charter schools with open arms. Seeing this, the lame duck Clinton Administration announced plans in the summer of 1999 to earmark nearly $100 million for cultivating more charter schools in America. Proponents argue that supporting this educational alternative introduces friendly competition, Ideally, it will brings out the best in public schools who must respond by becoming attuned to community needs and expectations.

Interestingly, at this point, no conclusive data exists proving that either charter schools or private institutions subsidized through voucher are qualitatively superior to their public counterparts. In fact, charter schools, as recent and largely untested inventions appear to be as much an educational risk as a surety. Yet parents rally around them. Americans are eager to *believe* that they are better.

Is popular disenchantment so great that we prefer to gamble our children's future on an unknown quantity rather than hand them over to the established schools in the area in which we live? A barrage of reports in the media telling us about declining test scores, disintegrating infrastructures, teachers failing minimal proficiency tests, and state and federal funding cutbacks has taken its toll. They have eroded our faith in the ability of community schools to perform the task assigned them.

Are the problems reported really so dire or is it something else that nags at us? As adults, our fears may not lie with the schools' potential to educate as much as the knowledge that they are physically and emotionally hazardous for children. Therein exists a strong part of the appeal of charter and voucher alternatives. Even if it's too early to tell, at least the possibility exists that these options may provide environments where students can concentrate on learning instead of being preoccupied with their personal safety while conditions continue to deteriorate around them.

Summary

Two of the three pillars of socialization have fallen from the triumvirate, and the third, churches, have slipped in stature under widespread apathy. The first, home and family life, are not what they once were. Supplying a mere fraction of support and structure they formerly did, children have suffered as a result. Schools, too, as the second in this triad, have strayed from their mission of giving younger Americans the knowledge and skills they will need to mature into bright, social, and principled adults. Too many years of poor facilities and declining academics are coming back to haunt the United States. Pile on top of that social conditions that transformed education into quasi–military camps, and the likelihood of either pedagogues or students being able to focus on learning grows ever slighter.

These institutions need to be revivified for things to improve. Americans must stop lamenting about their pitiful state and work to bring them back from the depths to which they sunk. Leaders of these social structures—educators, clergy, elected officials, and parents, who head them—have to decide that enough is enough. Apathy, shoulder–shrugging, and the I–can't–make–a–difference–by–myself rationalizing are no longer acceptable. Without exception, they must resolve that at least in the small corner of the world where they do wield some influence over youth, a measure of sanity and stability will be restored. It is past time to regain control over those runaway aspects of life which put youth in such a precarious position.

Cultural factors, too, have also had a hand in shaping the experiences of youth. It is these that we are now ready to consider.

4

Motifs and Moods of Popular Culture

A potent layer of influences on youth arises from a pervasive popular culture. Its reach extends across all social settings into out homes. Protection from its ideology as well as the technology it employs to promote its philosophy is nearly impossible. If once people recoiled from the notion of 'Big Brother', a controlling mechanism which invaded every nook and cranny where humans gathered and ideas germinated, recall that it was only fiction. In our postmodern reality, we have actually welcomed into our lives the devices that mold thought. Thanks to the presence of so many televisions, radios, computers, to cite a few, the philosophy of popular culture gained more than a foothold in every American household. The younger the age of the person receiving the input from such devices, the deeper the programming received.

Unsuspecting of its hidden designs, adolescents muster only the lightest immunity to popular culture. Nor do they perceive it as a threat. They had the misfortune of being born in an era that precludes normal emotional growth. Today, youth may be more susceptible than ever to prevailing cultural caprices precisely because of an unrelenting multimedia assault on their senses. Perceptual abilities that mature persons acquired during childhood to screen and select sensory input never had a chance to develop naturally in today's youth. If so, it's likely that the coping mechanisms adults rely on to sift through the barrage of signs and slogans and enable them to discriminate between fact and fiction are absent from the cognitive tool set of their children. In such distorted circumstances, teens would be acutely vulnerable to everything they encounter in the media of pop culture as well as socially in peer interactions. Parental voices, once the strongest in terms of teaching right from wrong, are now but two in a hostile sea. Having lost the chance to cultivate reasoning skills and practice sound decision–making skills, the alluring montage of pop culture images and messages arrayed before them exert a tremendous impact on pliable adolescent personalities.

Below we will examine three powerful forces animating the pop culture universe. First is "hip–hop", a subculture with its own codes and behaviors that radically differ from broader American society. Next, the narrative will consider the new hero mythology that pop culture spawned and kids fervently adopted. Issues of wealth and how it has clouded the judgement of adolescents will also be examined. Finally in this exploration of current social trends, we will open a discussion on the decisive role technology assumed in catapulting pop culture across the United States and beyond. As these streams converge, any resistance that the rare individual might offer in resisting its moods and motifs is soon encircled and annihilated.

Hip–Hop Comes to Main Street

Perhaps the most tempestuous among the winds of popular culture is hip–hop. The origins of this cultural tour de force lay in the *multiculturalizing* of the United States (see chapter 2). It is a public celebration of those who survived and transcended the minority experience. Originally a creative form of racial identity expression, hip–hop has transformed itself into a parallel culture, uniting youth chafing under adult rules with other minorities also oppressed by authority. Hip–hop's bursting on to the scene from its inner city Black roots in the Bronx or south central Los Angeles to main street USA, an incredible phenomenon in itself, invites consideration for the widespread following it commands among adolescents.

In its February 8, 1999 issue, *Time* magazine did an extensive feature titled "Hip–Hop Nation", on the emergence of hip–hop as a cultural wave sweeping the country. What began during the seventies as a reclaiming of urban communities by those who lived in them, has rocketed into something far greater than ever imagined. Christopher Farley, author of the *Time* piece explains:

> "Even if you're not into rap, hip–hop is all around you. It pulses from the films you watch (Seen a Will Smith movie lately, the books you read (even Tom Wolfe peels off a few raps in his best–selling new novel), the fashion you wear (Tommy Hilfiger, FUBU)...Hip–Hop represents a re–alignment of America's cultural aesthetics." (55–56)

A *USA TODAY* story aptly named "Hip–Hop takes the High Road", running on June 25, 1999, echoed these sentiments: "What's up with rap? Artists have gone from marginalized to moguls. Female stars are emerging. Its urban agitation is being embraced by suburban kids...(correspondent) Steven Jones traces rap from mean streets mind–set to mainstream." (1E)

If Farley and Jones happen to be right, and hip–hop heralds the voice of the young generation, it would profit those unfamiliar with it to learn more about it. As rap star Heavy D was quoted in the *USA* story, "'It's incredible the way it's influencing America, not just black America...You have suburban kids using everything from the fashion to the slang and its bringing people together without racial barriers.'" For better or worse, hip–hop represents 'the pulse of the street.' If before that pulse was determined by Madison Avenue advertising agencies, it has been taken over by street poets, musicians, and artists.

To begin, however, it must be noted that hip–hop and rap music are not necessarily synonomous, though they are often used interchangeably. Rap is a "form of rhythmic speaking in rhyme." Hip–hop refers to the broader cultural milieu that gave birth to rap and other gritty forms of urban aesthetics such as graffiti and break–dancing. Another angle on the link between Hip–Hop and rap came in a companion article in the same issue of *Time*. "Chuck D.," pioneering rapper and member of the notorious group Public Enemy opined, "Hip–Hop is the term for urban–based creativity and expression of culture. Rap is the style of rhythm–spoken words across musical terrain. It's the antithesis of country music but the two do pretty much the same thing—reflect upon their environments with stories and statements."

A site on the World Wide Web called "360 Degrees" educates the curious on the life, times, and moods of Hip–Hop culture. The homepage's creator remains anonymous, but s/he authored several essays on these topics which appear on the site. One of them, "The Politics of Hip Hop Culture," stressed how initially this movement had little social message or political content. Instead, Hip–Hop's main concern was promoting rap as a healthy means of entertainment and competition among Black youth. However, as rap grew its audience, spread outside the boroughs, and caught the attention of record executives, its focus shifted toward the political. The rage present in rap and other forms of hip–hop music resulted largely from increasing and unfriendly competition among rappers. In their bid to stay ahead of other group and generate sales, artists began to write more controversial lyrics. Record company executives, sensing the profit in tapping this inner city rage, persuaded rappers to up the ante in their lyrics.

Of course, hip–hop culture is larger than its music. How to act, dress, and speak are also covered by its unwritten creed. Although hip–hop originated in the African–American community as a device to separate itself from white America, it's anti–establishment propensities were further ignited by the antipathies all young people feel toward their elders. On its own, adolescence brings a time of testing limits and challenging authority. Embracing a vein of pop culture that reinforces the belief that school's not cool, that the ways of the street are the best teacher, and that only peers are socially important, undercuts traditional morality in a context that hits home with kids and their anti–authority inclinations.

Fred Durst, lead singer of the rap–metal band Limp Bizkit, gave an interview that sheds light on the mentality of rap and why it appeals to youth revolting against society's conventions. For a fuller reading of this interview, see *USA Weekend*, January 14–16, 2000, though the excerpts below speak for themselves.

Q: What are your songs about?
A: "Betrayal in my life, bad timing, learning from life."

Q: Your lyrics about women are harsh.
A: "I wrote a song and called my ex–girlfriend (ugly names) because she cheated on me and lied to me. And I expressed myself through that song. At the time, I definitely wasn't thinking that the record was gonna go platinum and a million people were gonna (mistakenly) think I think that about every woman."

Q: You've been accused of provoking some of the violence and rapes at Woodstock (II) last summer with your performance. Do you accept responsibility for that?
A: "No. Not at all. We are great guys (Limp Bizkit) with great morals. Rape is as terrible as anything someone can do…"

Q: You claim you've never read a book. Are you sure you haven't? Not even in school? By accident?
A: "That's right. When I was supposed to read one [for a book report], I chose *The Outsiders* because I had seen the movie."

Blatant contempt for the opposite sex, a denial of inciting anti–social behavior, and a mocking admission that books and, learning by association, are valueless in the estimation of a rapper. This is posturing that is not wasted on the teens who buy Biskit or any other hip–hop band's recordings. In the clothing kids wear, the slang they use, and the attitudes they display, adults can feel the dubious influence of Durst and fellow music impresarios.

Given the heterogeneity of the United States and its belated recognition of human diversity, the growth of hip–hop subculture marks a changing of the guard. As a form of expression forged in the experience of alienation, it shows that all youth, regardless of race or ethnicity, can identify and sympathize with this experience. But hip–hop is also about more than diversity. Born in cities, it can only be understood in its appreciation of urban themes. After the great population migration to urban centers during the twentieth century, it was inevitable that the focal point of America's culture shifted from its English, scholarly, and largely homogenous ancestry to the vibrant multicultural diaspora concentrated in cities. This realignment also altered the complexion of culture from high to mass, or popular form. People in these urban centers were the first to pull it down from the pedestal it rested on, melt it down, and recast it into their own.

A dilemma arises, however, in what this new face on the block can do for America. Rather than impressing upon its followers the pain of hardship, the struggle against systemic racism and oppression, and the ultimate flowering of minority culture, it squanders its creative energies on crass commercialism, the degradation of women, and a glorification of violence. Taken as a whole, hip–hop cannot help but pique the anxieties of those outside its experience, particularly adults. As adolescents are so quick to tell us, hip–hop does indeed cross all color lines. However, what it unites young people in is an antipathy toward of society and an implacable resentment of its order and institutions. Naturally, all authority, adults along with those who embody "the Man's" establishment, are cast as the ultimate evildoers and hip–hoppers as those whose ideology will break the chains of racial, economic, and age–based oppression.

New Mythology: Gods, Godesses, and Mortals

With the fading of religion from America's social scene, the absence of an established moral force has made itself painfully clear. Spurning traditional forms of worship and instead espousing an alternative mythology, pop culture created a new pantheon of demigods and deities. Celebrities have stolen the imagination of youth. A prerequisite for stardom and mystique these days is media coverage. Whoever gets it can claim divine stature. Whoever cannot, is soon forgotten.

Not surprisingly, the, the olympians among those exalted are actors, musicians and professional athletes. When the boyishly angelic face of Leonardo DiCaprio helps the film *Titanic* gross over a $500 million dollars domestically, he, for one, must be included in this elite. Latino crooner Ricky Martin who captivated young females across the nation with his 1999 mega–hit "Living the Vida Loca" might also place high on the list, unless, of course, he turns out to be a one–hit wonder, loses a fawning press, and drops back into obscurity. Every move actress Julia Roberts makes is scrutinized by the paparazzi, reported in the tabloids, and aped by an idolizing public. At $20 million dollars per movie and with a radiant, if toothy, smile, few can argue about her public appeal. After the release of her rather lumbering film, *Notting Hill*, a flood of tourists besieged that tony section of London, dreaming, perhaps, that Roberts or co–star Hugh Grant might just wander out of an area bookstore.

The younger crowd prefers music to celluloid heroes. Pre–and teenage girls mimic the dance and fashion moves of female pop singers like Britney Spears or Christine Aguilera. Boys with show business aspirations are rushing everywhere to form acapella groups like Boys2Men or N'Sync, hoping to cash in on the latest mass craze. The majority of boys, however, become star–struck not so much by show biz personalities as by athletes. Who among them doesn't revere basketball's Kobe Bryant or baseball's Ken Griffey Jr.? Children or teens, male or female, Hispanic, Black, or White, pop culture's overexposed celebrities spark tremendous enthusiasm among youth whether they pursue television, film, music, or athletic careers. Our kids want to be like *them* rather than us. Parents, grandparents, aunts or uncles, teachers too have dropped from the radar screen of cool. Average men and women who play roles in their lives obviously are not part of this august company. Even if they are not openly villified, the status of these former role models has taken a decidedly downward turn.

To be fair, it isn't just our kids to whom athletes have become compelling figures in this new divinity. Americans of all ages esteem them. When the National Basketball Association championship series is televised live to five billion people around the globe 151 countries, is it any wonder that the face Michael Jordan has become the most recognizable in the world? Perhaps because he is a father himself, Jordan seems to be one of the few superstar athletes who understands that people are watching him. His persona of cool good looks, polished manners and ethic of hard work is rare among athletes in being creditable. With his retirement from the game, however the example he set is receding into obscurity.

The flip side of sports worship reveals an altogether different and often ugly face. What happens when the object of affection is utterly undeserving? Could any adult, for instance, comprehend the attraction of a Dennis Rodman with his tattoo–adorned, multiply–pierced body, rainbow–hair, penchant for transvetism, and boastful legend of liaisons with assorted female pop stars and actresses? Parents cringe at the sight of him but kids can't seem to get enough. The same applies for any one of a plethora of sports personalities from "Stone Cold" Steve Austin of the World Wrestling Federation to now fading "Prime Time" now Deion Sanders of the Washington Redskins. Fame, wealth, shameless self–promotion and assiduous media attention—these seem to be the primary criteria for mythical status in pop culture. The only other precondition for popularity appears to be thuggish behavior. Professional basketball star Latrell Sprewell tried to strangle his coach, got suspended by the NBA, cut from the Golden State Warriors and subsequently rewarded with a multi–million dollar contract from the New

York Knicks the moment his suspension ended. Carolina Panther's wide receiver Rae Carruth became the object of a massive manhunt before being arrested in December, 1999, for arranging the drive–by shooting of his pregnant girlfriend who subsequently died. Baseball slugger Albert Belle of the Baltimore Orioles continually frustrates fans and reporters seeking autographs or interviews, typically lacing his refusals with obscenities and threats. In football, the NFL league offices have just passed a ban on 'throat–slashing gestures' mimicking homicide of this variety, which had been a favorite taunt of players after scoring a touchdown or making a quarterback sack.

As has become the norm, good is boring and bad is fun. Not many kids of school age could supply a coherent account of what Abraham Lincoln actually did for the country or when he lived in history but more than a few could you how Tiger Woods revived golf from its white–bread lethargy. Who can blame them? If you were aged ten, sixteen, or even twenty, who would interest you more? The culture swirling around them aggrandizes the self–indulgent antics of super–rich athletes whose only job it is to dunk a basketball, film stars whose only ambition is to look good, and musicians who rant, curse and scowl on stage. When they aren't busy performing, they get arrested on weapons charges outside of night clubs (like Eminem and 'Puffy' Combs).

By contrast, there is no one parents can point to who is even faintly as fascinating. Clearly, the adults that figure in a teen's day–to–day existence are not nearly as flamboyant or interesting. Very likely, they feel this and unconsciously resent it. That might explain the massive, manic fixation of parents on getting their kids involved in sports from a young age. According to *Time* magazine, over 40 million kids are now participating in organized sports from pre–school though high school (Ferguson, 1999). Sniffing the potential payoff ten years down the road if their kid rises to stardom, parents have begun to display increasingly irrational behavior parents at their sons or daughters games. The problem of parent–on–referee or parent–on–parent violence has become so widespread that organized attempts to address it have been made. For example, the city of Jupiter, Florida, now requires the parents of all little–league baseball players to attend a public preseason briefing on deportment during kid's games as well as signing a statement saying they will abide by certain standards of good conduct. Until this release is signed, the child cannot play. The National Alliance on Youth Sports (**www.nays.org**), based in West Palm Beach, Florida, developed and advocated an 11–point "National Policy for Children's Sports." Notable among these are three directly dealing with expectations for parents and coaches: #6–Parents Active Role, #7–Positive Role Models, and #8–Parental Commitment, this last item requiring parents to sign a code of ethics barring objectionable language and behavior. If parents are being asked to get a grip, less consideration has been given to how important youth perceive sports to be.

Working in an office, quietly supporting a household, leading the conversation at meals——such humdrum activities on the part of parents hardly fire a child's imagination. The benefits of plain hard work, raises for a job well done, or living an honest and temperate life, these are hardly the stuff that inspired teens, much less persuades them to follow dutifully in their parent's footsteps. Without star appeal, the lessons and values adults try to instill seem so out of touch with what our culture prizes that all their remonstrations barely make a dent on adolescent psyches. Today's heroes, for the most part, personify lifestyles that adults dare not think about for their offspring. Like all Americans, nonetheless, there are two things—wealth and fame—they find enticing and wish to see in their child's future.

Of course, all these pop culture avatars are not bent on leading youth astray. Michelle Kwan, Olympic figure skater, accepts her rise to role–model status. In a *USA Weekend* interview on October 3, 1999, Kwan stated that she has "…no patience with athletes who don't want to be role models. 'It's too late,' she says, 'you already are.'" How this particular 19 year–old knows something that escapes fellow celebrities many years her senior defies explanation.

However, as we might have surmised, this new congregation of gods and goddesses are image–deep. They are perfect caricatures for these times—extraordinary surface appeal masking grave imperfections. Scratch at the brilliant exterior and uncover rust and rot. Promiscuity, double lives, substance abuse, mental illness—the media bursts with stories about their seedier sides.

A splendid illustration of the obsession with media–made icons inundated us in the sordid saga of Monica Lewinsky. A hopelessly forlorn young woman, her one talent and subsequent ticket to fame was made embarrassingly clear to the nation, especially parents who had to explain to their children what exactly she did that caused such a flap. Apart from nearly bringing down a President, did Lewinsky actually do anything to deserve the spotlight that has remained focused on her since news of the scandal broke? She commanded a seven–figure book deal and six–figures for television appearances. Her biggest fan, Barbara Walters, named Lewinsky to her list of "The Ten Most Fascinating People of 1999," then blessed her with even more air time in a television special broadcast in November of that year. Whether this attention was ever warranted *ought* to matter but doesn't. Network moguls decided Lewinsky was newsworthy and so we were greeted by her black–bereted, smiling visage everywhere we turned. As a result, she emerged as another miscreant heroine of popular culture.

Americans remain undeterred. We prefer our heroes tarnished. It makes them more like us, the flawed, publicity–craving individual lost among the masses. Lionized by a media that creates larger–than–life legends around each 'star', the actual individuals behind the facade rarely deserve the adulation bestowed upon them. Still, without them, popular culture would be an empty temple in search of gods to worship.

Affluenza Runs Amuck

By and large, having never known exertion of labor, younger Americans display an amazing profligacy toward money. Popular culture does little to discourage it. Projecting a veneer of wealth, regardless of whether or not a person actually possesses it, stands as a cardinal rule of contemporary existence. We see it in their taste for designer–label clothing, exotic travel, unlimited cash allowances and credit cards, and late–model luxury cars. Few of these items remain beyond the reach of youth. Those that do can usually be attained a little pressure on parents. Everybody wants to be a millionaire, after all, as a rash of new television games shows reminds us.

The source of this wastefulness is not a mystery. Parents, stricken with remorse for failing to be the hands–on guides they should, pour cash and gifts over their offspring in a perpetual baptism into postmodern economics. If surplus wealth exists, current logic dictates that it should spread throughout the household without regard to age, status, or sensibilities. Consequences are clear. Flush with cash they did not sweat for, American adolescents wield purchasing power that exceeds their experience to manage. While many high school and college students hold part–time jobs, the income from them is marginal and does not begin to cover the lavish spending patterns parents enable with ridiculously extravagant allowances. Generations of adolescents without an inkling of the true value of money continue to emerge.

An article appearing in a national newspaper raised awareness of how far to extremes this taste for opulence has gone. Spring breaks have become an annual cultural rite among American collegians. Over the last few years, the rite has been widened to include high school juniors and up. (This is but another social trend showing the disengagement of parents from their kids' lives and a relaxation of rules against underage partying.) That said, reporter Kitty Yancey followed students planning their spring pilgrimages. Both the locales and amenities they are opting for boggle the mind. Florida is still the main attraction, but international destinations like Cancun, the Virgin islands and Europe are catching up. Among the higher–end examples mentioned in the article story were the eight students from Minnesota renting a seaside villa in Jamaica for $4,750 a week. This includes a maid, cook and security guard, but did not cover flight expenses or spending money. The manager of this Jamaican resort told the correspondent that more young people than ever are seeking upscale getaways. You wouldn't have to tell that to the owners of New York City's Fischer Travel because they already know. Young clients of theirs have arranged to charter 130–foot motor yachts (with a crew of up to 10) at a cost of $75–100,000 per week, "plus a hefty security deposit in case of party–hearty damage." According to Yancey, tour operators she consulted for this story indicated that with our blazing economy most students, not just the prep school or Ivy league crowd, are seeking swankier travel packages.

One has to ask, once more, where are the parents of these students? Surely, such costly excursions are being funded by sources at home. Making the not so safe assumption that some actually work, few earn enough delivering pizzas or working at the university bookstore to pay for this sort of extravagance. Only through the generosity of wealthy parents are such vacations possible. Perhaps the real issue is *why*. It's highly likely that these trips are viewed as a status symbol by the parents as well as the students. Around the office water cooler, they can brag to associates about where their kid took spring break as if it were them. As before, they have come to believe that this largesse, mindless of the message it sends, elevates their stature as parents. This is but another element of the perverse picture of family that now reigns in America.

Dated as it might be, I can remember cramming four friends, all about six feet tall, into a Ford escort as we headed on a shoestring budget for a week in Daytona Beach. Five us slept in a room with two beds at the Holiday Inn, skipped two of three meals per day, and languished all day for free on the sand to make the puny contents of our thin wallets last the whole week. Perhaps my reader shares similar recollections of spring–breaks–on–the–cheap. If so, our tales would be the butt of campus jokes by the *Conde Nast* standards of today's college students.

The distorting impact of affluence, or *affluenza*, a newly minted word to describe our demented pursuit of all things money can buy, makes its presence felt in another way. Credit, plentiful and effortlessly obtained, compounds the fantasy of undue riches in immature minds. Every year as the fall term starts, an army of vendors hawking textbooks, clothing and consumer services to apple–cheeked freshmen descend on campuses like locusts. Here at the University of Cincinnati, they set up festooned booths on the bridge outside the student union and yell to students passing by like carnival barkers. Loudest among them are representatives from the credit card companies. Let me defer to an article I wrote for *The Cincinnati Post* describing how students are baited and hooked. "The lure of immediate credit in amounts approaching $1,000 is hard for the (generation) X'ers with scant resources to resist. Produce an ID, fill–out a half–page form, and in a week your shiny new 'plastic' arrives in the mail. The process of obtaining these cards has grown so simple that economically vulnerable students wait in long lines to apply."

Unfortunately, in the frenzy to acquire these cards, students demonstrate a disastrous tunnel–vision about their newly procured wealth. No one tells them, nor do they bother to ask, about those unimportant items such as the interest rates being assessed or personal liability in the event of repayment problems. The prospect of starting life after college under a mountain of crushing debt doesn't enter their minds. Yet from within this mirage occasionally rises a prophetic voice. In this case, a warning was published in the student newspaper at UC by an upperclassman who had already learned the painful lesson.

> "Why is it that credit–card companies are so persistent in getting college students to sign up for their credit card?…The answer is simple. It's all about reading between the lines. If something seems too good to be true, it probably is. I learned this lesson the hard way because I fell into the plastic pitfall the beginning of my freshman year at UC. All they did was wave around a free T–shirt and I was up there filling out an application quicker than you can say

"IN DEBT!". It only took me five minutes to fill out an application that would hurt my credit for the next five years..." (DeRoss, 1999)

Abundant credit, generously endowed checking accounts, luxury trips and goods, and plenty of money available to them, adults have infected their kids with the same incurable affluenza bug they suffer from. In doing so, a grave disservice has been done. This and subsequent generations of young people are slowly being ruined by having the means to satisfy every yearning the second it arises. At the same time youth are learning to live carelessly on other people's money, they take no heed about the long–term hazards of such wastefulness. Credit cards and the crushing debt they conceal wait silently ahead in the future until that day of reckoning finally arrives with the first of dozens of phone calls from implacable creditors. All this at a time when life, after graduation, should be full of promise

Unswayed, pop culture, in its hedonistic leanings, encourages spontaneous self–indulgence. Youth, ravished by affluenza, fall victim to the pleasures of illusory wealth without regard to its ultimate price.

Reign of Technology

Electronic communication devices govern our existence. Cellular phones and pagers are carried by kids to school, by soccer moms in minivans, and businessmen flying across continents. Technology has become so indispensable to our lives that we've made it portable, never allowing ourselves to be beyond its long arms.

Throughout our offices or schools, desk–top computers, scanners, and fax machines dominate the environment. It's hard to remember a time when we learned or worked without them. At home, when we're not busy surfing the 'Net, we're glued to the big–screen, flat–screen, satellite, or high–definition televisions, perhaps with digitally–enhanced surround sound, located in each room where we nod at other family members and quickly lose ourselves in the moment's entertainment. When they tire of this family time, our kids retire to their rooms where they check their messages and return calls on the extra line installed just for them. If there are no calls to return, they can turn on the PlayStation game system hooked up to televisions in their bedrooms and play games until bed time. Parents, in turn, head briefly to the study or even the bedroom where we connect our laptops to an outside line, log on, check our e–mail and reply to any messages for the tenth time before we call it a day. Then, after slipping on our pajamas, we fall asleep while David Letterman or Jay Leno run through their monologues on the TV set in our bedroom.

Is this technology really satisfying? Can that mechanical voice announcing "you've got mail" substitute for human contact? Does the phone recorder blinking in red numbers that we have four or five messages make us feel more successful socially? Do the digital conversations we engage in via e–mail and chat rooms help us feel more connected to other human beings, even if their faces remain anonymous? Or does this technology, when all is said and done, only make us, like addicts, crave another fix to fill in for the interpersonal contact that once satiated our social desires?

No matter, technology is here to stay and indications are that it will continue to command a larger share of our lives. Admitting this, it begs acknowledging the types of technology dominating our surroundings. Television may be the elder statesman of the group but advances in broadcast technology (e.g.. digital images) have managed to keep it atop the hierarchy as the most popular medium in the history of the world. Computers and more specifically, the Internet are arguably the second most utilized form of technology today. More e–mails are sent each day than letters in the U.S. Post office and 15,000 new Web sites are added every day (Satran, 1999). Telecommunications and radio, sans imagery, don't generate quite the same level of excitement yet remain a fixture in regimen of every American. By any measure, machines have come to govern our interactions, and media–based technology particularly important to those of student age.

While television still reigns supreme given that 98% of American households have at least one, a cutting–edge technology that has ignited the passions of adolescents is the Internet. In the next chapter, we will spend time exploring the impact of television, and other visual technologies on the lives of American youth. For the moment, however, let us pause and consider this exploding cyber–influence.

Internet

At the nexus of the technological revolution looms an information superhighway, a network of computers linked electronically around the globe tabbed the Internet. From humble origins as a research tool linking a select group of American universities, the Internet has become the most powerful interactive communications vehicle ever known to humankind. From its inception in the 1960's as the Department of Defense's Advanced Research Project Agency (ARPA) mainframe system transmitting data to a handful of other defense computers, the Internet mushroomed into a visual, audio, and interactive medium that revolutionized communications, education, entertainment, and commerce.

As far back as 1997, 57 million people used the Internet "regularly" said the Census Bureau. Of that cohort, 14 million children over the age of 3 used the Internet. By October, 2000, America On–line, one of the biggest Internet–access service providers, trumpeted its achievement of supporting a client membership in excess of 25 million. As competition among computer service companies stiffens, the price of hardware, software, and Internet–connections will continue to drop. This guarantees that even greater numbers of families will buy computers for personal use and that children in such households will have access to the expansive domains of cyberspace.

Already, those of us past the age of thirty feel various degrees of stress at being left behind by the moving train of computer–comfortable youth whose dexterity and ease with technology leaves us green with envy. As Pavlik (1996) observed; "New media technology is the province the young, especially the worlds of cyberspace and multimedia technology. Teenagers are among the heaviest users of online communications services." Sons and daughters, nieces and nephews, the kid next door, all of them seem to have been born without that long-standing human aversion to automation. As a result, we oldsters turn to them to help us with every technical task from programming the timer on video cassette recorders to loading the latest Web–browser software onto our work stations at home. An outcome of being raised in the Information age reveals a reliance on technology that cuts both ways.

Unlike those of us who grew up in the twilight of modern culture, younger persons look as much to the Internet for social and cultural experiences as for educational ones. A student needn't bother joining a club or sports team at school when he can go home, log on, and chat with his phantom friends in an on–line chat room. Another student doesn't need to take the bus and visit the city's art museum when all she needs to do is locate the Louvre's virtual musuem and tour its vast collection from the comfort of her own living room. Peer interaction, reading about the coolest movies and television shows, and getting automatic e–mails about the most recent techno–trends and products can all occur within the intangible realm of cyberspace. Consensus could probably be formed that in themselves, these are not bad things. So why does apprehension still nibble away at the edge of our minds?

Perhaps because there is something palpably anti–social about the Internet. In the first focused study of the social and psychological effects of the Internet, a research team at the Human Computer Inter-action Institute at Carnegie Mellon University found that "people who spend even a few hours a week on line experience higher levels of depression and loneliness." (Harmon, 1999) In this two–year project, Web aficionados reported "a decline in interaction with family members and a reduction in their circles of friends directly corresponding to the amount of time spent on line." Between these and similar discoveries, researchers hypothesized that relationships maintained without face–to–face contact fail to supply the "support and reciprocity that typically contribute to a sense of psychological security and happiness…" Those who have reviewed this study say that levels of emotional distress will rise in proportion to American's increasing *digital isolation.*

All technology–resistant rhetoric aside, a fragment of our humanity seems to have vanished with the Internet's arrival. If interpersonal contact complete with handshaking, eye contact, nonverbal cues and oral communications described the past social venue of choice, it's been abruptly bumped aside by the indirect, circuitry–delivered, virtual encounter presently in vogue. Communications experts refer to this mode of exchange as *mediated.* Along with being able to influence the content of these messages, computer mediated communications approve and make acceptable a sense of the impersonal. Ironic, considering that Tim Berners–Lee, creator of the ballyhooed World Wide Web, averred that "The Web is more a social creation than a technical one…I designed it for a social effect—" (Satran, 1999).

The losing side in this tug of war between technology and tradition, naturally, are adolescents. Many adults, at least, can look back fondly on a childhood that included comforting relationships with parents, caring teachers who taught instead of metallic–voiced computers, and a home that provided havens—the dinner table, the bedroom, the den—where we actually talked to family members or found a quiet place to read or think. That world is only a dusty memory now, an experience certain to be buried in a history rewritten by technology.

<u>From the Mouths of Babes…</u>

If before parents provided structure and support in the lives of their children, it is becoming harder for them to do so under present social conditions. Popular culture takes no prisoners as it marches onward and presses more youth into its legions. Mothers and fathers have abdicated. Multitudes of children have been socialized by the media. Television, computers, and social trends have taken over child–rearing from parents and relatives. What do youth have to say about these tell-ing issues? Let us listen to what they told researchers about parents, schools, and related concerns that weigh on their minds.

The National Center for Kids Overcoming Crisis, a child advocacy agency, conducted a survey in 1995 that offers a snapshot of the atti-tudes of children in that 'little–studied' pre–teen, 10–13 age cohort. Their greatest overall concern was the death of a parent, with 65% mentioning it. By a ratio of 4–1, this same cohort said the person they would most likely seek out when facing problems is their mother. Con-tradicting this rosy picture, however, was the finding that a 47% claimed they had "no role model or anyone they want to be like when they grow up because no one is special enough." (1995, pp. 1–2). Also, two–thirds of those polled mentioned peer pressure as a concern, admitting that they would do something they wouldn't normally do if pressured. Despite these aberrations, pre–teens generally felt connected to their parents and still saw them as key to their own physical and emotional well–being.

Another national survey, encompassing pre–teens but also including a broader study population of 13–17 year–olds, hinted that with this older cohort strains with parents had begun developing and that peer influences and cultural diversions were replacing them. This *New York Times/CBS* poll of teenagers was conducted in the spring of 1999 and spanned a sample of 1,083 teens. Grouped by topic, here are the more illuminating facts:

Socially:

- 31% of all respondents said 'drugs' were the biggest problem facing youth today, with peer pressure coming in second at 21%

- 52% felt that their school had a "group of students" who seem to be especially troubled, anti–social, or prone to violence.

- 43% thought that it was "harder" growing up today than when their parents did

Academically:

- Of the biggest "problems where you go to school," these were listed by students in descending order: violence (14%), drugs (11%), popularity/cliques (10%)

- 78% reported feeling either "a lot" or "some" pressure from parents to get good grades.

    51% felt that the school they attended was 'somewhat' to 'not too safe'

- 58% said there are times they 'really want to talk' to their parents about but don't. Of this group 46% said it's because they won't understand

Media:

- 69% their parents set no rules about the amount of television they can watch

- 54% said their parents set no rules about the type of films they can see

- 63% said they use a computer 'regularly' at home, and 48% regularly access the Internet

- 47% said they regularly played video games at home

- Percentages of all respondents who have: their own telephone number (17%), TV in their bedroom (63%), computer in bedroom (12%), beeper or Pager (18%), cellular phone (10%)

Valuable insight can be gleaned from these findings. Growing numbers of kids are exposed to media in larger doses and for the most part feel it to be harmless fun. Findings also show that they do not feel it plays a role in inciting fellow students to violence (only 3% thought it did). This study sample also expressed conflicting opinions about parents—while they overwhelmingly credited them with teaching them right and wrong, they indicated that few rules were imposed on them by their mothers and fathers. Clearly, as children age, the influence of parents wanes, so perhaps that accounts for this split. In lieu of parents, friends emerged as the primary sources of support and encouragement for students, even though they recognize that peers may lead them to experiment with things they probably should not. Sharing media seems to be the preferred social scene for youth in their interactions with friends. Hence the reason why television, computers, video games, and phones consume much of their time and energy.

Spiritually, a vast majority, 94%, said they believed in God. This faith didn't necessarily convert into participation in churches or religious services, which drew the majority of students from 'a few times a month' to 'once or twice a year.' Perhaps, taking a cue from many adults, they describe faith as a deeply personal matter that does not require public justification or practicing. If the example set by politicians and parents is any indicator, this view of faith could be construed as an excuse to do what one wants only to seek atonement later. Public accountability for private actions, no matter the repercussions, doesn't enter into the equation.

If society abides by the premise that people are not responsible for their own misdeeds, which current events have made perfectly clear, and adults have taken the lead in modeling this behavior, can we really expect a higher standard from youth? On the contrary, they simply copy the attitudes of parents and leaders whose ethics display a remarkable elasticity. It also explain the cynicism they display in making many of the adults they know into role models.

Summary

The moods and motifs of popular culture impact deeply on American youth. Even more than family or school experiences, it has a hand in shaping the kind of adults that kids end up becoming. Through trends that speak directly to youth desires and experiences and an omnipresent media technology that ensures uninterrupted delivery, popular culture messages permeate young lives. As discovered, these themes are not necessarily ones adults would reinforce if given the choice. In this era of ever–shifting terrain and dissolving boundaries, it's no wonder that students are vulnerable to the pied piper of pop culture. In an otherwise dreary world of disappointing relationships with adults and ever–present hypocrisy in social norms and institutions, the lure of its Siren song is extremely difficult to resist.

5

Life in an Alternate Reality

One of the symptoms of the corruption and collapse of our popular culture is the insistence that we examine only the surface of any piece of art or entertainment...we should never dig deeper—to consider whether a given work is true, good, or spiritually nourishing...We routinely focus on superficial skill and slick salesmanship, while ignoring the more important issues of soul and substance.

——_Michel Medved_

Medved's words signal a metaphoric curtain rising on the next act in America's social decline. He correctly discerns that all that glitters is golden in the public's eye even if under that gilded veneer waits ugliness or duplicity. Our aptitude for seeing things as they truly are versus how they are represented appears to be ever more suspect. Appearances count far more than reality. Today, the _representation_ of an object often determines its actual nature.

In the last chapter, the narrative focused on _what_ social forces exert an influence over adolescents. This chapter examines _how_ popular culture exudes a strong and generally negative impact on them by blurring the line between reality and fantasy. As this boundary melts down, it becomes progressively harder for youth to develop and function normally. Consequently, their understanding of reality instead of dramatization, and implicitly, right versus wrong, has grown muddled. As things stand, the knowledge that crowns one a social success or condemns one a failure varies widely between settings—home, school, street corner, cyber cafe. Judgements based on values passed down from parents and teachers often clash with the unwritten code and other conventions of popular culture unquestioningly adopted by students. With the ascent of electronic media, proliferating symbols and mixed signals enfilade the perception of younger persons. On a broader level, this portends a societal crisis.

This pattern of confusion should scare us for what its suggests about the cognitive development of youth. Submerged in a culture saturated with vicarious experiences and escapism, the chances for them recovering a balanced sense of reality with all of its attendant obligations diminish. How, for instance, can they possibly relate to prosaic tasks like going to class, doing homework, or taking part in extracurricular activities when myriad diversions continuously beckons to them. Compared to the digital thrill rides supplied by television, Nintendo 64 gaming or the 'Net, such duties strike them as onerous. Learning, then, as an lifelong exercise of the mind, tests the increasingly thin limits of their patience even more.

For youth, differentiating between fact and fiction has become problematic. Things that we adults counted on as absolute seem far less sure to them. After all, intellectuals tell us that truth is relative now rather than fixed, a bequest of the 1990's intellectual "culture wars." Keeping in step, postmodern psychology requires that we divest ourselves of archaic philosophies about humanity. Weary from centuries of conflict caused by ideologies and dogmas, we have been persuaded to embrace a novel articulation of culture. Relativism—a sort of academic live–and–let–live–creed—showed us the way. In the United States, at least, the culture wars ended in a crushing defeat of traditionalism. Our Westernized, master version of history taught for years could not, the victors decreed, speak for all humankind. Under postmodern pressure, our children learned that there are in fact multiple perspectives from which to interpret the world and these viewpoints vary across regions, classes, age groups and technological frontiers. In short, the philosophical, religious, and humanistic foundations of Western civilization were abruptly dispatched.

With the demise of social and political homogeneity and the embrace of postmodernism's pluralism, the terrain of everyday life changed as well. Reality no longer provided a framework for perception. On the other hand, this proposition was inverted. Perception *became* reality. In other words, what we see, hear, feel and believe determined the conditions of being. In such a place, the broader technologies we rely on play a central part in shaping this reality. Today, electronic media supply the conduit through which we make contact with and experience our surroundings. It is primarily through these mediated, or simulated, encounters that children come to know the world. Social skills and knowledge, too, are increasingly acquired from technology–dependent exchanges instead of human conveyance.

Concrete or counterfeit, tangible or transitory, graspable or ghostly, these adjectives speak to legitimate concerns in the avenues youth pursue to obtain both personal information and social acceptance.

WHEN THEORY BECAME REALITY

The Culture Industry and Narcotic of Simulation

A German émigré professor whose essays on mass culture became prominent in academic circles offered a prescient perspective on the emerging American cultural scene. Beginning in the 40's, Theodore Adorno anticipated the rise of a vast and potent multimedia complex he dubbed the "culture industry." Radio networks, newspaper syndicates, and an embryonic Hollywood were the turbines driving this machine with the most powerful medium ever conceived, television, arriving a few years hence. Riding on the coattails of the advent of mass production in industry was a parallel development in the *mass production of culture* (Cook, 1996). By the middle of the twentieth century, millions of people listened to the same music, went to the same movies, watched the same television programs, and subscribed to the same periodicals. Sensing the profits to be made, media conglomerates emerged to fill this popular demand.

Hastening the growth of this industry was its level of market penetration. In a short span of time, with ever-widening reach, Adorno predicted that the culture industry would accrue the power to mold public opinion, challenge social convention, and impinge upon individual thought by cleverly blending news, information and entertainment. Thoroughly immersed, the masses couldn't help but be influenced by the content of films, programs and papers. Under constant messages and portrayals to conform, the capacity for independent choice evaporated. Under prolonged exposure, which was all but assured with the public's embrace of these media, people would eventually think less for themselves and gradually come to prefer the ideas presented in the avalanche of material they encountered. Soon enough, a 'dictatorship of a self-appointed elite' within these conglomerates would soon feel at liberty to make choices about advancing certain agendas, ideas and values to an unsuspecting audience. Unchallenged, this elite would wield exclusive authority to create or modify culture, without opposition, as the masses continued unaware to lap up what they were ladling out. In its late stages, the population would be held in its thrall and all hope for recovering freedom of thought, individually or socially, eclipsed (Adorno, 1972).

Adorno's work demonstrated amazing powers of prognostication for a man not native to the United States and one whose theories appeared decades before the communications revolution occurred. His intuitions on the growth and consolidation of separate news and entertainment concerns into media giants with world-wide reach proved uncanny. Consider that the largest of these purely entertainment entities today is Time Warner with revenues of $26.8 billion and a diversified empire that includes movies/television, cable TV programming, publishing, music, and broadcasting (Greenfeld, 1999). Other behemoths making the list were Walt Disney ($22.9 billion in theme parks, broadcasting, and entertainment enterprises) and Viacom/CBS ($18.9 billion). Their power can be felt around the globe. Saddam Hussein was reportedly addicted to Cable News Network (CNN) and rumor had it that he watched it day and night during the 1991 Gulf War for the updates on how his Republican Guard troops were faring against the Allied coalition. Battlefront communiques, it seemed, reached him faster through CNN than his own military channels.

A harbinger of what may yet lie ahead came in the announced coupling of American On–line and Time Warner Inc. in January, 2000. This mating of leviathans, worth $184 billion, stands as the most expensive takeover in history. If Wall Street analysts are accurate, it will also lead to further rounds of "furious acquisitions as traditional networks and media giants vie to embrace the Internet world." (Miller & Friedman, 2000). This Time Warner–AOL union serves as a textbook illustration of the mass communications principle of *convergence,* which describes how communication technologies, independent, but growing parallel of each other, eventually merge and the synergy produced by such a marriage ends up improving both far beyond their previous best. AOL, nominally the U.S.' biggest Internet access provider, suddenly has inroads to the more established cable television market. Given that the science to do it already exists, it won't be long before AOL taps into this rich consumer market through the cable ports Time Warner currently maintains in countless homes—the television set. Beware, Aldous Huxley's *Brave New World* looms ever closer.

If Adorno's musings scintillate, the work of another scholar actually alarms. Adorno, after all, critiqued modernism as he experienced it. Modernism since expired. A postmodern perspective on popular culture outlined by a French sociologist named Jean Baudrillard more accurately describes the essence of contemporary life.

In his 1981 book, *Simulacra and Simulation,* Baudrillard makes a forceful argument that the media of popular culture have completely devoured the intellectual sensibilities of humanity. He envisioned a perverse landscape in which the distinction between object and representation, thing and idea, were rendered invalid. "In their place, Baudrillard fathoms a peculiar type of existence constructed out of models or *simulations* which have no referent or ground in any 'reality' except their own." (Poster, 1988, p.6). Relying on McLuhan's maxim, rather than acting as a mode of delivery, the medium itself is now the message. What is being said has been subordinated to how it's being fed to us. The delivery system supersedes content. Even programs we are asked to take as factual mislead us. For instance, we can point a finger at television journalism "...which create the news if only to be able to narrate it."

Consider the production processes behind the evening news on television. Events being reported on; natural disasters, wars, political campaigns, all existed before these programs. What we see isn't so much a factual account of said event as a seamless, 30–second encapsulation of it. Peter Jennings, Dan Rather, or Tom Brokaw weave narratives and volunteer opinions on the event as skillfully edited film footage showing certain aspects of the story play across the screen. In this beautifully coordinated combination, they pique the viewer's interest and evoke a reaction. We talk about them with our spouses or friends as the important, perhaps only, developments deserving our attention that day. By inference, we conclude that nothing else worthwhile occurred this same day, otherwise it too would have made the broadcast. Yet before airing, producers have decided which events should and shouldn't be included in a half–hour broadcast. Are those left on the cutting room floor or staff conference table any less legitimate in being deemed newsworthy? Perhaps not to Jennings, Rather, or their executive producers, but to people in the vicinity of where the wars are being waged or the typhoons are wreaking havoc, they are the *only* news. What legislative debate took place on the floor of Congress in Washington or why the Nikkei stock exchange dropped ten percent in Tokyo, stories which may have preempted theirs on the news broadcast, matter not in the least to these unfortunates in harm's way. In its selection, omission, and delivery, then, the media is indeed creating news and manufacturing that particular day's vision of reality.

The panic inspired by the now laughable "Y2K" scare underscores this even further. From 1997 onward, with ever deepening dread, the United States was gripped by paranoia of impending disaster as the new millenium approached. Under a deluge of dire forecasts about widespread infrastructure failures, people were brought to the verge of hysteria. The media 'reported' on probable regional power grid shutdowns, banking system collapses, and food distribution problems precipitated by lost or inaccurate computer inventories. Computer navigational glitches aboard airplanes along with air traffic control radar also had high chances of failing too. In addition, terrorists, hoping to capitalize on our crippled communication and response systems, we were told, perhaps lurked in every major city, waiting to blow up revelers intent on celebrating this milestone. In response, thousands if not millions of citizens arranged for alternate power sources and even purchased portable generators. Many withdrew significant amounts of currency from their savings accounts. Others stocked up heavily on bottled water, canned goods and dry victuals. Friends and colleagues went so far as to cancel or postpone holiday trips in their understandable anxiety to survive this approaching armageddon. I hesitated to make plans myself. When New Year's Eve came and went, our nation and the world at large exhaled a collective sigh of relief. Relieved as we were, one couldn't help but feel the media was rather disappointed this once–in–a–thousand–year event that they had warned us so feverishly about didn't pan out into a world–wide web of catastrophe. The Y2K doomsday scenario was as pure a figment of media hype as could ever have been imagined.

Under such deceiving perceptual conditions, people sacrifice their ability for rational thinking because the map of reality they once counted on for reference points has ceased to exist. Replacing it is a world of simulation, an 'imaginary of representation' tainting all levels of encounter and confusing that which our senses perceive. In this age, reality has become skin deep, dazzling a society swamped with fanciful messages and counterfeit experiences that have no substance beyond pure appearance. "We live in a world where there is more and more information and less and less meaning." (Baudrillard, 1994, pp. 79–81). Advertising jingles, the image–montage style of music videos, and the spasmodic titillation of video games illustrate this. They contain minimal content apart from pleasing the ears, wowing the eyes, or exercising our reflexes as we manipulate a joy stick. Living in the moment is no longer sufficient. Our pleasures are now apportioned in nanoseconds.

Life as it once was has been eradicated by an endless "vertigo of electronic fantasy–images" (Aronowitz & Giroux, 1991, p. 66) duping the beholder into believing them to be tangible when in fact, they are only an elaborate smoke and mirrors act pretending to be real. Mesmerized by this array of shimmering mirages, discriminating between reality and this new *hyperreality* clouds our perceptual abilities. In its unquenchable thirst for ever more artificial outlets of experience, society has become "…the black hole into which all meaning simply disappears." Logically, as this hyperreality intensifies the gap between things authentic and simulated dissolves and all meaning collapses.

Baudrillard isolated a quintessential American institution, Disneyland, as the 'perfect model' of simulation. "It is first of all a play of illusions and phantasms: the Pirates, the Frontier, the Future World, etc. This imaginary world is supposed to ensure the success of the operation. But what attracts the crowds the most is without a doubt the social microcosm, the *religious*, miniaturized pleasure of real America, of its constraints and joys." (1994, p. 12). He concludes that we have subconsciously surrendered to the fantasy of Disneyland, not to mention other simulations, because they provide a duplicate existence we find far more rewarding than our actual lives.

Picking up on this thread, educational theorist Henry Giroux, explained the cross–generational allure of this Disneyland. For adults, these "theme parks offer an invitation to adventure, a respite from the drudgery of work, and an opportunity to escape from the alienation of daily life." Psychologically, Disney's power to captivate lies in its ability to "tap into lost hopes" and aborted dreams and satisfy the nostalgic cravings of people unhappy with what adulthood has brought them. To children, Disneyland is a "wish landscape" enticing them with a "more colorful and imaginary world." Through its multiple adventures, exciting rides, and larger–than–life characters, children not only escape the irksome rules and discipline of school, but get to lose themselves in a fantasy that assuages the "brutality and emptiness of everyday life." (1999, 5–7, 35). For both age groups, Disneyland provides a parallel universe preferable to the starkness of normal life. This inclination to exist in blissful but delusional conditions applies to other areas of postmodern life. Escapism has become America's preference. Television, video games or cyberspace are just a few of the conduits we used to enter this realm of fantasy. Creating and bending the circumstances of these illusory experiences to our will, that is, suspending our disbelief and losing ourselves in the act of pretending, makes them too powerful to resist.

Predictably, crises arise in the aftermath. Baudrillard believes that nowadays, "socialization is measured by exposure to media messages. Whoever is underexposed to the media is desocialized or virtually asocial." (p. 80). The implications of his statement are enormous. Unfortunately, they seem to have already been validated in the behaviors and attitudes displayed by youth. The majority of these have been absorbed from their exposure to sundry media. Smoking among teens, despite a wealth of data and adult warnings, is cool. Exercising, on the other hand, regardless of how loudly its benefits have been touted, doesn't much impress younger Americans. Pre–and teen obesity is at an all time high. Yielding to that timeless drive for peer acceptance, youth immerse themselves in the compact discs, electronic games, and television shows that are in vogue. Clothing has to be Tommy Hilfiger and athletic shoes Reebok, else our sons and daughters face the risk of being ostracized. Of course, which styles are 'in' and which are 'out' depends on the latest Gap or Foot Locker commercials they see. Habits, tastes, and styles, all of these are socially dictated by the media of pop culture.

In the next sections, we will examine the primary delivery systems of popular culture and evaluate their impact on socialization. Each does something unique. By themselves, perhaps, films or television do not prevent psychological growth. In confluence and over a lifetime, however, these simulations combine to derail normal mental development and sidetrack it into an alien land where rationality no longer applies.

CRISIS OF INDIVIDUALITY AND SOCIAL PATHOLOGIES

Blurred Identities

American suburbs overflow with middle–class white kids cruising around in hand–me–down BMWs listening to Ice T 'bust a rhyme.' African–Americans, young and older, are waging an ongoing war over their being "authentically black" when they excel at school, take management positions in white corporations, or fail any other racial litmus tests in the eyes of peers (Berry, 2000). Women, as usual, remain torn between juggling contradictory social expectations: that it's desirable to have a career and advance as far as you can as long as you don't compromise your womanhood and can balance a job with being a good mother and loving wife. Married, middle–aged, family men, aware that their best years are slipping away, often waver in resisting the temptations of beautiful younger women and sports cars, two prestigious trophies our society insinuates all successful, and virile, men should possess.

In this milieu of blurring roles and schizophrenic values, is it any wonder that the concept of *identity* grows ever more nebulous? The dictionary defines identity as "the condition that a person or a thing is itself and not something else; individuality, personality." Maybe this was the case once, but as society changed so did the meaning of the term. Kenneth Gergen, for one, describes this change. "As we absorb the views, values and visions of others, and live out the multiple plots in which we are enmeshed...we no longer experience a secure sense of self..." (1993, p.15). He thinks that as this process of social saturation continues, all of us undergo an 'erasure of individual self.' With their identities still taking shape, youth are the least immune to this saturation.

Flux in the contemporary world has altered the concept so much that social psychologists had a field day evolving a more current notion of identity. Christopher Lasch represents a school of thought that while already dated, coming from the 80's, begins to trace the mutation of individuality into its present dissociated state. Gergen, a modern–day guru of social commentary, gives us a more recent reading of the idea. His work speaks not only to what happened to the notion of identity but supplies a template for how its former parameters have been stretched, torn and reconfigured into something suited to post-modern America

As noted in *The Minimal Self,* Lasch articulated a number of truths about the mutating nature of individuality. Recalling that he wrote about the adverse effect of mass production and consumption on personality, Lasch believed that as Americans were transformed into consumers, things took a psychological turn for the worst. "The conditions of everyday social intercourse in societies based on mass consumption encourage an unprecedented attention to superficial impressions and images, to the point where the self becomes almost indistinguishable from its surface." (p.30). In this cultural cauldron of pictures, slogans, and soundbytes, the person lives not so much in an existence grounded in ideas as in impressions. Over time, these impressions coalesce together and become so internalized that preserving a separate, original sense of personhood apart from a socially–absorbed identity becomes impossible. Evidence of this process surrounds us in the middle–class, suburban white teens have adopted the clothing, attitudes and speech of Black rappers that reign over pop music and MTV.

If Lasch's insights tantalized, Gergen's *The Saturated Self* is the more complete in tracing the historical stages of "self" or identity. He compares and contrasts three distinct renditions of identity enabling us see how it has evolved to meet the times.

–The "romanticist" self: The individual has emotional depth and personal uniqueness. Derived from 19th century literature, s/he prized the capacity for developing relationships with other human beings. Traits such as passion, soul, creativity, and moral courage can be associated with the romanticized self. Profoundness and expression of feelings typified this type of person.

–The "modernist" self: Arising at the turn of the 20th century, romanticist views of the individual gave ground to a new profile. The "modern" identity saw sentimentality and the need to express it to others as remnants of the past. What defined individuality was "our ability to reason." People were, or should be, logical, predictable, and basically honest. A desire to inquire, learn and build reflected the natural order of our minds. The modern self valued intellect over emotion.

–The "postmodern" self: With both of the preceding definitions eclipsed by recent history, a new profile of identity evolved. The postmodern self "…is marked by a plurality of voices vying" to be heard and as they grow louder, "…all that (once) seemed proper, right-minded, and well understood is subverted." The postmodern personality exists "…in a state of continuous construction and reconstruction." S/he bears little resemblance to the sentimental being of romanticism, nor the enlightened rationalist of modernism, both of whose individuality arose from an internal center. In contrast, the postmodern self is purely a *social creation*.

This 'social creation' warrants closer inspection. In the present, a person's identity doesn't arise from personality traits passed down from parents or taught by them. Instead, it is mainly absorbed from external sources. Gergen coined the phrase *pastiche personality* to describe the contemporary self. In these surroundings, humans aren't capable of authentic emotional and cognitive development. Rather, their identities develop in a cut–and–paste composite. Beliefs, opinions, behaviors—these are picked up from various technologies and experiences. "The pastiche personality is a social chameleon, constantly borrowing bits and pieces of identity from whatever sources are available and constructing them as useful or desirable in a given situation." (p.150).

For Gergen, Lasch, et.al., the self can only be comprehended in a social context. When we listen to our children talking to other kids, we have firsthand evidence of how true this has become. The exclamations coming from their mouths surprise us in how contradictory they are to the opinions they share with us at home. What accounts for the discrepancy, we wonder. Applying Gergen's rationale, youth are simply acting like the social shape–shifters they need to be for postmodern survival. And though this ensures acceptance by peers, it doesn't make it any easier for them to develop personalities totally their own or free from unsettling influences.

Cult of Celebrity

My choice of the term 'cult' is intentional. For in it, I mean to suggest that our culturally–sanctioned predilection for celebrity–gazing has attained the dimensions of religious worship. Aware of pop culture's penchant for appearances, celebrities are the celestial objects toward which the attention of youth permanently inclines in the postmodern universe. Professional and amateur performers endowed with perfect faces or physiques, and either a show business pedigree or personal panache, are soon catapulted into that rarified air of celebrity so many Americans long to inhale. Of course, talent should make a difference. But is not a requirement.

Anyone reading this book already lives with a nagging paradox of postmodern life, although he or she may not even recognize it. Not unlike the technology–enthralled society in Vonnegut's novel, *Player Piano*, we are too distracted by automation's whirring and clicking noises, procession of flashing pictures, and surreptitiously dehumanizing influence of machines to notice the contradiction. It is this: we know more biographical information about sports heroes, movies stars, or musical artists than we do about the neighbor living two doors down from us. Worse still, there are many Americans who prefer it this way.

Where the elderly Mr. Wilson came from, his vocation, his hobbies and interests, these we can only guess at. If he ever was in love, had a wife, or fathered children, few others on the street know or bother to ask. Anything more than what we can deduce from visual contact—that lovely flower bed around his front porch perhaps means that he's fond of gardening—is off limits. Don't ask, conventional wisdom advises, and you won't have to be burdened. Nor would you then be obliged to tell him anything about yourself. Under the guise of respecting personal privacy, we have become a nation without neighbors.

Of course, in direct contrast, celebrity portraits and biographies are plastered everywhere. They jump out at us from supermarket tabloids, magazines such as *People, Teen People, Us*, and *Vanity Fair*, from Internet directories listing all our favorite stars and live–chats where, if we're really lucky, we can engage in an on–line discussions with our favorite star. With minor effort, we can easily find out the proportions of supermodel Christy Turlington, not to mention her likes and dislikes in dress, cuisine, whom she has been romantically linked to, and even the fees she commands by logging on to any of a dozen Web sites or shrines (in tech–speak) devoted to her. Ditto for Harrison Ford, Shaquille O'Neal, or Oprah Winfrey. Even the urbane television network, *Arts & Entertainment*, caved in to public pressure and the need to boost its ratings. Now it panders to popular whim with its stylish, larger–than–life accounts of public figures in its *Biography* series.

Interestingly, a pattern has emerged. In the United States, the dream of anyone overcoming their surroundings to achieve fame and wealth is not just cherished. It has become the fantasy of choice for an entire society. If it eludes us as individuals, then consolation can be found in paying homage to those upon whom fortune has smiled. Celebrities have been raised to the status of demigods because popular culture engenders a mystique and myth around their persons as ones who attained that intangible fantasy. A postmodern cultural creed hammers away at us that these actors, musicians, athletes, and even fashion models *must be* superior and therefore deserving of devotion. It may be that Christy Turlington *is* beautiful or Michael Jordan *did* defy gravity. The issue isn't that these people aren't superlative within the confines of their highly visible professions. Unsettling is the fact that sects of worship have sprung up around them or, at least, their representation in the media. We simply cannot see enough footage of them, amass enough biographical data, or stop analyzing the secret of what makes them special. Recognized by the media for these qualities, they possess the looks, the skills, and the glamour all Americans secretly wish they also had. They are esteemed as the personifications of perfection and therefore what the rest of us should also aspire to be. Each celebrity consequently inspires a cult of fans–followers who perceive them in an almost divine light. Once again, examples of this trend abound.

Another queer phenomenon that parodies popular culture's fascination with stardom is the instant prestige that accompanies celebrity reporting. Ingratiating pseudo–journalists chasing actors to every charity event or film premiere rockets them to star status. Mary Hart of *Entertainment Tonight*, Phil Maher of *Politically Incorrect*, and David Letterman of *The Late Show* owe their considerable fortunes to doing little more than shadowing every movement of celebrities or engaging them in glib but meaningless banter on the shows they host. Evidence or absence of talent on the part of the host doesn't matter. Fame by association, it seems, is good enough to bring riches and respect.

Assuming American's craving for celebrity data can ever be satiated, the next level of initiation into the cult is emulation. This is dangerously true for *adolescents already struggling with identity formation*. How many boys want to "be like Mike"? They inform their mothers that all they need to eat is Wheaties and to drink Gatorade, two products that Jordan endorses, and spend all their time on the basketball court instead of at the library doing homework. If not Jordan, then certainly some unworthy professional athlete inspiring boys to shave their heads, turn their arms into tattoo boards, and nag their parents into buying them the latest pair of Adidas or Nikes endorsed by this star they're agog over. More than a few pubescent girls dream of growing to six feet and becoming runway models. To bring them closer to this idyll, they eat frighteningly little and grow alarmingly thin. A John Hopkins University study released in spring of 2000 actually traced the growing undernourishment of Miss Americas during the last 78 years. If our daughters' immersion into the cult deepens, bulimia or anorexia may not lag far behind. Other girls, imbued with less height, may elect to follow the example set by younger female stars in surgically enhancing their still–developing bodies with breast implants as rumors insist teen idols like Britney Spears or Jennifer Love Hewitt did.

The people our children used to want to be like have vanished from the scene for very apparent reasons. Parents, grandparents, most adults can't compete with these new avatars. By comparison, the finest personal qualities of familiar adults who make up a child's world—kindness, honesty and reliability—seem excruciatingly dull. Raising children or going to work every day strike them as the worst form of drudgery. The grown–ups in their lives aren't as as tall, as chiseled, as muscled, as beautiful, handsome, witty, and definitely not as rich. Naive young minds have been completely seduced by a media which hangs upon celebrities' every syllable, covers them in nauseating detail, and proclaims their greatness.

Among the media missionaries spreading this new sect far and wide, a rapidly expanding network on cable television helping convert the masses steps up in the Entertainment or "E!" station. This network is a twenty–four hour a day, seven days a week, visual pageant for the cult of celebrity. Offering its millions of viewers a mash of star–profile programs like the bogus documentary series *True Hollywood Stories*, "E!" purports to be delivering what the public wants—behind–the–scenes coverage of Hollywood premieres, star-studded award banquets, or international fashion shows drawing the jet set, to name just a few. "E!" is tabloid print journalism transposed into a television medium. Well aware that its audience can never be fully satiated, it epitomizes the worst extremes of the cult of celebrity. Proof of this arises in acid–tongued comic Joan Rivers two–hour, *Fashion Revue* series that precedes every major award show (Emmys, Golden Globes, Oscars, etc.). In it, a panel of fashion mavens, led by Rivers and her dilettantish daughter, Melissa, spend one hundred and twenty minutes mercilessly critiquing the attire of each and every star on their way into the theatre hosting the event. Commentary ranges from sarcastic to plain cruel. Yet this program is inexplicably popular among young females and a perennial ratings coup for *E!* network.

Predictably, how deep and potentially deadly our obsession with celebrity can run sometimes manifests itself in criminal acts. Most readers can remember the murder of John Lennon in New York in 1980 by crazed fan Mark Chapman. Later that decade, John Hinckley, the would–be assassin of President Ronald Reagan, committed his dastardly crime in a deranged effort to attract the attention of actress Jodie Foster. Obviously these offenders suffered from various degrees of mental illness and do not represent the majority of people who follow the careers of favorite performers. However, there does seem to be a link, however vague and random at this point, between individuals' desire for star status and maladjusted behavior.

As with Eric Harris and Dyland Klebold, unbalanced minds seem especially susceptible to media messages, but incapable of weeding the fabrications or recognizing its inherent amorality. The videotapes they left behind showed they felt that Columbine would make them instant celebrities and this appeared to be a motivating factor. On the other hand, in their quest for notoriety, they conveniently skipped past the obvious criminality of the scheme that would elevate them there. Feeling alienated and outcast, this was the only sure path they had available to achieve stardom, infamous as it might be.

In his short story, "The Snows of Kilimanjaro," Hemingway's protaganonist, recalls an acquaintance named Julian, who thought the rich and famous were a 'special glamorous race of people'. When Julian discovered they were not what he imagined, it wrecked him. In a way, it is tempting to draw an analogy between this misguided character and many people living today. Like him, a lot of Americans naively believe that celebrities are superior beings. Nourished on this grand myth of popular culture, youth, more so than adults, understandably see celebrities as larger than life. Beautiful, fascinating, and wealthy, in unflattering contrast to parents and other adult acquaintances inhabiting their world, adolescents aspire to be like them. In that sense, they, too, have also been damaged by a fantasy.

If Julian's discovery of the truth ruined him, our inability to see past the glitter of fame and wealth threatens to destroy our foothold in reality. Adolescents have not lived long enough to see beyond veneers, through illusions, and have been handicapped by the deception. Given the cult's prevalence, there is reason to believe they never will perceive its origins in fantasy.

Rise of Voyeurism

A companion disorder to this infatuation with celebrity especially perilous for the young, and one induced by Baudrillard's "hyperreality", is the preference it instills for watching rather than acting. Life unfolds vicariously instead of personally, not so much as an old–style peeping tom leering through a bedroom window, but through the electronic eyes of a camera lens. Technology permits window–gazing without the fear of being branded a degenerate. Instead of being stigmatized, younger Americans have latched onto it in a twisted new approach to social interaction. Their lives, like those of their parents, apparently strike them as so monotonous and meaningless that the temptation to peer in on someone more interesting is simply irresistible. Actor or amateur, that the person being watched is even worthy of television or internet coverage qualifies them as an object for rapt attention. Instant celebrity via the magic of surveillance—this is a corollary of the digital age.

Enter the world of voyeurism, of visual eavesdropping. No risk of personal or social rejection exists. Anonymity is guaranteed. Pleasuring comes at a respectable distance. Today, technology enables us to live through the subject being observed. The Internet, chock full of streaming videos, audio plug–ins, web cams, and real–time chat boards where alter egos cloaking the user in obscurity prevail, abetted the onset of voyeurism. Undismayed, youth are the most prone to develop these voyeuristic tendencies since they are at an age when the world's forbidden taboos legally fall outside their reach yet beckon to them through various media. They grew up in a world where the most intensive experiences available to them don't come directly but indirectly through television, movies, and cyberspace. If adults still retain a scrap of memory of life before the media ruled, children and teens do not. The implications of this trend are neither happy or healthy.

Two evocative films, *The Truman Show* (1998) and *EdTV* (1999) provided stark vistas of a voyeuristic culture gone to extremes. The former artistically, the latter crudely, projected what would happen when the life of the individual is so totally violated by cameras recording every movement for observing hordes that the person can no longer find space to be human. Although by their respective ends, both films impart the moral that unchecked voyeurism will destroy individuals and relationships, they nonetheless let their heroes relish the limelight as much as despise it.

A real world instance of our bias toward vicarious living arises in a Web site aptly named *Voyeurdorm.com*. I saw it profiled on the cable news station MSNBC. Belligerent attorneys representing the enterprise vehemently insisted to the news anchor that *Voyeurdorm* was not a pornographic site where paying customers could watch six uninhibited co–eds living in the privacy of their own residence. For a monthly fee, clients could follow these female students as they wandered through their daily routines about the house. Mind you, this sounded like few ordinary residences—its inhabitants seemed to disdain clothing of all sorts. Of course, a couple dozen strategically placed cameras located in every place from the bedroom to a lower corner of the shower stall brought live video feeds directly to customer's home computer. Whether playing the piano topless, chatting electronically with loyal fans while wearing thong bikinis, or bathing, viewers were able to watch every move of its comely cast in their spontaneous splendor. All legal posturing aside, this site is merely an Internet equivalent of a peep show where patrons can indulge in flesh–driven reveries without risking the public embarrassment of being seen entering a strip club. In a strange juxtaposition possible only in this day and age, the very technology they rely on to enter into this forbidden realm protects them from unwanted invasions of their own privacy.

The objectification of female sexuality reverberates as a powerful theme in pop culture. It is also one ideally suited to the tastes of the voyeur. Perhaps this is nothing new. Television and motion pictures have been exploiting the female form for decades, the Internet simply made it more discreet. However, what is new and dangerous is the increasing presentation of *juveniles as sexual objects*. Specifically, if media portrayals were to be believed, adolescent girls ooze sensuality and sexual sophistication. On the Web, pornographic sites advertising images or video of teenage girls are flourishing. On television, dressed provocatively and wise enough to manipulate the boys and men (even their fathers) around them, post–pubescent girls get depicted as wily and willing (see most any the WB's or Fox networks's teen dramas). In film, this updated Lolita theme resounds through Oscar–winning *American Beauty*, art–house favorite *Cruel Intentions*, or the offbeat *Jawbreaker*. Of course, since it is always the young heroine who selects her lover and the circumstances under which they will couple, the viewer is maneuvered to believe the female is doing the using rather than being used. This projection of sexual power among teenaged girls eliminates any inklings of impropriety or guilt in the beholder.

So prevalent is the perception of American girls as sexually–charged even they have been contaminated by it. Cosmetic surgeons are busier than ever doing chin sculpting, liposuctions or collagen injections into lip tissue on adolescent females. More amazing is the fact that parents condone it by funding these operations. Years back, we all heard tales of the debutante from the Hamptons or Beverly Hills who wanted and got a nose job on her sixteenth birthday. Now, it is not uncommon for parents to sign releases for their daughters in high school to get breast implants, or so a plastic surgeon friend of mine sheepishly admitted. Girls want to look like the glamorous models and starlets whose images decorate magazine covers and movie screens, after all.

A less lascivious, commercially–motivated version of voyeurism becoming a theatre of the absurd appeared in January, 2000. It was then that the story broke of the "DotComGuy" (*USA Weekend*, January 2). A 26 year–old man legally changed his name to the above handle. In a publicity stunt suited to these times, this man walked into a Dallas home equipped with nothing other than a computer. He boasts that he won't leave the house until 2001. His aim: depending exclusively on the Internet for his sanity and survival. In the mean time, however, cameras will broadcast his movements to the public 24/7 via his Web site. Ordering in all furniture and groceries, he will be free to chat live with viewers around the globe. Nor are visitors to his house prohibited, so friends, family and "celebrity guests" he hopes, will occasionally drop in. DotComGuy admits that his motives are mercenary, but one also assumes that the dubious renown connected with his becoming a "virtual" hero to the techno–generation and potential windfall that promises supply added incentive. Probably the best thing that could happen would be if no one subscribed to watch. As of June of 2000, thankfully, nothing more has been heard of the Dotcomguy.

Vantage point not withstanding, the voyeuristic experience only imitates reality. The universe it tries to tempt us with is synthetic, an approximation, and regardless how vivid its detail, nothing can make it real. Yet because it creates the feeling in the viewer that they are not only privy to a taboo world, but somehow personally involved with the person or subject they are watching, this illusion nourishes them. Michael O'Neill said in *The Roar of the Crowd*, that there is "…an immediacy about the moving images, an intensity of directly felt experience," (p.38) which sustains the illusion and the observer's fixation on it. For a while, at least. The curse of the voyeur is his fleeting pleasure. Whatever comfort or companionship he feels from the encounter, it does not last and the need for increasingly frequent and more intense viewing episodes slowly consume him. We see this pattern in young people. How quickly they tire of the channel they are watching or the Internet site being visited. Always a higher level of stimulation in being sought.

If the Internet provides the fastest passage into the voyeur's world, television runs a close second. "Reality programming" is the current buzzword in the industry as well as a prominent theme for a new batch of shows. (Levin, 2000). Until recently, executives pushing reality programming, like those at Fox network responsible for the *Who Wants to Marry a Millionaire?* fiasco, typically ended up with egg on their faces. Despite this debacle, other networks heads remained undeterred. A later attempt at reality programming debuted on CBS' *Survivor* during the summer of 2000, wherein 16 mismatched people were stranded on a tropical island with scarce provisions and only their ingenuity to save them. The last remaining contestant of this group won one million dollars. This time, network executives hit the jackpot. An estimated fifty–two million viewers tuned into the finale, setting a record for being the most watched show ever in summer series television. Never mind that the winner turned out to be an utterly unscrupulous businessman whose "Machiavellian determination" (Gorman, 2000) won him the money and blasted him into the stratosphere of popular culture. Love or hate this man, his instant celebrity ironically provided America with yet another contemporary anti–hero for mass consumtiom. Given its incredible success, especially with the younger viewing demographic, *Survivor II* captivated millions, assuring a place of honor in television history. Nor does one need crystal–gazing to foresee a III, IV, and V.

Apart from its darker emotional implications, the voyeuristic disorder breeds a related malady. It kills the impulse to act for one's self. Like O'Neill observed, using technology as a window into the experiences of others forces the beholder into passivity. Viewing is "…an act of personal receiving rather than social exchange." (p. 48) It dampens the desire to seek out interpersonal encounters. We withhold the vitality and warmth they require of us. In turn, the emotional sustenance we draw from shaking hands, looking directly into another person's eyes, or hugging them when saying goodbye are denied us. Such detachment in obviously unhealthy for children. Warmth, compassion, and concern are preconditions for normal growth and development. With prolonged exposure, voyeurism reduces the human mind to the equivalent of a caged rat in a lab experiment pressing a lever to get yet another food pellet, except the individual keeps pressing the left side of his mouse as he points and clicks his way from one scene to the next in seeking an ever higher level of viewing stimulation. It fosters a isolating sense of *digital depression*, or being wired to everything but finding companionship nowhere (Pavlik, 1996). Investigative reports have shown that several of the teen school shooters were described as loners who spent inordinate amounts of time playing games, surfing the 'Net, or chatting with cyberfriends rather than other kids in their neighborhood. Sheer coincidence? I think not.

In adolescents, still other complications can occur. Generally speaking, the younger the person, the worse its effect. Along with a decay in their psychological and social well–being comes an atrophying of their physical fitness. Lax grooming, poor personal health, insufficient exercise, even obesity, often accompany as symptoms of this digital wasting. Reaching the goals projected for youth in the federal government's Healthy People 2010 program (**www.health.gov/healthypeople**) seems highly improbable. For example, in spite of a program target goal to reduce teen smoking, the number of young smokers actually rose from 28% to 36% during the 90's. But who needs to fret over lung capacity or the exertion of movement when the need for fellowship can be gratified by sitting for hours in front of a computer monitor or television screen? As the use of technology widens, our sons and daughters may well be overcome with a wider paralysis.

Implications

Brilliant minds have put together a disturbing composite of postmodern society. Although some, like Adorno, died years ago, the importance of their work has not been diminished. He correctly foresaw the ascent of mass media and the gradual erosion of human intellect. Closer to the present, Baudrillard delivered a bleak reading of an existence in which we have surrendered our independence of thought under the spell of a media blitz whose primary effect was to choke individual initiative while diverting our attention to hollow diversions. Until now, it was formerly assumed that the media mirrored reality, "…whereas now they are coming to constitute a (hyper) reality, a new media reality, 'more real than real,' where 'the real' is subordinate to representation." (Kellner, 1989, 68). As a media construction, the properties and borders of the reality we once knew cannot be trusted. Because hyperreality has infiltrated our lives to the degree that it has and covered its tracks so well in merging information with entertainment, no one seems to have noticed. Nor is it likely that many people would even object to this artificial world. It's simply more enjoyable.

By and large, broader segments of the population content themselves with living indirectly through celebrity surrogates or other public figures whose lives, they are repeatedly told, offer so much more than their own. While still capable of functioning at a low level—mechanically attending school, going to the office, catching up with family members on the weekends—they save their energies for other pursuits. Too often, however, their passions are roused only by one form or another of entertainment.

Congruent with those who assert that we are losing in the war against media subterfuge is Neil Postman, author of *Amusing Ourselves to Death*. He refers to the present as a *peek–a–boo* world. The 'ensemble' of electronic media and recreations we now rely on imposed this condition, bringing with it a world "…where now this event, now that pops into view for a moment and then vanishes again. It is a world without much coherence or sense; a world that does not ask us, indeed, does not permit us to do anything; a world that is, like the child's game of peek–a–boo, entirely self contained." (p. 77).

If Postman hit on something valuable and ours is a time where quick–hits rather than substance have become the foundation of reality, can we pinpoint an American institution that captures this essence? And of all uniquely American institutions, is there anything that represents culture better than the great cities of the United States and the symbols we associate with them, like New York, the Statue of Liberty and Ellis Island, or St Louis and the Arch to the West? Of these bustling metropolises, landmarks to our ambitions and aspirations, might there be one in particular that reflects our present preoccupations. Yes, avers Postman, as he shares his choice with us:

> "Today we must look to the city of Las Vegas as a metaphor of our national characters and aspiration, its symbol, a thirty–foot high cardboard picture of a slot machine and a chorus girl. For Las Vegas is a city devoted entirely to the idea of entertainment, and as such proclaims the spirit of a culture in which all public discourse increasingly takes the form of entertainment. Our politics, religion, news, athletics, education and commerce have been transformed into congenial adjuncts of show business, largely without protest or even much popular notice. The result is that we are a people on the verge of amusing ourselves to death." (pp. 3–4)

Amuse is a relative term. Its use here should not produce smugness as much as kindle alarm. As will soon become clear in the next chapter, Postman, Baudrillard, and Adorno all arrived at the same inescapable truth. The allure and beguilement of entertainment rules the present character of American society. Thus, the subject matter of these enter-tainments are surely worth investigating at closer quarters.

Summary

Theory can inform us and help explain how things reached their present state. How youth inherited a world created largely out of media synthesis should be eminently clear to the reader now. What this simu-lated reality has done to individual psychology should also seem less obscure. Everything from identity to ideas are influenced by a popular culture whose dominance over their lives continues to grow. Rare is the teenager or young adult whose personality, values and views are not incorporated from seductive sources outside of him or her. While ado-lescents have always been susceptible to both peers and fashion, a com-pletely different scenario exists today. An unavoidable mass media assured that they now emerge as products of a cultural factory that con-ditioned every maturing boy and girl into its accepting its own perverse representation of reality. Swiftly, quietly, without much notice, it has managed to crush almost all opposition.

At least this what the theories set forth in this chapter lead you to conclude. Does "real life" support such contentions? In the narrative ahead, our focus will move past abstractions into actual demonstrations of this process.

6

Media Technologies and Techniques

"The...dam movies. They can ruin you. I'm not kidding."

—_Holden Caulfield, The Catcher in the Rye_

Y ounger, life–inexperienced individuals have been badly disoriented by artificial representations of reality. A panorama of entertainments amplified by technology has seen to it. Adults, for instance, retain the ability to distinguish between the phantasms of the scrolling video game wherein a computer–generated villain is vanquished with machine guns, lasers, or cluster bombs versus the means a real person might use to settle conflicts. Artificial experiences and mechanical reactions have not fully consumed them. With kids, we can't assume the same to be true. For Eric Harris and Dyland Klebold of Columbine infamy, it certainly wasn't the case. To be sure, there are others like them out there.

Although mainly informal, a widening body of research indicates that today's adolescents, having been deprived of the intellectual, social, and moral grounding which past generations of youth received, run into some difficulty in separating artifice from reality. In its assorted modes, technology offers encounters so life–like that for some these have become preferable to interactions with other people. Supporting this media machinery are the adapted, some would even say

141

mutated, perceptual powers of our youth. Plainly, youth now respond to very different sets of stimulation than adults once did.

While watching a panel–format news program not long ago, the name of which escapes me now, one of the guest 'experts' proposed an interesting idea on why youth may be more susceptible than ever to the insidious cultural messages transmitted by electronic media. He suggested that having literally grown up in front of computer and television screens and the electromagnetic fields they generate, perhaps a biological change had taken place in children unknown to us. What if at a cellular level, he conjectured, the brain's early hard–wiring had been altered in ways not yet measurable by modern medicine? This mutated neural network would assimilate and process information far differently than before. It would function less like a thinking, feeling organ and more like an unemotional but intelligent machine. Unhindered by socially–imposed contrivances such as values or conscience, this new type of brain might account for the behavioral aberrations we have been witnessing in younger persons.

For the moment, this expert's opinion smacks more of Robert Heinlein's or Isaac Asimov's futuristic fiction than science. Still, enough logic undergirds it to dismiss it out of hand. Cognitive psychologists might have something worth studying here. True or false, this notion was no less fascinating.

This chapter is about media and the things it whispers into young ears, fills dilating eyes with and pounds into forming personalities. While I don't earn a living as a media critic, I, like any thinking American, can tell the difference between harmless amusement and toxic reinforcement. The latter rules. One need not be a trained deconstructionist to see that what is being doled out as entertainment suitable for all ages is not even remotely that. And to those who argue that long–term contact with such programming does not actually alter attitudes and behavior, preferring to lay the blame 'on the home,' for example, they obviously must not live or work in close proximity to adolescents.

Note the term used above—programming. An odd coincidence, perhaps, but the fact remains that this is exactly what these exposures do. Thus, the real question is not are youth affected by these media, but *to what degree?* Searching for answers gives this chapter its focus.

In the pages ahead, we will look at the activities which skewed the perception of American youth. In a society as undisciplined as ours, with abundant wealth, omnipresent diversions, and slight adult supervision, leisure–time pursuits have become the focal point of many lives. Naturally, with the ongoing communications revolution, the majority of these recreational outlets involve interaction with the media. In addition, a fledgling youth culture that took first took flight on these media is coming home to roost. These factors converged to produce generations of adolescents—technically sophisticated on one level, psychologically debilitated and socially irresponsible on another—like the world has not seen before.

TECHNOLOGIES OF SIMULATION

"Television: chewing gum for the eyes."

——Frank Lloyd Wright

Television and the Loss of Perspective

No other mode of communication has served the interests of popular culture so loyally as television. It has become a dietary staple for the entertainment–starved masses around the world. Since its debut at the 1939 World's Fair and gradual invasion of homes across the nation, its intrusion into our lives has stirred much debate. Proponents laud its utility in offering the public free news, information, and entertainment. Critics attack it for its corrosive influences, specifically over impressionable younger viewers, who quickly find themselves immersed in a sea of inappropriate programs.

Regardless of positioning, we can agree that television is the 'meta–medium' of the information age—a vehicle providing not just knowledge, but knowledge about how we know what we do. With one present in almost every home in the United States, its supremacy is unchallenged. Given this reach, its domination over mass culture cannot be disputed. In a novel angle on this linkage, I defer to Neil Postman. "Twenty years ago, the question, does television shape culture or merely reflect it?, held considerable interest for many scholars and social critics. The question has largely disappeared as television has gradually *become* our culture." (1985, p. 79)

As far back as 1968, parents worried about such a scenario formed the Action for Children's Television advocacy group to promote responsible broadcasting. Its founder, Peggy Charren spearheaded a lengthy crusade that triumphed in 1990 with the passage of The Children's Television Act of 1990 by Congress. In theory, this legislation set "...federal requirements for educational children's programming and restricting commercials during kid's peak viewing hours,"(Kiesewetter, 2000). Impolite as may be to challenge the life's work of Charren, even a short survey of program listings during the so–called protected "prime time" slot confirms broadcasters are neither complying with the spirit or the letter of this Act.

If quality of exposure doesn't alarm, perhaps quantity will. The time television consumes in the lives of Americans should concern everyone. A.C. Nielsen Company found that the television is switched on *7 hours and 12 minutes per day* in the average U.S. home (*TV Free America*, 1998). By the age of 65, the typical American will have spent *nine years* of his life watching television. As a further sign of its ascendance and subsequent erosion of family dynamics, 66% of us admit to watching television during meals. Discussions at the dinner table have been supplanted by rapt attention to reruns of *Seinfeld*.

According to a separate study commissioned by the Kaiser Family Foundation (11/17/99), children aged 2–18 spend an average of nearly *five and a half hours per day* using media—television, computers, reading, video games, and listening to music. Of this, "Watching TV" topped the list of media used daily, with kids reporting an average of 2 hours and 46 minutes devoted to the tube. Sixty–five (65%) percent of children 8 and older reported having a television in their bedroom, suggesting that maybe adults do indeed let television babysit their kids. Also of interest among the Kaiser findings was the fact that 49% of child respondents said there were no parental rules governing what they watched. As we will shortly see, considering what the networks choose to air, this dearth of rules could be costing America dearly.

Television today is so littered with programs of nonexistent value that plucking an example out of the heap is akin to plunging your hand into an anthill and hoping to pull out an insect or two. In truth, the current schedule of programs does not even matter that much. Remove them today and the creative geniuses at the networks could manufacture equally objectionable replacements by tomorrow. The Big Three networks—NBC, CBS, and ABC, persist in pelting us with moronic sitcoms (with the same formulaic premise: youthful, mismatched roommates living in a New York City apartment, who sit idly by all day at home or in the nearby coffee shop and incessantly, though comically, complain about career or relationship woes appealing to either incurably bored or hopelessly dim viewers.) Of course, the parade of young–adults–in–the–city shows run primarily when these networks aren't padding their lineups with the eternal triumvirate of police, courtroom or medical melodramas.

Fox, arguably the lowliest of all the commercial networks, seems to exult in trashing all standards of decency with a menu of outlandish and offensive offerings designed to tweak the adrenal glands of younger viewers. After debuting with *Cops*, moving up to the *World's Wildest Police Videos* and its own spin on the carnival sideshow—*Believe it or Not*, Fox surpassed its own miserable standards when it began broadcasting *Shocking Behavior Caught on Tape*, a vile show clearly oriented toward a young audience. My wife and I inadvertently stumbled across this repulsive program after dinner one Saturday. (It ran, by the way, ran from 8–9 pm, the second half of the designated prime–time slot when plenty of children are among its audience at home.) Appalled at what I was seeing, I grabbed the memo pad we kept near the telephone and jotted down descriptions of what was appearing on the screen. These were some of its more objectionable segments:

- Spring–break teens partying on a beach, after binge drinking, coax a few of their peers to strip down and have actual sex in front of a crowd roaring its approval while someone catches it in videotape. This same video was used as evidence to prosecute the teens for public intoxication and lewd behavior. despite the taped evidence, the teens vehemently denied engaging in these unlawful acts when questioned in court by the public prosecutor.

- Hotel surveillance cameras catch the bride and best man of a wedding party secretly rendezvous in the garden of the hotel only a few minutes before the ceremony. Video shows the bride–to–be starting to lift up her dress while the best man unbuckles his belt as a prelude to…Only the sudden and unexpected appearance of the groom at the edge of the courtyard prevents this illicit liaison from consummation.

- A middle–aged, male neighbor asked to house–sit for a family gets taped rifling through the underwear drawer of the family's teenage daughter and stealing her panties after the homeowners have noticed such items seem to be missing whenever they return from their vacations.

- Footage from a party of young adults divided into two competing teams with their own uniforms (t–shirts), show them setting up two garbage cans, and in the background, two kegs of beer. Team members start guzzling beer with the sole intention of vomiting after bingeing. The contest is won by the team whose members fill their garbage can with regurgitation first.

Offensive as this show was, it doesn't appear to be too out of step for Fox which savors its pariah status and markets itself as a viewing alternative for youth.

Championing the youth movement on the airwaves are upstart networks such as Warner Brothers (WB). Overflowing with unwrinkled and unschooled thespians, its founder and CEO Jamie Kellner, who professes himself to be the only middle–aged person at the network, confirms that in their slate of programs they are not "…in any way, trying to get people that are 40 and 50." (Hughes, 2000). Instead the WB runneth over with beautiful, young faces which "attracts that coveted teen audience." It works. Viewers have a tough time changing channels with the human eye candy that regularly strolls across their screens and makes these shows so compelling. Consistent with this philosophy, Warner Brothers' fall 1999–2000 prime–time lineup included nine weekly programs oriented toward teens or young adults. Many of them dominate all rivals in the their given time slots. In this motley crew are three shows revolving around vampire–staking, demon–fighting and witchcraft–dabbling as a bonding rite for adolescents; *Buffy the Vampire Slayer*, *Angel*, and *Charmed*; four teen melodramas; *Dawson's Creek*, *Popular*, the critic's darling *Felicity*, and *Roswell*, pitting benevolent teenage extra–terrestrials against a malicious team of FBI alien hunters, and two shows allegedly portraying modern family life, 7th *Heaven* and *Safe Harbor*.

Apart from the last two, whose depiction of parents swung from inadvertently helpful at times to dumbly dismissive at others, these programs have either no significant adult characters or caricatures of them. Parents spout irrelevant platitudes or unfairly administer discipline, that is, when they aren't wallowing in mid–life crises, sexual dysfunction, or philandering with neighbors or co–workers. Other adult relatives, usually grandparents or uncles and aunts appear sweet but impotent, easily hoodwinked by the most transparent teenage lies. Older siblings, unless they are co–stars in the program, typically bully and beat down their younger brothers and sisters. Teachers fare even worse, sleeping with students (check the first year episodes of *Dawson's Creek*), lamenting their own lost youth or voicing their regret for pursuing education as a career in front of their silently embarrassed classes.

School officials usually get depicted as the dregs of humanity, deserving of any and all misfortunes. For instance, the 1998–99 season–ending episode of *Buffy* crashed to a cathartic end when the loathsome principal of Sunnydale High was devoured by a sixty–foot serpent, which had been the part–human, part–demon town mayor until moments earlier. (This broadcast, by the way was nobly postponed by WB executives when its original airdate fell just a few weeks after the Columbine slayings.) In programs where higher education is involved, professors typically appear as bookish egotists bent on destroying the delicate psyches of innocent undergraduates, while deans and fellow administrators' guiding motive invariably seems to be fattening the university's endowment by whatever means necessary even if that means compromising the principles or integrity of the institution.

Police, clergy, and remaining adult figures rounding out the ensembles in these youth–centered melodramas are invariably cast as either heavies or extras, incidental to the plots, periodically useful but mostly unimportant to the outcome. The producers of these shows like WB chief Kellner, obviously believe that children possess all the knowledge they need to survive in some inner font of knowledge and that it is only through these arduous teen tribulations that they tap into this reservoir and discover their self–worth. When all is said and done, it is always the kids who outshine the bewildered adults in their lives as the true sources of wisdom. If any advice is sought along the way, peers provide it and their counsel, naturally, proves to be the sagest. As adult eavesdroppers on this alternate reality of teen television, we can perceive the silliness of the story lines and the misleading wisdom imparted. But can our children? Over years of reinforcement, what does watching these performances do to them and their ability to believe in and trust grown–ups? You make the call.

Strange problems and abnormal solutions, vulgarity, iconoclasm, and stereotyped images of adults as boors, buffoons (see Fox's new smash *Malcolm in the Middle*), or just plain bad people aren't the only thing wafting on the airwaves. Sexual content and racy themes abound, not only but particularly on the cable networks. Less restricted by FCC rules, they regularly flout permissible viewing standards. *The Playboy Channel* exists to showcase soft–core productions developed by Hefner enterprises. Cinemax, a subsidiary of Home Box Office (HBO), offers films ranging from bawdy to explicit for sophisticated adult audiences. Home Box Office, which touts itself as a family entertainment enterprise, despite its *G–String Divas*, gave us the enormously popular *Sex in the City*, though it had the false modesty to wait until at least 9 o'clock on Sunday night to air it. In this program, the 'sex columnist' Sarah Jessica Parker dispenses advice as well as heading a nubile cast of other lovelies in their experiences with "…foot fetishes, faking orgasms, vibrators, voyeurism, men who scratch themselves in public, gay straight men and straight gay men." (Mansfield, 2000). Reacting to the praises showered on her by 14—year—old fans passing by the place she's being interviewed, even Parker confides that such viewers are "too young" to watch her hit program. Commercial or cable, whether the formats are comedic or dramatic, the fact remains that adolescents sift nightly through dozens of viewing options that include situations unsuited to their maturity. The "v–chip" technology designed to give parents the power to block select transmissions cannot possibly cover the continuum of inappropriate programming.

If prime–time fails to live up to its billing, day–time television offers slight reprieve. Soap operas revolve around dramatizations of wanton greed and lust, albeit with immaculately groomed, gorgeous actors. Along with the soaps are a melange of talk shows dealing with topics unfit for children's consumption. The madhouse atmosphere, ribaldry, and sheer grotesqueness of *The Jerry Springer Show*, encapsulates all that is wrong with day–time television. Yet left unsupervised, as a friend with two sons confided to me, kids on summer or holiday recess from school will actually set their alarm clocks so as not to miss the scandalous antics of *Jerry Springer*. For any child warned by his mother not to watch this program, it sparkles like the forbidden apple in Eden.

There remain a handful of television networks dedicated to offering programs of educational value. *The Learning Channel, Discovery Channel,* the *History Channel* and the venerable Public Broadcasting System stand as oases of intellectual resistance in the vast desert of popular culture. Glimpsing any of their offerings, however, it becomes painfully and quickly clear that the demographic segment these stations seek to draw upon are thirty and older. Unless they were given an assignment by a teacher, kids and teens wouldn't give these channels a thought when they have a free candy store full of tripe available at the touch of a button on the remote control.

Regarding television, the scales are weighted so heavily in favor of its promotion of pop culture ideology does anything more need to be said? A final group of networks and programs on them tells us all we need to know: the Comedy Channel and *South Park*, ESPN and ESPN2 with their '24/7' glorification of sporting events and athletes, or ABC with its new ratings coup, *Who Wants to be a Millionaire?* In a gesture worthy of them, Fox's lastest rip–off, or spin–off if you prefer, was *Who Wants to Marry a Millionare?* In it, a real estate magnate picked his bride from a "harem of 49 other candidates". Their nuptials were staged on national television, complete with religious vows, wedding gowns, chamber music and teary eyes. A *USA TODAY* editorial (2/18/00, 15A), derided this stunt as a "fraud". Rather than having anything to do with a an exchange of sacred vows or commitment to a relationship, it was "about television during the February (ratings) sweeps and a magical moment it was too. A new mutation was registered, sort of like the discovery of a three–headed pig, disturbing yet riveting." This observation offers an excuse heard everywhere these days. We may be simultaneously repelled and drawn to what we see on screen but somehow we just can't bring ourselves to turn the set off. When such abominations air during prime–time, as this program did, we can bet that our children are transfixed alongside us. Is this a media diet we want to raise them on?

Theodore Adorno, whose groundbreaking work was explored earlier, was quoted as stating that television was the 'boldest form of wish–fulfillment.' In this, he implies that television permits the viewer to enter a world of the wildest fantasies where his or her cupidity can at last be satisfied. He conjectured that television now substituted for the unconscious mind and gave us an arena to release those hidden desires we formerly encountered in sleep. We no longer need bother to dream. If we dream now it's with our eyes open and glued to the screen. For it is there that our deepest wishes find expression and fulfillment.

"America's long–running romance with Hollywood is over. Few of us view the show business capital as a magical source of uplifting entertainment, romantic inspiration, or even harmless fun. Instead…, the dream factory has become a poison factory."–M. Medved

Teenagers and the Cinema

According to film industry data, 14—24 year olds make up the single largest cohort of the movie—going public. If the past is any indication and informs the present, youth exhibit a special fondness for horror movies and comedies. Smelling the potential for profit, Hollywood seems happy to oblige them. Regarding the first genre, the present rule has become the more gore, the better. With the comedic variety, the fewer boundaries left intact the stronger its attraction to the sophomoric tastes. Consider the following facts.

Two of the highest–grossing slasher films of the 1990's targeting adolescents were *Scream* ($140 million) and *Scream II* ($101 million), per the Internet Movie Data–Base (**http://us.imdb.com/search**). Although spared the delight of viewing the sequel, I rented the original from the video store, intrigued by the buzz it had gotten. Brimming with an ensemble of frenetic young actors, loaded with sharp–edged metallic instruments, and literally dripping with blood, *Scream* appalled adults but delighted teens. In fact, these two installments did so well that a *Scream 3* was released in early 2000 and the $35.2 million it netted in its debut weekend set a new record for the 'slasher franchise.' (*Yahoo! News*, 2/6/00). The success of these celluloid massacres has been so pronounced, that Hollywood's studios scrambled to churn out a rash of copycats (*I Know What You Did last Summer, I Still Know What You Did Last Summer*, etc.), all of which made robust sums between the theatre and video cassette rentals.

Emotionally, viewers of any age can sympathize with a movie character being terrorized or whose life is being threatened. Bruised and bleeding, each injury done to the film's protagonist makes us wince in pain and fear too. Our fear is archetypal, as is the drive for self–preservation. Thus, when the cornered hero or heroine finally strikes back and defeats their attacker, we, too, breathe a sigh of relief and perhaps enjoy a vicarious moment of triumph at seeing this adversary vanquished before us. Predicated on human emotional response, the formula is simple, cathartic, and ultimately enjoyable.

What appears to have changed is the *expectation of violence* younger audiences bring to the cinema. Whether on a date or with friends, for hours before, a sense of anticipation builds that tonight's scary flick will outdo in bloody scale the one viewed last Friday. Scenes in which supporting characters meet their ends actually elicit boos and catcalls if the film cuts away before the hatchet gets buried in a forehead, the bullet fired sprays brains against the wall, or the grisly sound of a knife slicing open a stomach can be heard. (One wonders if a veteran of Verdun or Stalingrad, placed in the back row of a theater today might pale at the sights our kids routinely cheer in these sanguine visual encounters.) Teens have been conditioned to revel in the graphic and gratuitous. Each subsequent scene needs to be bloodier than the previous one or fails to elicit the hormonal rush the observer expects. This bloodlust even applies to the quasi–historical films like *Saving Private Ryan*, a Steven Spielberg epic that won multiple Oscars. When I saw it at the theatre, I sickened at battle scenes where limbs went flying and chest cavities tore open. On the other hand, accustomed to such brutal depictions, several teens around me whooped and back–slapped their approval while I fought off nausea. How inured they appeared to be is a disturbing sign of the times. It is also symptomatic of how desensitized youth fed a menu of carnage—in arcade games, television, and realistic movies—have become.

One such movie reputed to be a favorite of Eric Harris and Dylan Klebold may have served as diabolical inspiration for their killing spree at Columbine High. *The Basketball Diaries* included a graphic scene in which a bent–on–revenge misfit played by Leonardo DiCaprio savagely repays the peers who tormented him for being different. In a slow–motion dream–like sequence, a ruthless DiCaprio, donning a long black trench–coat returns to a class whereupon he produces a concealed shotgun and cold–bloodedly murders the jocks. Mere coincidence? Not likely.

Another lucrative genre of films are those accurately labeled by critics as "gross–out comedies." In the summer of 1999, the gross–out quartet of *Austin Powers: The Spy who Shagged Me, Big Daddy, South Park the Movie*, and *American Pie*, pulled in a whopping half–billion dollars domestically. The magnitude of their success caught even industry insiders unprepared. Not for long, however, as the studios quickly churned out more of the same. Actor Adam Sandler, made a multi–millionaire from his spate of stupidly crude comedies from *Happy Gilmore* to *The Waterboy*, has taken to producing similarly repugnant films for friends like Rob Schneider and his *Deuce Bigalow, Male Gigolo*, another box–office bonanza for the studio.

Tom Doherty, professor of film studies at Brandeis University, examined the peculiar popularity of these movies in an article he penned for *The Chronicle of Higher Education*. He pondered the question of whether or not this is simply the next step in director's creative expression or a new "cultural crisis." Trained academic that he is, Doherty argued both sides of the issue with dexterity. On the one hand, he celebrated the license that filmmakers enjoy to flout conventionality by making pictures that take 'bathroom' behavior from the locker room to the silver screen, if only to challenge the moral crusaders who rail against this entertainment cancer. On the other hand, Doherty wondered aloud what might come next. "How far the sequels will go in ratcheting up the gross–out quotient can only be imagined…" At some point in the near future, "the gross–out scenarios will crash through the comedy zone and morph into pure spectacle. Increasingly, the antics are staged not to inspire laughter, but wide-eyed wonder, whether tinged with amazement or disgust."

I confess that disgust rather than amazement better represents what I felt much of the time while watching the comedy hit *There's Something about Mary*. The scrotum–caught–in the pants'–zipper depiction, the beating up of her mentally retarded brother episode, and the semen–as–hair–gel scene left me, well, grossed–out. Unsure what I was supposed to feel, I confess emitting a few nervous giggles at these moments while my juniors in the theatre hooted with glee. Unlike theirs, my stilted laughter did not come from amusement as much as not knowing how else to react.

Michael Medved, respected film critic and author of *Hollywood vs. America* (1992), spoke out more directly. "The pattern of honoring ugliness has become so pervasive that it suggests that such shocking work is honored because of its hideous elements, not in spite of them." In excoriating what he labelled a 'preference for the perverse,' Medved continued: "The message in the movie business seems to be that portrayals of cruelty and dementia deserve more serious consideration, more automatic respect, than any attempts to convey nobility or goodness." (25–26)

It isn't accidental, Medved asserted, that the film industry manages to undercut traditional values and social norms. Marshalling hundreds of movie titles and descriptions to support his claims, he identified two institutions that have suffered systematic degradation through consistently negative portrayals; 1) religion (founded on fear and repression) and the clergy (tortured, miserable) and 2) parents (self–absorbed) and family life (dysfunctional and restrictive) The evidence he amassed was so overwhelming that it swept the field of any opposition. Compounding a bad situation is the industry's penchant for perpetually upping the ante in terms of on–screen offensiveness. Illicit and explicit sex, pointless violence, bitter irony, rampant hypocrisy, psychological disillusionment, and foul language, all of these constantly push the limits of taste to tawdry extremes.

Consistent with the dramatizations presented on television, films also choose to portray adults, specifically parents, as pitiable and tragically flawed. *American Beauty*, which pulled in rave reviews from critics and won four Oscars including Best Picture, offers us cinematic microcosm. *American Beauty* traces the spiritual bankruptcy of family life in the suburbs focusing on the disintegration of the father played by actor Kevin Spacey. Trapped in a loveless marriage to status–conscious and frigid Annette Bening, forever at odds with his own daughter, facing poor career prospects, and gripped by a mid–life crisis, Spacey escapes his desperation by fantasizing about a relationship with his teenage daughter's beautiful friend. Although its this secret passion that both condemns and redeems him as the movie progresses, *American Beauty*, while a compelling film, requires the maturity of adulthood, especially middle–age, to fully appreciate. To the adolescent viewer, it merely makes parents look pathetic and family life a hopeless mess.

Taken against this celluloid backdrop, are not Doherty's and Medved's analyses consistent with the musings of Baudrillard who asserted that in the age of simulation, repetitive exposure to convoluted re–creations of life will require ever–higher levels of intensity or debauchery in consequent encounters to pacify the experiencer. More pressing than that, how will we know when these exaggerated on–screen depictions begin to influence actual behavior? There are symptoms that this is what we have begun to see among disturbed teens who reached this frightful state ahead of the curve and committed sexual, domestic, and violent crimes.

Needless to say, there are those like Jack Valenti, president of the Motion Picture Association of America, who vehemently dispute the role of films in encouraging anti–social conduct. According to its charter as it appears on the MPAA Homepage (**www.mpaa.org**) this organization exists to "serve as the voice and advocate" of the American motion picture and home video and television industries. In the wake of the Columbine massacre, Mr. Valenti was summoned to testify before a Senate panel debating the "21st Century Media Responsibility Act of 1999." In testimony given over several weeks, Valenti resorted to the usual jab–and–feint strategy. On May 4, 1999, Valenti harangued the Senate with his declaration that America must reinvigorate its "moral shield"—of home, church, and schools—to safeguard youngsters from corrosive cultural influences. In a miserable attempt to imitate one of the founding fathers, Valenti went on record saying, "…if that moral armor is sturdily assembled, and fitted in the early years, no momentary lapse will dissolve its bindings." By June 7th, wearying of the proceedings, Valenti altered his tactics to invoke the Constitution in defending the free speech and creative freedom rights of the entertainment industry. Legislation notwithstanding, the outcomes were predictable. Valenti and the oligarchs of Hollywood asserted their artistic privileges, promising to change nothing.

Popular culture has seized control of the movies and engineered them to meet the mood of the times. Films reflect a society on the edge of a precipice. *The Virgin Suicides, The Fight Club, Pulp Fiction*, all are films our kids can easily access at video stores or on cable and a litany similar entries—just as dark and deranged—is endless.

Video Games and Rehearsal for Killing

Mere mention of game titles supplies a *caveat emptor* in telling players all they need to know about the content—*Streetfighter II, Duke Nukem, Bushido Blade, Ace Combat 2, Carmageddon,* and *Mortal Kombat,* the latter of whose success was so great that it spawned several cartoonish action films. The wide appeal of video games to American youth well documented. It places second in the roster of most popular forms of home entertainment, just behind television and racked up astronomical sales of $5.5 billion in the United States alone in 1998 (*Time*, May 10, 1999).

One researcher speculates that what makes these games so enticing is that "video game players, in contrast to television viewers, exert control over what takes place on the screen." (Goldstein, 1998, 59–60), and in turn this power over events, real or simulated, has shown to actually reduce stress levels. The pleasure kids derive from being in command during this play makes logical sense compared to other areas of their lives—at school, in the home—where they must submit to circumstances outside their ability to manipulate. The real world demands concessions to annoying adult rules and authority. The game world does not. There the player has ultimate power. The affects can be intoxicating.

Investigations into the lives of the teenaged gunmen in both the Columbine case and the Paducah, Kentucky school shootings fanned a furious debate about the impact of blatantly aggressive video games on adolescent psychology. In both instances, the shooters were frequent players of games whose sole objective was to kill. Are these simulations providing a harmless entertainment avenue for normal kids to channel their hostile energies and constructively loose pent–up anger? Do they merely sharpen hand–to–eye coordination and motor reflexes and end at that? Or might they actually be nudging borderline minds toward violence by providing rehearsal sites where they can hone their marksmanship and engage in indiscriminate, if make–believe, manslaughter?

The American Psychological Association issued a press release from its web site (**www.apa.org**) on April 23rd, 2000, citing two studies which showed that violent video games *can* increase aggressive behavior. Appearing in the April issue of *The Journal of Personality and Social Psychology*, the studies concluded that such video games "may be more harmful than violent television and movies because they are interactive, very engrossing, and require the player to identify with the aggressor." Tracing the impact of games like *Doom*, *Wolfenstein*, and *Mortal Kombat*, researchers generalized that "…young men who are habitually aggressive may be especially vulnerable to the aggression–enhancing effects of repeated exposure." (Anderson & Dill, 2000). In an unrelated yet interesting finding, lower academic achievement also emerged as an outcome of excessive game–playing.

While it must be acknowledged that no irrefutable evidence exists to support a link between video game murder and real–life acting out, the APA data does infer a reasonable cause–and–effect relationship. Others are more outspoken on this connection. Leading this camp is a controversial figure, retired West Point psychology professor and founder of the Killology Research Group, Lt. Colonel David Grossman, who recently published *Stop Teaching our Kids to Kill*. Mincing few words in an interview with a local reporter, (Kiesewetter, 1999) Grossman was quoted saying, "Certain types of these (video) games are actually killing simulators, and they teach our kids to kill." Proof of the pudding, he argued, manifested itself in the deadly marksmanship of riflemen like then 14–year old Michael Carneal, charged with the Paducah, Kentucky middle school shooting. Carneal hit eight students with eight shots, an incredible feat that would be difficult for a trained combat soldier to match. Games such as *Doom, Mortal Kombat*, and *Time Crisis*, are providing to our children military–level training in chilling detail, Grossman claims. Although his book was released prior to Columbine, reports from that crime scene attribute eerily similar marksmanship to Eric Harris, who was known to wile away countless hours playing his own customized version of *Doom*.

Even if you dismiss the rest of Grossman's contentions, some of which involve broad leaps of logic, he makes a legitimate point on the shocking desensitization of parents and children to an activity considered to be *play*. Decrying the increasing level of tolerance to games of annihilation, he speculates what will come: "As soon as violence is introduced it becomes a toxic substance. It's a murder simulator. You wouldn't tolerate a rape simulator, would you?" Indeed, the line between what now reigns as acceptable entertainment as opposed to that which would have been deemed reprehensible only a few years ago has certainly blurred.

Exposing student–aged youth to violence is not the only unseemly influence supplied by video gaming. A report, "Blood, Gore, Sex and Now: Race; Are Game–Makers Creating Convincing New Characters or 'High Tech–Blackface?" (Mariott, 1999), featured in the *New York Times* draws attention to other problems. Apparently, the next generation of video games offer more than digitally sophisticated graphics and characters with exaggerated personal attributes. Characters in them have become racial caricatures. African–American athletes, for instance, in these games are prone to "prance and dance", emit "James Brown–like screams", wear "gigantic Afros", walk in a "catlike stroll", and 'talk trash' to opponents. Among this new variety of ethnically diverse heroes are stereotyped characters of Mexican, Polynesian, Croatian, and Indian origins.

From most vantage points, the value of video games is doubtful. Despite their billing, they do not provide a healthy recreational outlet to youth. At their best, they present adolescents the chance to develop hair–trigger reflexes in coping with threatening people or situations. Shoot first, ask questions later, is the mentality. Obviously, in the world of videodrome, this is the best approach to confrontation and conflict resolution. In society, it is the worst possible strategy our children should be learning.

Jeffrey Goldstein offered an intriguing psychological explanations on the irresistibility of video games. "Intense, repetitive play may result in an altered state of consciousness, referred to as '*flow*' (1998, 63). If Goldstein and the data he cites is valid and the game script being rehearsed over and over is homicidal in its intents and puposes, the impression it makes on this 'altered state of consciousness' may well account for the mad, misanthropic actions of an Eric Harris or Michael Carneal.

Cyberspace

"Cyberspace. A consensual hallucination experienced daily by billions of legitimate operators, in every nation..."

—— W. Gibson, *Neuromancer*

Cyberspace contains infinite unknowns. Author William Gibson who gave the world this term, declares as much in the above quotation from his novel. Films like *The Matrix* enhance its mystique. In itself, cyberspace poses a conundrum—having no depth or dimension, it manages to exist everywhere, all of the time. Can so mysterious a realm ever really be accurately mapped or properly understood? If its expanses cannot be plumbed, why are we so certain that children should have unlimited access to it at school and home?

The average user spends 7.1 hours a week on–line, two times longer than what they devote to reading (McCafferty, 1999). Constructively used, only a fool would deny there are unparalleled learning opportunities in cyberspace. New informational and scientific thresholds are being crossed each day. Yet somehow, intuitively perhaps, we feel there are things to be apprehensive about in its uncharted regions. Paranoiacs, conspiracy theorists, hate–mongers, cultists, pornography panderers, and crackpots have found the perfect haven in cyberspace. It established a sanctuary from which to propogate the most odious material with virtually no risk of repercussions apart from attracting fellow malcontents and misfits. And in spite of feeble attempts to filter what enters our homes through it, adults should not suppose that their children are safe from its extensive reach.

Chat rooms, for example, justifiably make many adults nervous. These exchanges are on the one hand faceless and blind, yet on the other hand, deeply personal and intimately revealing. If kids naively enter into these encounters trustingly, others do not. With self–created sobriquets, identities can easily be concealed, and self–disclosures fabricated. Such communications occur thousands of times a day and involve many of our sons and daughters. If your city is like mine, you periodically read stories in the news about a middle–aged pedophile who arranged to meet a 13 year–old school girl he met on–line, only to get arrested when a wary onlooker at the mall noticed the unlikely pairing and phoned the police.

While devoted Web surfers and computer savants extol online chatting as the trendy social forum of Generations X, Y and beyond, an impartial observer can recognize the implicit hazards. Anonymity, deception, and freedom to say things that cannot be verified by interpersonal inspection—these are the trademarks of Internet chatrooms. For these reasons, quite possibly, e–mail communications, have become a favorite mode of interaction for another fringe element of users. *Cyberstalking* has emerged as a new form of electronic molestation. An academic colleague in the criminal justice program here at the University of Cincinnati found that almost "25 percent of stalking cases reported by college women surveyed involved stalking by e–mail." (Fisher, 1999). In the worst instances, cyberspace brings together sexual predators with their unsuspecting victims. The Kansas man with the handle Slavemeaster and penchant for sadomasochistic sex, was linked by authorities to the murders of at least five women he lured to meet him after chatting on the Internet. (Gillam, 2000)

Ironically, cyberspace offers both the best and the worst of popular culture. Digitized libraries, virtual museum tours, instant access to news headlines, and user–friendly directories of educational and recreational information—these reflect the good. Almost half of the research used in this book was done from a computer workstation in my office at the university. To those who know where to look and how to find knowledge resources, cyberspace offers infinite opportunities. Racist Web sites, quack science and philosophy prettily packaged, and ongoing electronic invasions of our privacy by persons or agencies you would never let come in the front door—these represent the bad. Making this thin line even more precarious is the realization that we cannot possibly monitor each and every moment our kid accesses the 'Net. Aware that it can contain academically useful information, we don't wish to ban this medium from our houses and in the process, deny him technical knowledge and skills his peers are acquiring. Citing a Kaiser Family Foundation study, 69% of kids between 2–18 have a computer at home, with 16% saying they have one in their bedroom. If we widen our scope, 42% claim to use a computer every day either in school or recreationally at home. Much of the time kids are on–line, they are not under parental or teacher supervision Yet as adults, we know that at fairly frequent intervals, our son will invariably stumble into content or contacts would make us cringe.

As a case in point, the degree to which obscene material has infiltrated cyberspace gives everyone but its vendors cause for concern. With technology made affordable, pornographic homepages continue to replicate. Amateurs are even getting into the act. At the university which employs me, we had to implement a new policy on the "proper use of technology" because a number of students were creating personal homepages with unsuitable material and/or hyperlinks to commercial adult sites. "Sex is a virus that infects new technology first," said one prominent technocrat (Van der Leun, 1993), and his words ring in our ears as we sift through the dirty referral e–mails every AOL or Prodigy subscriber receives each week. Sparing the innocents, younger children, from these messages and sites is no small task. Over time, it becomes a battle we cannot win.

As covered earlier in this book, the Internet exploded on the scene in the 1990's though its antecedents have been around and employed in research capacities since the sixties. Now it is so ingrained in the fabric of postmodern life that thinking back to an era when it wasn't part of our daily experience eludes us. Glancing ahead, Bill Gates spoke admiringly of what the future may hold; "Generation I—children born after 1994 who may never know life without the Internet." (McCollum, 1999, 1), Excited by the prospect, Gates expects great things from this cybergeneration. "They will think about the Internet in a far more profound way than some of us…" and will live "…in a world where everything is on line and that will be be taken for granted." On hearing Gate's words, one need not be a Luddite to wonder whether this totally "on–line" world is necessarily good or even desirable. In the frantic haste to 'get wired', few are those who stop to ask what the final destination may be.

Cyberspace is unfolding in exponential leaps. No one, not even techno–wizards like Bill Gates or Tim Berners–Lee can tell us what revolutionary breakthroughs will happen next. Despite IBM Big Blue's 1998 victory over chessmaster Garry Kasparov, artificial intelligence, or thinking machines, remain a few years off. Voice–activated computer response is already available on the store shelf. Live–feed video has existed for several years, interactive chat rooms even longer. Undoubtedly, the goal of these innovations and those to come is to impress us with a totally *life–like* experience. Approximating reality down to the most minute detail so that the user no longer notices qualitative differences between the simulation and the walls of his house appears to be the ultimate objective. Each technological advance, minor or radical, makes cyberspace more compelling and brings us that much closer to a true virtual reality.

Unencumbered by the usual adult resistances, kids and teens acquire computer skills much more rapidly and as their proficiency increases so do their level of comfort. This very ease with technology among youth puts them deeper under its spell. Symptoms of this addiction manifest themselves in their behavior. The longer they dabble in cyberspace, the less satisfaction they draw from these simulations and the more hours they spend trying to regain that exhilaration. An essay posted in the cybermagazine *SF Teen* (as in San Francisco), maniacally admits to the compulsion. According to its teenage author, surfing the Web for the first time 'heaven on earth'. After "It's really fun", this teen says, "I can't get enough of it. It's addicting—like a drug! I must have more! More! More!!!" (Burgheimer, 1995)

Clearly, any such addictive behavior harbors unwanted side effects. Like the other technologies of simulation discussed thus far, cyberspace dampens a person's hunger for social experiences. A study released by the Institute for the Quantitative Study of Society at Stanford University in February, 2000, found that more than a third of adults complained that the Internet detracted from their interactions with family members or friends. If parents felt this way, and we know they aren't nearly as facile as their offspring with computers, doesn't the same or worse apply to children? Are not younger browsers also missing out on valuable quality time with adults? A different study conducted by University of Chicago cautioned that increasing isolation and alienation may be repercussions of excessive Internet use, but this tells us nothing we don't already know. Nor does a Carnegie Mellon University report done in 1998 found higher levels of depression among cybersurfers than in the general population.

Finally, Clifford Stoll, author of *Silicon Snake Oil* and *High Tech Heretic*, wrote that the cyberworld burgeoning around us will usher in a lonely and dehumanizing existence. "The Internet, rather than bringing us together, isolates us. Rather than empowering, it enfeebles." (Keller, 2000). By now, obtaining a general consensus that cyberspace breeds loneliness, depression and social withdrawal would be easy. The injury it does to youth psychology is still something of a mystery, however. With the exponential growth of cyberspace, it's too soon for researchers to diagnose the long–term effects of human immersion in cyberspace's infinite domains. We have only circumstantial evidence and a gut feeling to make us wary. Maybe it is enough.

If and when the cyberworld envisioned by Gates and Berners–Lee does come to pass, however, no one talking about it today can fathom the Pandora's box it might open. In the interim, the virtual experiences it makes available can function as powerful aphrodisiacs on minds unprepared to offer any resistance.

Pop Music: Messages and Mayhem

Hip–hop culture and its voice, rap, reigns supreme atop the north American music charts. According to *Time* magazine, rap unseated the previous title–holder, country music, in units sold, accounting for 81 million compact discs, tapes, and albums in 1998. Overall, its sales

increased a whopping 37% between 1997–98. Any attempt to disregard it as the lyrical musings of a marginal subculture within American
society stalls under the weight of these figures. Its persistence under
withering criticism from people running the rainbow of political and
religious views, African–American and white, demonstrates its resilience.

Interestingly, what began as a Black, artistic rejection of social
oppression migrated to a much broader audience in the alienated
masses of white suburban youth who account for 70% of rap music
purchases. As rock music did for earlier generations of adolescents, rap
heralds a contemporary rite of passage. As a form of teen rebellion,
what could antagonize parents, particularly in suburban white families,
more than a son or daughter playing rap music everyday at eardrum–
perforating levels in their bedrooms or cars? From its debut, rap has
railed against authority in creating a forum for street corner poets cap-
turing the struggle to survive an unjust society. Teens of all races, naturally, can empathize. If, however, there's more to this picture than
what meets the eye and rap music impinges deeper upon adolescent
psychology than just acting as an irritant to parents, we must examine
its content. What messages permeate its thumping beats, street slang,
rhymed exclamations? As a late thirtysomething academic, I had only
the vaguest ideas about its true content.

Browsing the Web for answers, I alit upon at a site that educated
me. It was titled "The Rap Lyrics Home Page" (www.geocities.com/
Broadway/2682/). This site had catalogued the lyrics of over twenty–
five rap stars on a song–by–song basis. Reading the lyrics of over two
dozen tunes, I found that I could place each in one of five general cate-
gories depending on its subject: 1) the joys and perils of drug abuse, 2)
the lure of cash and street–smart ways of making it, 3) the rule of violence and murder, 4) the degradation of women, and 5) the futility of
living in a racist society.

In themselves, these themes speak of an experience shared by a marginalized segment of American society. On that basis alone, they need

to be heard and understood by those doing the repressing. Problems arise when one looks at the words and imagery rappers use in spinning their gritty odes to the hardships of urban life. By any impartial standard, they could be deemed pathological in their disregard for human life, unrequited hate of society, and flagrant deprecation of females. They also espouse of an ethic that qualifies as sociopathic in its endorsement of 'by whatever means necessary' in seeking personal domination over a lawless environment.

Following are excerpts from a few tracks, enough to give the reader a sampling of how viciously these ideas are voiced. A warning must be issued to those are offended by language usually considered profane or otherwise offensive. To feel the intended impact of these lyrics, I did not compromise this research by minimizing their rawness through paraphrasing. What appears are those lyrics penned by the artist(s) in their original, unedited form.

Bone Thugs–n–Harmony's song "Mo Murda"

Let em know who the boss is, so nigga, you wanna get tossed in the river?

> *Nigga, put em in the mud, see them pump blood...*
> *You know, nigga, we can't be bluffin,*
> *We bang insane. When I put one to your temple, mo murda,*
> *Then blow out your brain.*

–The Wu–Tang Clan's song "C.R.E.A.M." (Cash Rules Everything Around Me).

It's been 22 long hard years I'm still strugglin,

> *Survival got me buggin, but I'm alive on arrival,*
> *I peep at the shape of the streets and stay awake to the ways of the world*
> *Cause the shit is so deep*
> *A man with a dream with plans to make CREAM which failed:*
> *I went to jail at the age of 15*

A young buck sellin drugs and such who never had much...
Handcuffed in the back of a bus, forty of us...
But as the world turns I learned life is hell
Living in the world no different from a cell

–Ice–T's song "New Jack Hustler"

With cocaine my success came speedy, Got me twisted, jammed into

> *A paradox, Every dollar I get, another brother drops,*
> *Maybe that's the plan, and I don't understand, God damn—you got*
> *Me sinkin in quicksand, But since I don't know, and I ain't never*
> *learned,*
> *I gotta get paid, I got money to earn... Cool out and watch*
> *My new Benz gleam, is this a nightmare or the American dream?*

–Snoop Doggy Dogg's song "Serial Killa"

6 million ways to die, choose 1, It's time to escape, but I don't know

> *where the fuck I'm headed up or down, right or left, life or death I see*
> *myself in a mist of smoke, Death becomes any nigga that takes me for*
> *a joke.*

–Dr. Dre's song "Bitches Ain't Shit"

Bitches ain't shit but hoes and tricks...

> *Lick on deez nutz and suck on the dick,*
> *Get the fuck out after you're done*
> *Bitches ain't shit but hoes and tricks...*

Fury, desperation, alienation, self–loathing and a whoring of female sexuality suffuse these lyrics. In trying to estimate their effect, can listeners can separate the music from the messages? Are kids able to enjoy the pounding cadence of these songs without singing along to the words and subconsciously assimilating the ideas woven into them? Some say no. In the *Time* cover story ("Hip–hop Nation") cited in

Chapter 2, author Chris Farley collected several opinions on the matter. A Black record–store employee named Marlon said, "I'm hip–hop every day…I don't put on my hip–hop." Katie, 22 and white, adds, *"You do develop a sense of self through it.* You listen and you say, 'Yeah, that's right.'" (author's italics)

Since no research exists in this area, we can only guess at how profoundly rap music affects the actual behavior of the hip–hop generation. That it glorifies the 'code of the street', a savagely twisted notion of live and let live—is plain enough. It is certain that the actual artists seem unable to distance themselves from their own messages. The arrest in a New York club of rap mogul Sean Puffy Combs and his escort, Latina singer Jennifer Lopez, for allegedly shooting at three other patrons (*Yahoo News!*, 12/28/99) provides a case in point, as do the police–catalogued incidents of assault and murder between rival rappers over recent years. White rap star, Eminem, whose homophobic, homicidal and obscene mutterings are emitted during interviews as well during his raps ("Christine Aguilera gave me head!"; *Rolling Stone*, 6/12/00) was busted outside a suburban Detroit club on weapons charges in the summer of 2000.

Family, schooling, and the individual's choice to rise above circumstances of poverty or sink deeper into their grip are issues largely ignored by rappers. In rap mythology, the only real way to make it comes from hustling drugs, using women for sex, and exhibiting a willingness to kill. If there is anything socially redeeming in it, this author was unable to locate it. Still, to be fair, it must be stated that the sampling of songs reviewed does not represent the entire hip–hop genre. The work of Lauryn Hill or Will Smith, for instance, mesh jazzier or reggae sounds with lighter rap rhyming (about relationships, self–esteem, or children). Their work bears little likeness to gangsta' rap, the best–selling vein in this genre.

Those of us working with young people notice hip–hop's influence on student dress, talk, and social organization. I, for one, cannot walk through the campus commons without hearing the F–word punctuating every third sentence, not in a hostile utterance but in casual conversational use. Other hip–hop coins–of–the–realm like yo! (hi, look, listen), homeys (friends) and aw–ite (all right, cool) pepper student parlance. Simply communicating with them required my colleagues and I to learn the basics of the lexicon many of them have adopted. In this era where reality is being dictated by entertainment, rap joins its own formidable voice to the media din that permeates postmodern life.

Yet rap cannot be made the scapegoat for all disturbing trends in pop music. Acclaimed poet and Virginia Technical University English professor, Nikki Giovanni, takes this position too. In an interview with an area newspaper, she chided those who criticize rap music. In an inferred comparison to rock music, Giovanni argued that rap defuses violent impulse by providing an outlet for the anger and frustration Black youth live with. 'The people who don't get it, maybe they just don't like to hear the truth,' she suggested. It's better for these kids to wear baggy jeans and backward baseball caps than black trench coats with rifle loops sewn into their linings was her argument.

Giovanni's point is valid. There are other whirlpools in the popular musical maelstrom that also wreak social and emotional devastation. Starting in Seattle, a movement known as "grunge" cut a wide cultural swath among disaffected white youth during the first half of the nineties. Nirvana, arguably the most revered of grunge bands, played dirge–like songs about drug abuse, psychic self–mutilation, and the futility of living. In a terribly but tragically fitting end, the singer of this band and messiah of the movement, Kurt Cobain, took his own life by swallowing a vial of pills. Grunge, gratefully, never really recovered from this blow and its angst–fueled fire fizzled afterwards. Female artists also commanded a share of the musical spotlight in the grunge. decade. One band aptly named Hole, was fronted by (the widow of Cobain) Courtney Love, a confused, corrupted woman prone to recount lurid details of her life as a teenage prostitute in the band's early albums.

Closer to the present, a raucous group called the Offspring released a song on their 1998 *Americana* album entitled "The Kids Aren't All

Right." In poignant words, we hear from these troubadors that things are seriously wrong with youth today.

When we were young the future was so bright

> *The old neighborhood was so alive…*
> *Now the neighborhood's cracked and torn*
> *The kids are grown up but their lives are worn*

How can one little street

> *Swallow so many lives…*
> *Fragile lives, shattered dreams…*

Jaime had a chance, well she really did

> *Instead she got on speed and lost her kids*
> *Mark still lives at home cause he's got no job*
> *He just plays guitar and smokes a lot of pot*

Jay committed suicide

> *Brandon OD'd and died*
> *What the hell is going on*
> *The cruellest dream, reality*

The pointedly anti–social and misogynistic messages crammed into the music listened to by teens today are making themselves felt in some very ugly ways. Already raucous behavior at concerts or "raves", spontaneous all–night music and dance parties, stimulated by club drugs such as Ecstasy or Special K, have reached new levels of intra–and interpersonal abuse.

Epitomizing this chaotic scene is a ritual ideally suited to these times given the monikor of moshing. In spaces cleared directly in front of the stage, or mosh pits, concert goers engage in a free for all of unrestrained chest–thumping, head–butting, arm–swinging, and kicking. People are hurt regularly but as long as the injury is not too severe, moshers claim to get a rush from drawing blood or having their own drawn. The sheer frenzy and release of the experience keeps them coming back for more. With participants typically drunk or high, moshing awakens their true Bacchanalian instincts. Primitive as this ritual is, it has descended into something even darker. At Woodstock '99, a three–day outdoor festival held on the thirtieth anniversary of the original event, numerous females reported being raped or otherwise sexually assaulted in or on the fringe of the mosh pit. Victims told police that these attacks took place in full view of the moshing males, many of whom cheered or joined in rather than helping *(US News & World Report,* 1999). Rioting, looting, destruction of property, and sexual predation now attend these musical festivals.

Whenever crowds collect for mass spectacle, from sporting to theatrical events, audience members straddle a thin line between rational behavior and mob frenzy. History tells us this is nothing new. The Nika revolt in 6th century Constantinople killing 30,000 people started as a brawl over whether the Blue or Green team of charioteers won a race fairly. That violence belonged to a savage era. We want to believe that the human species has evolved over the last thousand years. In this day and age, lawless behavior in public places should earn instant social condemnation. It did for a while until something primal was reawakened and released by our postmodern forms of recreation.

MTV: Media Fusion and Delusion

The marriage of two tremendously influential media occurred in the inception of a network known as Music Television, or MTV. Debuting in 1981, MTV soon became a standard bearer of pop culture as well as a fixture in the lives of American youth. It also manufactured a fresh generation of anti–heroes whose amoral antics were amplified by the fusion of these two dominions of pop culture—television and rock music.

To this day MTV, above all other networks, reigns supreme in its sway over youth. From its early days, it supplied a free–form arena to artists seeking to test broadcast boundaries. Recall for a moment the fuss that surrounded Madonna with her intentionally irreverent *Like A Virgin* video. Then there was Michael Jackson's controversial crotch–grabbing scene in his *Black or White* video. By today's standards, where next to every video centers on graphic sexual simulations, grind–dancing, or dramatizations of gang–violence, these slices of 1980's life seem downright tame, even quaint, indicating the degree to which our expectations have been lowered. The fact that Allan Bloom alluded to MTV in his conservatively cranky *The Closing of the American Mind* in 1987, as a "nonstop masturbational fantasy" seems like a gross exaggeration in retrospect. Critiquing the music and the videos, however, diverts us from examining MTV's cultural impact.

By the mid–90's, MTV departed from its rock–n–roll format and shifted to a focus on urban chic and the embryonic hip–hop scene. With this change in orientation, MTV blazed a trail for rap music and hip–hop culture. It exported it into the living rooms of households across the United States. Sensing their parents' revulsion, suburban kids ate it up. Management at MTV also decided to broaden the network from its modest beginnings as a video jukebox into a full–fledged programming source. A number of in–house productions were developed that focused on aspects of popular culture enticing to youth.

Presently, one of its most popular shows is *The Real World*. A program rife with more delusion I've never seen. *The Real World* is anything but. If integrity meant anything in the media, this program would be titled *The **Unreal** World* for its unrelenting fantasy element. In spite of its contrived drama, this series works valiantly to seem like a documentary. Ostensibly, it traces the lives of five or six adolescents as they struggle to make it in the 'real' world. Forget that they are invariably ensconsed, free–of–charge, in a million dollar beachfront home on Oahu or cavernous apartment in San Francisco overlooking the bridges, bay and Sausalito, residences that would strain the income of a cardiac surgeon. (The 2000–2001 season opened with new cast members arriving at this year's digs, an ostentatious antebellum mansion christened "Belfort" in New Orleans.) Each segment includes one of more of the cast dallying into reckless drinking, drug abuse, gender bending, sexual promiscuity, or some other juvenile forms of experimentation. One gets the impression that apart from these escapades the cast would die of boredom and kill its audience with the same affliction. Pretending to give every episode of this series a moral, the characters are invariably shown gathering to talk after their individual melodramas, where they discuss the consequences and assure their housemates they have learned and been changed by these experiences.

Noticeably absent, of course, are adults. In the real world most of us inhabit, adolescence is a time of anticipation and learning. Mistakes are made. Friends disappoint us. Dreams reveal themselves to be constructed of an ethereal substance. But always in the background waits the reassuring presence of adults. Parents, grandparents, counselors and teachers—all of them offer us advice, guidance, and support as we struggle through those years. Because, however, the producers created a bogus parallel reality rather than an authentic 'real world', and MTV executives have decreed that the optimum environment is free of anyone over twenty–five, the omission of adults from this program turns out to be strategic.

If this program fails to impress upon my reader the dubious value of MTV's own 'reality programming' endeavors, try something on the lighter side. Of late, it has been running its popular *Sping Break Uncensored* series. Imagine *The Jerry Springer Show* meets the hip–hop crowd during Mardi Gras–type interludes and you have an idea of what's in store. Bare breasts and genitals routinely escape from flimsy bathing suits as hordes of partying, sun–baked, and hormone–raging students engage in stupid and humiliating antics encouraged by some or another Gen–X celebrity host. An episode that I chanced to see placed one couple at a time in the back of a Volkswagen Beetle. The goal was to strip naked and switch bathing suits, boys into bikinis and girls into shorts, as quickly as possible while cameras just outside the rear and side windows caught everything on tape. Whichever pair, and there were numerous volunteers, pulled this exchange off in the least amount of time won. In their haste to win, more than a few contestants emerged from the car with body parts normally hidden from the sunlight on full, if unfocused display before the camera. In the background, drunken peers in the audience yelled lustily. Believe it or not, this event was far and away one of the tamest aired.

Ironically, during my own holiday breaks during college, I can recall my parents yelling at me to turn off the MTV. They railed about it being trash and rotting my brain. Male musicians wearing an earring and eye–liner and female singers murmuring risque lyrics while hiding under a mane of feathered Farah hair—they were the norm. That was the Eighties. By today's standards, they were practically as mild as the Fifties.

Fallout from Simulated Reality

It would be untrue to say that a body of evidence existed demonstrating a firm a link between media saturation and anti–social behavior in youth. There is none. This absence, however, should not be taken to mean that a correlation fails to exist. It merely shows a lack of investigations into this important area.

Research or not, it does not diminish from what I'm attempting to do in this book. Simply because statistical data is slight at this phase doesn't preclude the possibility of a conceptual connection between what youth are routinely exposed to in popular culture and the bizarre behavior they manifest in consequence. In fact, this whole book rests on the premise of causality. By deconstructing the myriad myths and distortions, that pop culture reinforces, the sheer weight of evidence suggests the likelihood of cause–and–effect.

If we are willing to consider theoretical arguments (recall Baudrillard's), the first and most prevalent byproduct of simulation is its fostering of *delusion*. Let us briefly revisit Postman who supplied commentary on this very phenomenon:

"There is no more disturbing consequence of the electronic and graphic revolution than this: that the world as given to us through television *seems natural*, not bizarre. For the loss of the sense of the strange is a sign of adjustment, and the extent to which we have adjusted is a measure of the extent to which we have been changed. Our culture's adjustment to ...television is by now all but complete; we have so thoroughly accepted its definitions of truth, knowledge and reality that irrelevance seems to us filled with import, and incoherence seems eminently sane." (p. 78–80)

Worsening an already dismal situation is the fact that children and teens know no other way. They were literally raised in front of television. Consequently, we are "...now into a...generation of children for whom television has been their first and most accessible teacher and, for many, their most reliable companion and friend." Thus, their faith in what it shows them and how it teaches them to think is absolute. With the exponential growth of the Internet, Postman's argument could easily be extended to this new medium as well as others besides television.

With their perception skewed from a delicate age by images of objects that vary from misleading to deliberately wrong, youth approach life with a set of beliefs and expectations bearing faint resemblance to reality. Education, careers, income, and self–reliance automatically accompany certain stages in growing up. The investment of time, effort, and discipline it takes to secure these things are rarely of ever dealt with in the media. Rather, movies and television would lead them to believe that these things magically appear when the day comes that they are ready to leave home and their parents.

Take a second glance at how television typically depicts young lifestyles and the seeds it sows in the immature minds of its audience using MTV's *Real World* again. Each season the show starts afresh with a diverse group of adult–wannabees moving into plush surroundings they did nothing to deserve. Within its fantasy parameters, viewers are asked to take this largesse for granted. The necessity of paying for such housing through a career that required years of schooling and grueling hours on the job never enter into the equation. On MTV and many other shows, it just materializes. Perhaps this partly explains why eyes grow wide and mouths gape when students move away from home into their first college residence hall or apartment. Cramped, sans designer furnishings, and often in drab sections of the city, this cold blast of reality contradicts all their expectations. If the internal data university officials possess saying that housing as a crucial factor in the satisfaction of first–time entering students, that may be why the attrition rate of college freshmen outdistances all other class levels combined.

Over the course of a lifetime, such immersion in fantasy make it progressively tougher to develop and function normally. Life in the real world, adolescents gradually discover, is not at all like it's portrayed on television or in the movies. This realization is not a comforting one and can result in a range of reactions from simple disappointment to bitter disillusionment. In severe cases, such as the stories told by Eric Harris in his videotaped legacy, this disenchantment becomes so extreme that it takes on a terrible alter ego of its own.

Another psychological principle supporting the notion that behavior can indeed be affected by the input we receive from our environment is termed *priming*. This term and its implications are thoroughly developed in psychologist John Bargh's *The Automaticity of Everyday Life*. In a related article published in *The Chronicle of Higher Education*, Bargh explains how priming is employed by advertisers and fellow purveyors of pop culture to plant psychic messages designed to prompt precise behavioral responses. For many years, priming was employed to get an individual to buy a specific brand of product—athletic shoes, cigarettes, cars, etc. Thus, its effectiveness has been documented over the years. One need not be a trained empirical researcher to notice that the Joe Camel cartoon pitchman for that brand of cigarettes helped to boost smoking among teens, or that adolescents purchase more overpriced Reebok and Nike athletic shoes than any other age group. But what happens if we remove advertising from the picture? Are films, television programs, video games, or computer experiences somehow exempt from sowing ideas that might elicit other urges and impulses? Can priming take place only in sloganeering or marketing? Or might it also result from exposure to any media presentation priming us to a particular idea?

Since priming actually "activates concepts in our minds that affect how we behave," according to Bargh, it seems plausible that it any encounter with media *could* work to prime the beholder. Toward what end, becomes the critical question. As he observed,

"Whatever we do—walk down the street, watch television, or talk to another person—the objects, people, sights, sounds and smells we experience trigger various concepts in our minds…Once something that we have perceived activated a mental concept, the concept stays active for a while. During this period, it can affect our thoughts and decisions, even if they are entirely unrelated to whatever activated the concept in the first place." (1999, B6).

Mightn't this explain, partially at least, what we have been witnessing lately in society? Are Americans, pinned under an avalanche of disturbing media representations, being unwittingly primed to commit wantonly anti–social acts? Given the fantastic scope of some of these actions and later defenses of I–don't–know–what–made me do it, the mere thought induces a shudder. Yet how else can we account for the mild–mannered postal worker or stockbroker who snaps one day and shoots his supervisor along with a half–dozen other workers? And these are adults. How can children gorged on a diet of hostile or perverted archetypes be less impervious?

Harkening back for a moment to the 'Lost Children of Rockdale County' (see Chapter 3), we have at least one documented occasion where what teens watched on television prompted deviant behavior. In this case the deviance took the form of sandwich sex (three participants) or orgies (more than three) initiated by 13 to 16 year–olds.

Interviewed by psychiatrists after the Rockdale story broke, the teens rationalized their participation saying they were merely "imitating what they saw on the Playboy Channel" (Blum, 1999, 2). While we mustn't be so naïve as to blindly assert that television was the solitary influence on them, it clearly provided inspiration for this specific episode. Questioned as to the right or wrong of this behavior, they told psychologists that if it was being shown on television, it couldn't be anything adults weren't already doing. Restrictions imposed by parents or taboos held by society didn't warrant a second thought.

<u>Implications</u>

Under pressure from parenting, education, and child advocacy groups, the so–called V–Chip device was invented to prevent children from viewing unsuitable television programs. Similarly, if there was nothing to fear, the U.S. Senate wouldn't have bothered to debate a bill entitled the "21st Century Media Responsibility Act of 1999" after the Columbine slaughter ignited fears about the cultural pollution of youth. If we felt confident that cyberspace was exclusively beneficial, Internet access–providers such as American On–Line wouldn't trouble to publish an elaborate set of protocols on its home page called Parental Controls designed to limit a child's ability to use e–mail, enter chat rooms, or access adult Web sites.

Collectively, the effect of media simulations on children encounter across the terrain of daily life ranges from ambiguous to toxic. Whether visual, audio, or hybrid technologies, this much is absolutely clear: the messages contained in popular media are inconsistent with those sent by parents at home or educators at school. Youth are forced into confronting parallel, often diametrically opposing perspectives. One set, advocated by adults, encourages responsible behavior, clings to traditional values, and rewards individuality within the fabric of society. The other set, as it encapsulates pop culture morality, subverts all of that.

A film running briefly in theatres across the country in 1999 brilliantly captured the nuances of these troubled times. *Election* starred Matthew Broderick as an award–winning high school civics teacher in a small Nebraska town. The plot was elementary: an overachieving, do–gooder played by Reese Witherspoon sets her sights on being elected class president. Pretty, smart, and manipulative, Witherspoon has an affair with another teacher, a (married) friend of Broderick's which is soon discovered by school authorities and leads to the friend's dismissal. Silently enraged at her smug self–righteousness, Broderick vows to prevent this juvenile upstart from winning the election and adding another laurel to her already bulging resume. In the mean time, discontent with his own domicile, Broderick soon goes from consoling his friend's wife to sleeping with her, sometimes fantasizing about the high school girl he despises, Witherspoon, during intercourse. Back at school, in a flash of evil genius, he recruits the captain of the football team to run against his nemesis. When his candidate is defeated by the barest of margins, Broderick discards the two ballots during his official count that would have assured Witherspoon's victory. Found out the next day, Broderick is forced to resign in disgrace. He soon leaves his wrecked marriage and unhappy life, heading for the forgiving streets of New York. There he finds happiness as a museum tour guide. Witherspoon, unaffected, goes on to a scholarship at Georgetown University and a career a Congressional aide.

The resounding moral of this film is that teachers, like all adults, neither abide by a higher standard nor are hindered by any qualms of conscience. When caught in compromising positions, they too revert to a porous ethical code that permits them to save their necks, if not their respect, under tribulation. Its director goes to great lengths to portray them as sad, sympathetic and fatally flawed. Even when we understand their motives, they cannot be trusted to act as students and administrators should expect of them. On the other hand, *Election* takes pains to stress that students, or youth in general can be forgiven any and all misjudgements. They are, after all, only doing what they have seen the adults around them do and therefore are exempt from blame for their own misdeeds. Popular myth revels in this fabrication and weaves it into almost every form of entertainment geared to teens and young adults. Conscience or crimes, apparently, are a creation of and curse on adults alone.

Summary

Films do not shoulder the burden alone for the worst of popular culture, but they do little to showcase its best. Instead, most entertainment "…panders to the lowest common denominator…" of public standards (Giroux, 1999, 3). Along with television, video games, cyberspace and musical trends in youth culture, they combine to transform life into an artificial experience where former values no longer apply and formerly unimaginable social expectations continue to unfold and gain acceptance.

Every place still–opening eyes turn sordid material awaits. A cascade of bogus Messages and false images washed over youthful perception. All the efforts taken by Parents, teachers, and other concerned adults to instill values and decency in children Are ruthlessly undercut by a dizzying media melange that tells them the opposite. Thus, young minds are rapidly jaded. Innocence lost forever. Any prospects for turning the tide in the war against popular culture die the instant a television is flicked on, a videotape begins to play, or a computer screen brings up an adult Web site. As long as these media and the instruments that transmit them into our homes remain a fixture in the lives of otherwise bored and unsupervised teens, the outcome of this struggle is a foregone conclusion.

As the American family fell apart and mass entertainment continues its downward slide, there may yet be one last chance for redemption. Throughout U.S. history, education has played a major part in shaping culture—from increasing literacy rates among the rural population in the 19th century to breaking barriers against racial injustice via desegregation in the 20th. A metaphoric and literal beacon, it has often illuminated the path out of darker, troubled times. It is there, then, in education's potential to evoke social change with far–reaching cultural ripples, that we put our hopes.

7

Education Meets its Match

"Mom, I kind of thought it was cheating, but why would Dr. Karch do that?"

——a student in Maryland asking her mother why the school principal provided answers to state education assessment tests (Thomas & Wingert, 2000)

Eight hours a day, nine months of the year, teachers toil away. Unappreciated and certainly underpaid—by $8,000 a year at the start of their careers and $24,000 by age 50 as compared to other college–educated professions—(Steinberg, 2000) theirs is a demoralizing job. Despite this lack of recognition, and increasingly dogged by scandals like the one quoted above, they exist as an uncelebrated cadre of professionals on whose narrow shoulders the destiny of American society may literally rests. And education will be the instrument.

In _An Aristocracy of Everyone_, Benjamin Barber picks up and magnifies the Deweyan notion of education as a catalyst for cultural transmission and social welfare. Through years of schooling, or 'apprenticing in liberty,' youth are versed in the rudiments of citizenship. If the United States is to maintain its preeminence, education must emphasize social responsibility vis–a–vis community involvement, in addition to academic excellence. The two are intertwined, not mutually exclusive, since both work for the interests of democracy. In Barber's opinion, education can only be seen as a success when it cultivates a sense of civic duty as well as intellectual growth. In such a scheme, teachers serve as the vanguard of progressivism. For it is they who, knowingly or not, have accepted the incredibly complex mission of penetrating the vast smokescreen of misinformation and myth spread by popular culture. Consider the opponent they are facing.

Contemporary culture leaves telltale marks on the minds and manners of youth. In its words and gestures, popular culture instills doubt about adult wisdom and order, capitalizing on a view of parents as absent or disinterested figureheads in disintegrating family structures. It feeds the illusion among kids that money is abundant, easy–to–come by and able to procure happiness, health, and even justice. It represents teachers as sullen and unreliable individuals trapped in careers they secretly loathe. It promotes socially–contracted attention deficit disorder through incessant exposure to visual, audio, and virtual montages of information, all of which dazzle the eye but offer no substance to the mind. It clouds, deceives, and spoils through sexual, violent, and fantasy simulations ubiquitous in its media. It exults in sadistic or burlesque films designed to shatter boundaries of convention, revels in profane, misogynistic music, and recycles idiotic or amoral television programs . Finally, popular culture subverts those timeless traditions of individuality responsibility, common ethics, and spiritual creeds yet leaves nothing to fill the void other than its own bizarre cosmology of fetishes, cults and once exotic pleasures.

Can educators possibly be prepared for this monumental challenge? Or are they, like so many parents, overmatched in pitting themselves and their ingenuity against a culture laden with diversion and dissolution. Furthermore, have they been buffeted into submission by the same fierce cultural winds as their students? And, if so, does this impair or negate prospects for learning? In the coming chapter we will address these issues.

In the United States, education has always drawn tough assignments. As it did in the past with desegregation, Americans count on it more than they know to take the lead in addressing social inequities or cultural crises. In the case of racial integration, rationality triumphed over prejudice and ours became a better nation as a result. The battle education is waging to win over the minds of young people today poses an altogether different problem. It isn't about defeating an obvious, ugly adversary such as bigotry. The challenger on this occasion is subtle as well as overt. It already commands a huge following among youth, the very population we want to rescue. Thus, this will be the hardest task schools ever confront. Can education restore the equilibrium of a society in slow but steady decline? Or will popular culture continue to hover like a dark shadow over this and coming generations? The outcome of this epic struggle may well decide whether posterity inherits a world of light or returns to a new intellectual dark age. The stakes are really that high.

A New Boom: More Students and Education's Rising Profile

In spite of repeated attacks on its quality and our society's interest in finding alternatives in charter schools or subsidy programs such as tuition vouchers, public education in America is far from its nadir. Fifty–three million children were enrolled in K–12 (kindergarten through high school) education in the autumn of 1999. Birth rates assure this trend will continue. Consider these facts from *Baby Boom Echo: No End in Sight*, a 1999 report issued by the U.S. Department of Education:

Between 1989–2009:

1. Elementary school enrollment will rise by 4.7 million, secondary enrollment by 3.6 million and college enrollment by 2.8 million

2. Public high school enrollment will increase by 29% while full–time college enrollment is projected to rise by 26%

Between 1999–2009:

3. The total number of public and private high school teachers is expected to rise by 75,000, a 6% increase, while a total of 2.2 million public elementary and secondary school teachers will be needed to accommodate new students and replace retiring teachers

After 2009:

4. Unlike the decline after the first baby boom where births dropped, the number of births will continue to increase slowly for the next 10 years and rise further through 2028

Important inferences can be drawn from these data. First, adequate facilities must exist to accommodate the surge of students the report labels as the baby boom 'echo'. The sheer numbers of youngsters who will swell the nation's schools between 1999 and 2009 are unprecedented. Yet existing educational sites hardly seem equal to the task, aged and decrepit as they are. Following decades of dereliction, vast financial appropriations at both the state and federal levels will be needed to offset this obsolescence and, if the past is any indication, funding to repair existing schools or build a new infrastructure had better be generous, not piecemeal or at a trickle. The Educational Excellence for All Children Act of 1999 aspires to do precisely that. A companion piece of legislation, the School Modernization Bill, provided for $25 billion in bonds available to states and school districts over the next two years to build and modernize up to 6,000 public schools.

Second, and also addressed in the Act, teacher preparation and certification programs need to raise the bar in attracting the best and the brightest to replenish the ranks of a graying cohort of experienced teachers. Creating 'mid–career pathways' for seasoned teachers in order to keep them active in the profession is another goal. Raising academic standards in the classroom and making teachers more accountable for student learning outcomes bring additional expectations to bear on schools. Finally, colleges will have to improve teacher training programs and invigorate curricula as they take the lead in training this next cohort of professionals. Fundamental as these items appear, current realities show how desperately an overhaul is needed. In a *US News & World Report* (8/3/98) essay called "Dumbing Down Teachers," John Leo explained how 59% of 1800 prospective teachers in Massachusetts flunked a 10th–grade literacy test. A synopsis of the teacher–training curriculum obtained from the University of Massachusetts–Amherst included these courses among a host of similar entries: Diversity & Change, Black Identity, Classism, Racism, Sexism, Jewish Oppression, Lesbian/Gay/Bisexual Oppression, Oppression of the Disabled, and Erroneous Beliefs. Leo's verdict: "Among other things, the 59 percent who failed often couldn't spell simple English words like 'burned' and 'abolished.' Apparently they went to school without knowing much about anything and then came out the same way. But at least they are prepared to drill children in separatism, oppression, and erroneous beliefs." Leo's irascibility isn't necessary when the facts speak volumes.

Third, this fresh crop of educators better be schooled in the latest instructional techniques to reach students who grew up immersed in media technology. Lectures, in–class drill, and essay writing will not work with today's students. John Rosemond, a family psychologist whose parenting column runs in national syndication, touched upon this growing problem and its spread in our culture. Addressing the epidemic proportion of attention–deficit–disordered children diagnosed today, Rosemond has few reservations about identifying the culprit—television. In a recent column, he wrote: "The constant 'flicker' of television compromises the brain's ability to properly develop the structures necessary to a long attention span." The machine–gun imagery riddling television, hyperactive heroes dashing frenetically through video game grids, or the constant sensory shifts enabled by the pressure of a finger on a computer mouse, all have contributed to the mental impairment of youth. Thus, the cognitive processes the latter bring with them to school are incompatible with traditional pedagogical methods of rehearsal, recitation, and rote. Interaction with computers, self and group discovery, and linked–assignments, requiring applications of multiple media to complete a class project, these must be included in any teacher's classroom repertoire for them to have a fighting chance.

It is clear that public education from kindergarten through university has its work cut out for it in the years ahead. School experiences for adolescents will require a particularly intelligent plan to offset the increasing impact of negative cultural influences. As a whole, is education practically or philosophically ready to meet these imperatives? Ready or not, teachers, professors, and administrators must be prepared to stand alone as islets of resistance against a raging river of popular culture. Do they understand this burden and, if so, how will they cope with it? As for students, is there any prospect of educational salvation for them? We will find out shortly.

TEACHERS AND ACADEMIC ENVIRONMENTS

If by this stage in the discussion, through the preceding chapters, we have accurately identified the *zeitgeist* of popular culture, it poses a significant problem for education. Seizing upon and reproducing anything that is low–conceived, pop culture proudly dons an anti–intellectual demeanor. Reveling in surface, reviling substance, it celebrates a dumbed–down mentality and even enjoys denigrating the importance of school.

Movie mega–star Bruce Willis appointed himself spokesman for this camp in an interview with *USA Weekend* (February 11–13, 2000). Chiding the worth of a college education, Willis didn't hesitate to admit that he would advise his own children away from it unless they expressed a wish to become a lawyer or a doctor. He condescendingly insisted that he has never considered finishing his own B.A after dropping out of Montclair State College near his New Jersey home. As for the actual degree, Willis told the interviewer, "It's just a trophy. I have some bowling trophies I think would be worth about the same thing." These are the careless words of a man commanding twenty million dollars per film, one whom countless people see as an icon and whose statements in this article alone were read by hundreds of thousands of Americans, and who has fathered several children of his own. Yet in his self–serving opinion, people are better off without too much schooling. Fame and riches, obviously, do not procure common sense or intelligence.

Education has fallen out of favor in youthful eyes for a variety of reasons. Reading, reflection, study, of what practical use are these in the media age? Isn't the sum total of all knowledge available at one's fingertips on the Internet, cd–rom encyclopedias, or even television? Plodding through these vestiges of education makes scant sense to our techno–literate children. Given a choice, they opt for learning that is decentralized, informal, and at its optimum, in a classroom–without–walls format. Education has developed into the new cottage industry—kids acquire knowledge from dozens of knowledge factories and sources other than teachers. Today, peers, Web sites, and quasi–educational broadcasts provide what teachers once did without the rules or regimentation of class time. If, perchance, escapism, entertainment, and simulation distract students treading this virtual path, well, it is still more appealing than books, homework, or study hall.

Time–honored forms of art, literature, music and knowledge have been squeezed from the cultural arena. Ornate, scholarly, and high–minded, they are anachronisms in today's gallery of the perverse. *Popular* culture, as its names suggests, has been usurped by the masses and it is their tastes, moods, and caprices it now caters to. Students certainly understand this, which accounts for their antipathy toward these older and largely overlooked expressions of culture. They don't seem to be alone. Sadly, there are growing numbers of adults who have not only rejected the lore of the past, but have actively embraced the aesthetics of the postmodern present. A procession of exhibits demonstrating this tendency wait just ahead.

School Cultures and Troubled Teachers

"I know what it was like to be at a school that gives preference to athletes and ignores conflicts among students. I saw the athlete's harsh treatment of students who did not fit the 'norm.' I saw the faculty look the other way when athletes misbehaved." (Marquez, 1999, 17).

This statement is from a Columbine High School insider, a surviving 1999 graduate whose view of the situation, if authentic, implicates at least some teachers as moral accomplices in the horrors that occurred there. News of high school and colleges athletes earning special treatment from school officials is nothing new. It surprises few of us. However, when their deeds become so malicious and frequent that fellow students discern a pattern of persecution, as Marquez does, the risks heighten Worse still, this disorder cuts both ways. If all but outcasts among the student body have been conditioned to worship sports heroes, which in America we have, teachers and administrators probably have been affected as well. Just as youth today are enchanted with athletic celebrity, maybe the inverse is also true—that adults, even educators, show favor to adolescent athletes who achieve glory on the playing field irregardless of their arrogance and bullying off of it.

Along with high schools, universities indulge in a chronic habit of covering student–athlete misbehavior. Turning a blind eye or spinning it through the athletic department's press officer, if anything, they reward players through stipends and grants, non–academic scholarships, pseudo–employment, and gifts from alumni, voluminous NCAA restrictions notwithstanding. A brief glance at the abysmal graduation rates among athletes at Division I–A institutions and one starts to appreciate the magnitude of the problem. Expectations applying to all other students, outcomes like intellectual growth and or acquiring a sense social responsibility don't even factor into the relationship between athletes and universities. Corps of coaches, advisers, tutors, and 'friends of the university', i.e., community boosters and donors, collude to help the sport set circumvent academic rules codes of conduct.

In chapter 3, mention was made of the sad saga of former NFL running back James Brooks. In addition to legal woes stemming from missing child support payments despite having made millions over his career, another tragic element in his story came to light. He is functionally illiterate. Despite having been awarded a bachelor's degree from Auburn University, his attorney said this deficiency bars him from higher–paying, professional positions. With the press trumpeting this humiliating failure of higher education, the current president of Auburn, William Muse, invited Mr. Brooks back to complete an adult literacy program. Muse courageously committed the university to covering the cost of Brooks finishing the program from his cell if serving a jail sentence prevents it. Embarrassing as his position may be, it's doubtful Brooks stands alone among the ranks of one–time college athletes who did not deserve a degree. Furthermore, in fairness, it ought to be noted that Brooks is part victim as well as villain. Years of teachers and coaches who knew his secret yet passed him along for his athletic mettle bear the blame for his predicament. America's infatuation with athletic prowess at any price hurt not only Brooks but many forgotten others.

Nor are the psyches of educators impervious to other ignoble influences of these times. Scattered among them are instances where teachers have begun to display incredibly poor judgement that reeks of pop culture inebriation. Thirty miles up the road from my office in a sleepy little hamlet called Franklin, Ohio, a high school English teacher gave this criminally stupid assignment to her class. She asked students to answer two questions in the journals they kept for her course: 1) If you could assassinate a famous person, who would it be and how would you do it? 2) If everyone you knew should die in a tragic accident and one person could live, who would you choose and why? (*The Middletown Journal*, 10/16/99). As soon as parents of students enrolled in this class got wind of the assignment, it provoked a firestorm of criticism. Given recent events, how could this instructor even consider such issues as classroom fare, insert them into a learning context and yet not see the recklessness of this assignment? In short order, this misguided individual was suspended without pay and subsequently reassigned. A public apology by the principal of the high school followed. How coincidental that this event came on the heels of Columbine when we finally had to stop denying popular culture exerted an impact on people's behavior. Going one step further, is it possible then, that teachers, like their impressionable young charges, are also picking up on and and responding to the nefarious vibrations echoing through society?

One more hair–raising demonstration of this frightening trend arose with the suburban Ohio superintendent who suggested that all teachers in his Reading school district be armed with handguns to tighten school security. Pistol–packing pedagogues, he thought, might well deter student–initiated violence (*Cincinnati Enquirer*, 11/12/99). Gratefully, a still–rational school board severed his contract after a furor of protest from angry parents and community leaders, though not until conceding a buy–out clause on his contract paying him $165,000.

Outside middle America, another case that made national headlines earlier in the mid–90's, concerned Seattle teacher, Mary Kay LeTourneau, already married and a mother, seducing a 14 year–old student. She ended up having two children by him. Even in court, she refused to renounce her conduct and instead used the witness bench as a tearful platform from which to proclaim her undying love. What the behavior of these teachers and administrators seems to indicate is that if students are confounded, educators aren't necessarily making it easier for them. Distorted perspective, horrendous judgement, and baldly inappropriate conduct are becoming more common among adults as well as kids. When teachers violate the public trust by behaving so, forcing schools to lose their aura of moral invincibility, the last sanctuary existing in the United States has been violated.

Threatening to further upset the balance of an already fragile relationship are ambiguous media portrayals of teachers. The USA Network aired *The Mary Kay LeTourneau Story: All–American Girl* on January 30th, 2000. Characteristically, it cast her as a confused, love-lorn woman on the one hand, but a widely misrepresented and sympa-thetic folk hero on the other. Covered extensively in the preceding chapter, it's enough to say here that television shows and films consis-tently depict teachers and professors unflatteringly. Over time, and with what they are seeing, students begin to believe in these portrayals. Interestingly, the damage may be bilateral. Just as their students may be affected by popular culture, there is room to speculate whether or not the *self–perception* of educators has also been hurt media represen-tations stereotyping them as corrupted and corrupting. Have they become self–fulfilling prophecies?

In an environment like this, can teachers still serve as effective men-tors in the lives of their students? Theoretically, maybe so. Practically considered, I am not so sure. Perhaps only a handful of them have been tainted and the sensationalized media coverage they garner makes the crisis seem far more acute than it actually is. Nonetheless, clear symp-toms of the virulence of popular culture have manifested themselves. Sad as it may be to say, where one teacher has been infected, there are sure to be others.

Coup de'etat of Technology and Overthrow of Teacher Authority

Technology has infiltrated the classroom so thoroughly that recall-ing a time before its arrival challenges the memory. Students enrolled in schools today cannot even conceive of pre–media technology instruction. The infiltration process, however, was not clandestine but given with the express consent and blessings of our elected leaders in Washington. Commencing in 1996, the passage of the Snowe–Rock-efeller Amendment to the 1996 Telecommunications Act earmarked over $4 billion dollars in federal monies to be spent on putting "the Internet into every classroom in the country." (Hundt, 1999). Toward this end, its impact has already been felt: in 1994, 9% of all classrooms were on line. By the close of 1999, that figure rose to 54%. Cooperative partners in this technological drive are schools themselves. Supplementing government appropriations, American educational institutions were estimated to have spent approximately $5.53 billion on technology during 1999 alone.

In this made rush to wire every classroom and create new computer labs, few have bothered to stop, survey these installations, and speculate what technology actually means for schools. An assumption exists that technology enriches education by leveling the academic playing field. Visible evidence supports this view. Indeed, more public schools than ever before have increasing numbers of computers available to pupils. On a broader level, it is true that technology democratizes learning, that in theory, access to computers removes disparities in access to knowledge and information for all students without regard to socioeconomic status, race, or color. Wider accessibility benefits lower income students who have lagged behind affluent peers, redressing the "digital divide" threatening to split America into a society of technological haves and have nots. *Falling Through the Net: Defining the Digital Divide*, a Department of Commerce study released in July, 1999, found that 60% of households with incomes earning $75,000 or more had Internet access while this figure plummeted to 10% for those earning less than $20,000. If economic injustice handicaps some students from enjoying the fruits of technology at home, schools seem determined to function as the great equalizer among social institutions. Computerization, we're repeatedly told, will provide the catalyst. In this push, teachers are also striving to increase their own competency with electronic media. According to a study commissioned by Market Data Retrieval as reported in *The New York Times*, over 54% of teachers use the Internet 'for instructional purposes' during class sessions, 65% have e-mail addresses, and 69% use a computer daily (Mendels, 1999)

But, returning to the opening question, what about the status of the individual teacher in this unstoppable push of technology? Where does she or he fit in? In this reengineered educational assembly line where machines rather than people contain and control knowledge, student's perceptions of teachers have radically changed. In short, teachers have been supplanted by technology. They are no longer respected as arbiters of knowledge. Their authority has been coopted by electronic media. Ingrid Banks, a college professor, lamented this changing of the guard. "I understand the importance of using new technology in teaching, but...I am troubled by the prospect of being asked to teach on–line or televised courses. I fear that they would *obscure or even erase my presence from the classroom.*" (author's italics). In many circumstances, instructors merely function as desktop support technicians, wandering between members of a class, solving minor software glitches or keystroke errors as they lead students through Web–based course assignments. This departure from being knowledge purveyors to computer lab assistants redefined the traditional nature of the student–teacher relationship.

If indeed knowledge is power, a maxim of modernist history, and teachers no longer possess it, they have also ceded a significant portion of their authority over students. Diana Oblinger explains how this comes about:

> "In a traditional setting students access courses, expertise, or information through a hierarchy. Students begin their search for information or knowledge in one place (teacher) and gradually go from office to office or course to course to acquire progressively more detailed information. Their path resembles a hierarchy. In a web–enabled world, hierarchical channels are no longer required, Everyone can communicate with everyone else." (1999, 24)

Therefore, in this web–enabled world, the teacher has become dispensable for learning. In turn, the delicate balance of power in the classroom irrevocably shifts in favor of students, many of whom matured with and digested technology their teachers attempted to learn late in college or only during crash courses at professional development workshops. No longer respected as the ultimate source of wisdom, their lectures, instructions, and behavior management efforts carry far less weight with youth. Their leadership position has been sabotaged by technology and students much more adept with its applications than themselves. Little wonder that some pedagogues like Banks fret that "Instead of letting technology drive teaching, we should think about ways in which technology could supplement—not substitute for—what we do in the classroom." Poor Professor Banks seems not to understand that it's too late for that. Technology won't be relaxing its grip on us any time soon and turning back the hands of the clock to an era already being recalled with nostalgia even more unlikely.

In our haste to integrate computers into education we never considered its impact on a fundamental dynamic of learning—the crucial relationship between teachers and students. An unexpected consequence resulted. Students shifted their allegiance from teachers to technology when it comes to seeking information. Exercising this new preference, youth have removed teachers, like parents, from their time–proven role as mentors on the path to adulthood.

Demise of Discipline

Decreasing public respect for the function of teachers, prompted by depictions in the media, prompts a related quandary for education. Discipline, a precondition for learning, is defunct. When students have rarely been asked to abide by it, at home or in prior academic experiences, order suffers and chaos gains a foothold in schools. What killed discipline should intrigue us.

In the United States, an increasingly legalistic and litigious society brought about the circumstances for its decline. In court, students have successfully sued for everything from the right to have prayer eliminated from school functions to racial quotas being banned as criteria for medical school admissions (recall the *Bakke* decision). Although courts were once reluctant to involve themselves in educational disputes in partial fear of encouraging a flood of frivolous lawsuits, this has changed in recent years and indeed the dam has burst. On another level, postmodernism's fanatical celebration of diversity and subsequently 'individual rights' at the expense of social cohesiveness promoted this unfortunate trend. Schools, wary of legal reprisals and costly lawsuits for enforcing traditional (modernist) codes of conduct began to falter under mounting pressure and disciplinary standards relaxed. Violations of these standards drew progressively lighter sanctions over time. By failing to maintain a hard line on academic and behavioral expectations, the cycle was completed. Discipline was stripped from classrooms and schoolyards. Consistent with the musings of popular culture, once unshakable ideas about obedience to regulations weakened considerably. Students, as we have seen, now wield a host of rights that must never be abrogated by school officials.

Knowing they have only the token support of principals or districts, teachers have been rendered ineffectual in commanding deference from difficult pupils. Back–talk, profanity, confrontation, and even threats of bodily harm are commonplace among student responses to teacher directives. College faculty tell similar tales about obnoxious, hostile students who ignore requests to comply with their instructions and routinely disrupt lectures, lab work or group assignments. An associate in the Biology department told me of a student who kept talking during his lecture on dissecting an animal specimen. When he politely asked her to stop, she replied with a string of curses, then grabbed her backpack, knocking the specimen tray on the floor, and stormed out of the laboratory while vowing to pursue his rebuke with the dean. Loutish behavior, yes, one–of–a–kind drama, not really—scenes like these and worse can be found in classrooms across the country everyday. It's tempting to say it's the inmates who are running the asylum these days. Self–discipline appears to be running in dangerously short supply. Americans acclimated to asserting their rights don't seem as comfortable living up to the responsibilities that accompany them.

Let us use truancy as an illustration since it's a massive problem for public schools throughout the United States. According to *The 1997*

Condition of Education annual report compiled by the U.S. Department of Education, on any given day, 9.8% of all "central city" high school students were absent without excuse from classes while 8.6% of their suburban peers missed school. For middle schools, this figure dropped to a slightly less alarming 7.0 % in city districts and 6.3% in suburban zones (National Center for Education Statistics, U.S. Dept. of Education). That same year, statistics indicate that 46.4 million students were enrolled in America's K–12 public educational system. It doesn't require mathematical genius to calculate from these figures that millions of students skip school each day. Additional data compiled by the Education Department shows that the majority of truants are habitual offenders. What consequences do these students face?

Punishments from the schools equate to a slap on the wrist, for most. Suspensions for absenteeism seldom occur. Expulsion is hardly a legitimate option these days since public institutions are obligated by state statute to educate all students residing in their service areas (unless convicted of felonies). At its most severe, repeat offenders are assigned to penal study halls or given after–hours detention. Holding a student back for missing too many days is an abandoned practice since it will likely provoke a legal challenges from the family of the student being failed.

With educators' hands tied, communities have begun experimenting with other measures to discipline chronic truants. In Cincinnati, the "Target Truancy" initiative was introduced. Detailed in a (2/22/00) news segment on NBC television affiliate, WLWT, in the program city police are used to round up class–cutting teens who tend to gather in obvious places like bus stops or shopping centers. Police take these students home where their guardians learn of the offense. If the parents are away at work, the student is detained at local precinct headquarters until parents come and get them. The idea behind this effort was to embarrass parents and students sufficiently to deter future absenteeism. The gamble did not pay off. It backfired. Instead of contrition and a pledge to mend errant ways, what the authorities received were a rash of protests from parents incensed at being called away from work to pick up wayward children. Some complained that there was nothing that they could do, the child was uncontrollable, the schools were to blame, and how dare they be bothered with such matters when the school and municipal leaders did not provide a solution.

As we have witnessed in so many instances, conventional wisdom has been stood on its ear. In the convoluted logic of postmodern life, parents need not take responsibility for wayward offspring while corrective actions taken by schools are heavily restricted. Naturally, youth emerge unscathed. In a marvelous reverse of tradition engineered by popular culture, the pendulum has swung so far in the other direction that teachers are the ones under the thumbs of students. Unable to exude authority or assert control, they are being victimized by class bullies. With their stature eroded, toothless disciplinary policies, and parents alternating between apathy and antagonism, teachers have been targeted by frustrated and troubled youngsters as the only adult figureheads who cannot fight back. This truth means elementary and secondary school teachers will be in for a particularly rough ride in working to accomplish the mission they were trained for.

Campuses as Social Agencies and the 'Entitlement' Myth

Low–cost medical treatment and health care, along with wellness programs and well–equipped recreation centers. Child care for student–parents provided by the host institution. Free birth control clinics and contraception. Individual or group psychological counseling. Sponsored support groups for single parents or divorced students, gays and lesbians, victims of substance, sexual or domestic abuse. Assorted opportunities for credit and nominal–fee personal banking. Subsidized housing, on and off campus. Cheap meal plans. Subsistence on federal and state funding in the form of low interest loans and grants in–aid (a.k.a., financial aid).

If this sounds like a description of a welfare state, one of the socialized nations of Scandinavia or perhaps the People's Republic of China, think again. The services listed above are provided to almost every college student at almost every public university in the country. My employer, the vast University of Cincinnati, is no exception to this new rule. Under similar social pressures, a growing number of suburban high schools have closed ranks with their inner–city cousins in providing these services to teenaged students. Extending Hillary Clinton's concept, the school of today has indeed become a village of overlapping support systems.

What led to this transformation? Simply put, schools and universities assumed the dimensions of full–blown social services agency because that is the expectation placed upon them by the public. Home and family let them down and churches are largely gone from the social scene. The only viable institution present to pick up the slack is education. Their mission to educate is no longer seen as enough. It is also important to remember that contemporary culture is driven by the mass satisfaction. Skilled as consumers and accustomed to getting their wants immediately gratified, Americans demand more and more not just from businesses but from government–supported agencies in their communities. One can detect this consumerist trend in growing habit of referring to students as clients or customers. The wave of interest in assessment and outcomes through performance criteria is another indicator of the commercializing of education. Legislators and taxpaying parents must see a demonstration of sensitivity to constituent wants. Education, too long exempted from accountability for its product, has suddenly been put on notice.

There is still more. Pampered in an era where personal needs eclipsed any concurrent social commitments, students are fairly bursting with knowledge about their "rights." As I've discovered during the exercising of my duties as a student affairs dean, they are quick to point out they are *entitled* to the amenities listed in the opening paragraph. This sense of being owed is so embedded in the adolescents I come in contact with that my colleagues and I at the university I have nicknamed them "the entitlement crowd."

With this belief in entitlement comes a companion militancy. If the conveniences mentioned earlier don't exist, students soon threaten to take themselves and their tuition dollars somewhere else. Never mind that a sizeable portion of this tuition bill is footed by the government in the form of Stafford loans or Pell grants. A student questioned why income earned from a summer job was spent on 'concerts, clothes, and movies" instead of saved for college boldly remarked, "'…that's what student loans are for.'" (Decker, 1999). That taxpayers don't mind underwriting a four or five year stint at college mirrors the new expectations. At least twice a week acidic complaints come before me from students about transferring to another university if additional parking spots aren't added, if the cafeteria doesn't start staying open until 2 am like Taco Bell, or we don't drop their $5 co–pay per ($75/hr. charge) counseling session at the counseling center on campus.

Afraid of being stigmatized as indifferent to popular expectations, high schools and colleges are falling over backwards to accommodate them. Slipping into the same conundrum as in other areas of postmodern life, education caves into increasingly selfish and unrealistic agendas and in the process compromises its primary purpose. Never designed to be a comprehensive community agency, resources that might otherwise have been allocated toward teacher training, instructional materials, or facilities improvement are being diverted to auxiliary functions. Students are pacified. But educators can see the writing on the wall. Ever–expanding support services are consuming money that could, and rightly should, have been dedicated to attracting or retaining the best faculty as well as academic program development. Regrettably, this pattern toward entitlement shows few signs sign of abating.

Impetus for it partly derives from present–day legalities. Worried about infringing on students' rights, administrators have back–peddled from any position requiring the drawing of a line not to be crossed. Syndicated columnist Walter Williams, himself an economics professor at George Mason University, minced few words about his feelings on "student's 'rights' gone wrong" the literal title of his column on May 2, 1999. "Today, kids have *rights*, and teachers and principals must heed *due process*" (1999). His inference is clear; students hold the power, while educators content themselves with the procedures. Aware that ensuing legal battles over sanctions for misconduct or locker inspections might not be worth it, educators countenance attitudes and behaviors that in the past would not have been tolerated. In consequence, we have reclassified the social mission of education away from training children to be temperate citizens to never satisfied clients.

Another adverse but perfectly predictable outcome of the entitlement trend manifests itself a reckless disregard for others as well as the community. Renowned sociologist Amitai Etzioni has referred to this as "excessive individualism" which comes at the expense of communities and one's obligation to them. It is a tune familiar to us all. Indoctrinated from a young age as consumers, we take and take but give nothing back to the familial, social or cultural benefactors supporting us. Frankly, it does not require a behaviorist to tell us that youth accustomed to getting everything they want when they want it will probably not react well when asked to return something back to the neighborhood they live in or the school they attend. With a culture that insists upon and guards an array of individual rights, students believe that gratification is a one–way street. This attitude even applies to educational endeavors.

OBSTACLES TO STUDENT LEARNING

If by this stage in the narrative questions linger about the detrimental effect of popular culture on a student's educatability, they should shortly be put to rest. In a lengthy essay published in the American Academy of Arts and Sciences cerebral journal *Daedalus,* Robert Hampel addresses several aspects of popular culture and their intervention in the lives of adolescents. Provocatively titled "A Generation in Crisis?" he concentrates primarily on electronic media. These media, he contends, systematically neutralize not only students *willingness* but their *aptitude* to learn. In a moment of shining simplicity, Hampel puts his question to us in these words: "How does pop culture affect academic achievement? The habits it encourages are at odds with the skills necessary for thoughtful analysis and understanding." Recalling the comments of Bruce Willis opening this chapter, those of metal–rap band Limp Bizkit's lead singer Fred Durst as cited in the last chapter, or countless other pop icons cited before, they echo a theme that runs the length if this work. Popular culture sneers at scholarship or any intellectual activity, preferring to extol street smarts and successes achieved through them. With their natural antipathy toward schooling aroused, youth warm to this message

Hampel also enlightens us with a second astute observation. Although he names television as the prime offender, in the context of his article it is clear that his indictment extends to most electronic media that count youth among their audience. "Television is antithetical in other ways to what is necessary to use one's mind well. If learning is often sequential and linear, viewing has no prerequisites, no progression of skills after the simple processing of pictures and sounds is acquired." Television, videos, games, and the Internet, all of these image–based systems allow for non–reflective interaction. They do not necessarily require thought. When students have been raised on such fare, it's implausible they would eschew it in favor of educational processes that hinge on thinking and reasoning to comprehend the material presented.

Fellow educators concur. Perry Oldham emphasized the mounting difficulty teachers face in trying to foster student learning. In an essay published in *Education Week* journal, Oldham asserts that an unfair competition has the deck stacked against education. Cultural distractions are too widespread and stunningly packaged for students to pull their eyes away. Popular entertainment, from professional sports to the tripe television doles out are continually running interference, preventing students from developing the mental discipline and academic skills they will need for schooling as well as life itself. Congruent with the anti–popular culture opposition, Oldham declares that until access to these diversions is curtailed, student performance in the classroom will continue to suffer.

While computers and cyberspace gained ground, the undisputed champion of all media is still television. As such, it has drawn the most flack for distracting and deceiving young Americans. Advocacy groups, like the Washington D.C.–based TV Free America (**www.tvfa.org**), compiled data on its homepage which support this position. Two correlated findings tell the story:

- Hours per week of television watching shown to *negatively affect academic achievement*: 10 or more

- Percentage of 4th graders that watch *more than 14 hours per week* of television: 81%

Compounding the detrimental impact of television is its reluctance to be employed for educational purposes. An Annenberg Public Policy Center at the University of Pennsylvania research study released in June, 1999, showed that even of the small assortment of children's programs classified under Federal Communications Commission guidelines as educational, 21% still had little or no learning value.

From these investigations and earlier narrative, we have deduced that interactions with media are hardly beneficial. Television, films, and other media present views of reality that are rife with distortions, delusions, and plain lies. Schooling, in general, and teachers, in particular, have been singled out for ridicule by popular culture. They are treated with a mix of contempt and pity in most dramatizations. Nonetheless, it may be that the biggest obstacle of all arises in the conditioning students received in their lives outside of school. Today, educators are forced to cope with students programmed to respond only to persistent non–intellectual stimulation. *Reflex* won, *reflect* lost. Although the masses do not mourn the vanquished, society will soon be paying the price for this victory.

The Changing Face of Literature

While generous space in this book has focused on electronic media and its exalted spot in the pecking order of youth interests, print is not entirely dead. The immense popularity and sales of the *Harry Potter* fantasy books for smaller children illustrate this well enough. Yet the central issue isn't whether kids are reading, it is *what* they are reading. Just as television, movies, and cyberspace thrive on in salacious topics, so does postmodern literature for youth. In a general sense, we already covered those "celebiographicals"—books written about or by teen sensations in music and drama. In a society obssessed with celebrity, personal stories are gobbled up on everyone from skating idol Tara Lipinski to actor Leonardo Dicaprio, with kids doing most of the buying. This material hardly qualifies as literature, however. It is on that body of youth fiction or serious writing directed toward adolescents, that we will spend the next few moments.

As art imitating life, children's fiction has taken a stark and somber turn. Apart from the *Harry Potter* fantasy series, content for younger readers is fairly bursting with situations and imagery previously restricted to adult audiences. Julia Duin, a columnist for the *Washington Times*, wrote an unnerving expose on the sobering state of books for teens. In her 12/17/99 article, Duin reported that today's teen fiction is beset with scenes of violence, rape, mental illness, animal torture, and occult practices. These topics, according to relaxed publishing industry standards, it seems, have now been deemed suitable for young adults ages 12 and up. If Duin blanched and parents balk, literary critics feel differently and applaud this genre of so–called 'reality–based' fiction.

An editorial running in one metropolitan newspaper supported Duin's sentiments on the morbid quality of adolescent fiction.

"Among the hot teen books described are *Dancing on the Edge*, a NationalF Book Award finalist and winner of the Parents Choice

Award in 1997. It open with a Ouija board séance and tells how the heroine was cut from her dead mother's body in order to be born. The heroine, whose grandmother is a medium, starts casting love spells on her friends and then sets herself on fire. She recovers from mental illness in the end.

Another is *I was a Teen–age Fairy*, published in 1998 for the 12–and–Up set. It talks about pedophilia and how a teen–age model is lured into drugs, sex, and alcohol.

Another, entitled *Deal With It*, explains lesbian sex, how to find abortion clinics and how to diagnose your own sexually transmitted disease."

(Cagnetti, 2000, A20)

Personal politics and prejudices aside, should you disagree with the above position on these issues, the fact remains that such subjects are quite distant from what used to pass as suitable literature for young readers. Ann Tobias, a literary agent specializing in children's fiction and cited in the editorial above, refers to the present fad in publishing as "four D books": focusing on divorce, drugs, death, and dismemberment.

For those who concede that teen literature may indeed be ominous, but children's literature (under 13) is still unsullied by morose fascinations, they need to take a closer look. Consider the *Bobby's Back* horror series widely read by 11 and 12 year–old males. The first installment in a series of four introduces the reader to Bobby, a "young man who seeks murderous revenge on a group of five people (four of them are female) who teased him when he was a child." (Lewis, 1998). Some miserably misguided author actually wrote a book about a boy who murders to avenge being picked on? Is this really fantasy? Or is it the life of Eric Harris as recounted on his pre–Columbine videotapes? Resemblance aren't just uncanny. They are alarming for how they implant the idea, even as fiction, that revenge is sweet and murder its best redresser.

If you happened to be born in the sixties, as I was, you grew up in a time where most every middle–class household owned a set of *Encylopedia Britannica*. When we weren't using them for school work, my sisters devoured *Nancy Drew* mysteries and I wiled away countless hours during the summer with *Hardy Boys* detective books which I traded with friends who owned volumes I did not. In between, we somehow managed to discover lighter classics like *National Velvet, Sounder,* and by our mid–teens, meatier prose like *The Catcher in the Rye* or *To Kill a Mockingbird.* When I wanted to live dangerously, I yielded to my cravings for science fiction, starting with *A Wrinkle in Time,* progressing to *The Martian Chronicles* and wrapping up with *Dune.* With parents who also read for pleasure, the spindly wire magazine rack in our house always brimmed with copies of *Life, Look, Time* and *National Geographic.* Excitement built up over our weekly trips to the library. Mothers in the neighborhood took turns chauffering our gang to this wonderful place. My sisters, friends and I all had library cards issued to us not long after the training wheels had been removed from our bicycles. Even as kids, we took this luxury for granted and I can't imagine my childhood without the books I so loved being part of it.

Recollections like these belong with other artifacts from this forgotten civilization in a museum. Such memories might as well have come from a century ago. Contemporary culture could never abide by reading material that opens young minds to learning and other intellectual benefits.

Here and now, adolescents may be treading water in an ocean of words but absorbing little knowledge from this exercise. That is because *accessing* information has been confused with *processing* it. The two are not the same. This is evident from the declining performances turned in by students on reading and writing skills tests. For education to make a difference, information must be weighed, analyzed and talked about. In the now defunct age of typography, this is what we used to do. Teachers helped students navigate through their reading of texts. Students asked questions or for clarification and instructors provided explanations. Knowledge was presented in sequential components and coherently explained. Linear thinking dominated rather than scattershot exposures to random bits of data. Books progressed from the simple to the complex, and our thought processes paralleled this pattern.

In *The Gutenberg Elegies, The Fate of Reading in the Electronic Age,* Sven Birkerts addresses this loss and what it means for the literacy of subsequent generations. He perceptively notes that reading as it used to be done for learning; focused, repetitively and intensively, has been replaced by reading of an extensive, fleeting, and superficial nature. In the electronic age, all subjects might be within one's grasp, but few, if any are ever mastered. Just like people are trained to expect a fresh image on their televisions every six seconds, they bring that same expectation to their encounters with the written word.

Culture–Induced Attention Deficit Disorder

A fundamental problem for youth raised in the media age occurs in the disabling of their powers of concentration. Continuously under siege by rapidly changing pictures, sounds, and perceptions being fed to them on television or computer screens, they have been handicapped in their ability to focus on a single, stationary object. Any item that doesn't 'morph' into something else within several seconds and keep them entertained cannot retain their interest. Regrettably, the ascent of these media signaled the death knell of educational endeavors which relied on the student's capacity to pay rapt attention, follow the logic of a math problem or the plot of the story they are reading, and cogitate on the experience as it's unfolding. In today's world, the mental emphasis has shifted from "deliberate information analysis and critical thinking to quick information accessing…" (Fidler, 1997, 116).

Our postmodern surroundings depend on continual quick–hit stimulation. Cruising the Internet, kids can amuse themselves as long as they have a mouse and an inclination to point–and–click on one hyperlink after another. On television, the image changes every nine seconds, on MTV, which practically patented the video montage format so widely used now it makes some of us dizzy, the images switch every four seconds (Hampel, 1998). Compact disk players exist that can accommodate up to twenty CD's at once, another barometer of how swiftly our interest wanders when the stimulation doesn't live up to its billing. The hand–held remote control unit that accompanies every television, video cassette player, digital video disk (DVD) unit, and stereo system reinforces this point. Allowing us to change entertainment directions with the press of a button, it has become an indispensable part of our tech–heavy culture. Domestic arguments, fights between siblings, and even homicides have been committed over who is controlling this all–important device.

A unique talent mastered by Americans is that of visual grazing. Remote control at the ready, people perpetually and mechanically flick through the seventy or eighty channels offered by cable servers in the search for programming that appeals to them. Unappeased, they forward to the next station, pause just long enough to catch a glimpse of that show and then resume scanning for something better. The Internet makes this roaming habit even more effortless. Point and click, point and click, and point and click until an object worthwhile finally pops up on the monitor. In itself, this habit reveals something important about the grazer. It indicates that they are not satisfied with any of their options. Pacification is unattainable, and therefore, so is pleasure. Channel changing has become an involuntary reflex for their discontentedness. The search for new perceptual material never ends. Even when found, its appeal is extremely short–lived and the search soon renews.

Educators have noticed this culturally–conveyed contagion. In the classroom, they fight against it daily, although the struggle may be in vain. In an article aptly called "Feeding on Fast Food and False Values," that appeared in *The Education Digest*, Helmut Manzl explores this unequal contest. Both elementary and secondary school students today, he said, exhibit much shorter attention spans and carry an expectation of immediate gratification, due mainly to their lifelong experiences with the media. The result are learners who become bored quickly, fail to develop study habits and discipline, and expect instant and painless education. Onerous as it is to them, students can't flick to another station or escape by clicking on another hyperlink when the adult lecturing at the head of the class begins to bore them.

These same student frustrations apply to university–level teaching. Educators are now warned to remember that "…your students have spent more of their lives channel surfing than reading; they are not capable of absorbing more than commercial–length packets of information." (Douglas & George, 1999). How we can entertain any hopes of significant learning taking place during so short a span of time leaves us wondering. At a faculty retreat sponsored by the University of Cincinnati in 1995, professors were appraised of techniques to keep students focused in class, since at best, research showed they had a mere *20 minutes* before students began to lose interest. Actually, that may be pushing the envelope. The authors quoted at the opening of this paragraph recommend *7 minutes* at a time. Symposium facilitators counseled faculty to rotate their instructional methods quite frequently if they wanted to have an impact (Salvato, 1995). At this rate of decline, one can't help but speculate what the maximum student attention span will be in another ten years. Will it have to be reckoned in seconds rather than minutes?

Accustomed to and ruined by nonstop environmental stimuli that change in a heartbeat, American youth have been cognitively disabled. The basic ingredients of learning: coherent and sequential presentation of knowledge, faith in the teacher as interesting and informative, concentrated mental focus, and critical thinking and problem solving in students, these are increasingly remote outcomes for educators to attain.

Education and the Internet

How has the Internet affected education? Will it bring an efficacy to the way students learn?. Will it aid students with intensive academic support software in honing reading, writing and math skills? Or does it threaten instead to remove the need for reflective thinking by making the answers available on user–friendly, topic–heavy Web sites? More to the point, is the wealth of information available on the Internet an effective replacement for content once presented during class instruction or researched in the library? There is reason to believe not. For as one college professor put it, "...the Web is replete with as much bogus material as accurate information."(Gandolfo, 1996, 27).

Many teachers and education advocates agree. *Time* magazine ran an investigative report called "Lost in Cyberspace" on the heralded connection between education and the World Wide Web in its April 26, 1999 issue. Popularly praised as a formidable learning tool, the Web, it seems, suffers from a bipolar disorder. While a portion of its "back alleys," esoteric and difficult to find, can be "brilliantly educational", mostly it seems to be a "stunning advance" in presenting primarily personal views, biases, and occasionally crackpot theories as hard science. With no one to patrol it or fact–check (as occurs in print media), a preponderance of unsubstantiated and untethered ideas float randomly through cyberspace. Empirically unsophisticated students gladly pilfer this information for school papers and projects, unaware of its dubious pedigree. Of course, there also lingers the question of substance. The Internet disposes a cornucopia of data at our fingertips without assuring any profoundness. John Skow, author of the *Time* article, reiterated this concern in his commentary on conducting on–line research. He compares it to taking a toddler for a stroll. Awed, initially, "...Pretty pebbles and deeply meaningful small sticks present themselves, but seldom proceed in a straight line. There is always some beguiling irrelevancy to be clicked, which is good. Often, however, the...pilgrim discovers to his surprise that there is not much depth of information." As we have seen, in many aspects cyberspace is an ethereal domain.

Furthermore, as we embraced technology and incorporated it into schools, we forgot to address some essential issues on how students learn. Ed Neal, director of faculty development at the Center for Teaching and Learning at the University of North Carolina, redirects our attention to these key matters. Using the Socratic method to make his point about the outcomes of computer–based instruction, Neal queried:

> "What did the students learn and how well did they learn it? Did they simply acquire factual information, or did they learn to analyze, synthesize, and exercise critical judgement about the subject matter. Did they learn to write clear, grammatical, logical prose? Did they learn tolerance for other viewpoints and how to defend their own opinions in a rational way? Can they apply what they know to other areas of their work and life? Did their learning last beyond the end of the course?" (1998, N41)

Assuming the Internet to be the primary instructor now, it is highly improbable that it fully meets the objectives implicit in these questions. Not just because technology, per se, is incapable of providing a deep and lasting intellectual massage, but also because of the behaviors our reliance on it engenders. With education stripped of its mainstay—dynamic teacher–student interaction—its technology–heavy environment now requires students to sit for hours before a computer in "'mental states approaching suspended animation'" (Trout, 1998).

Even among schools or universities who supply students with cutting–edge computer facilities, anxieties persist about how far the craze for technical rather than human instruction will go. Given the growing market demand for distance learning along with that nasty little inconvenience of having to physically attend school, will faculty gradually be phased out in deference to a "Web–based 'Course–in–a–Box' approach to teaching" (Bothun, 1999) This format displays everything from an on–line syllabus listing course goals and schedule of assignments to the location of the class real–time bulletin board, to linked Internet sites where additional information can be obtained. Will this preference for technology as the delivery system of choice for learning eventually lead to Curriculum–in–a–box and after that Diploma–in–a–box or Degree–in–a–box?

Youth credentialed in such a manner may be superbly techno–literate. But should we expect the same level of proficiency in their interpersonal and social skills? Educational technology delivers a technological education. A longstanding expectation for education is its preparing young people for social intercourse and responsibility. Learning in the vacuum of cyberspace fails to fulfill that crucially important task.

Conclusions

In *The Learning Society*, Robert Hutchins defined education as "the deliberate, organized attempt to help people to become intelligent." Surveying the contemporary landscape, do any of us feel confident that helping youth to become intelligent is still within our powers as adults? Much as I wish to hope so, a bitter truth gnaws away at me that it may not. Quite honestly, we cannot be sure that schools do anything deliberately these days, much less attain their academic objectives. With priority given to meeting a mounting social agenda, school systems can no longer devote adequate time to crucial tasks like refining the structures and methods which foster learning. The present philosophy of public education has abandoned academic concerns and shifted toward an emphasis on fixing social problems. Rather than teaching, simply getting themselves and their students safely through each day brings a rewarding feeling to many educators. If this has indeed our preoccupation, can we dare claim that a process as intricate as 'helping people to become intelligent' falls within our receding powers?

In America as in most democracies, it has also been accepted that the chief ambition of education is to prepare younger generations for constructive participation in society. Neither the United States nor its way of life will endure if it fails this assignment. William Damon, director for the Center on Adolescence at Stanford University, isolated three imperatives that must be met for the civic training of American youth to be complete. "Positive engagement with civic life" begins with the development of 1) intellectual abilities such as critical reasoning, literacy, and a knowledge of the past, 2) moral grounding and the exercise of traits like honesty, a concern for justice and personal responsibility, and, 3) a practical commitment to and involvement with community organizations (e.g. the Big Brothers/Sisters program or Habitat for Humanity). Contrast these precepts with the discussions that occurred earlier in this chapter and decide for yourself whether or not you believe education is fulfilling its social and political missions. Intellectual competency among students, except for the basic skills needed to operate technology, is near at low ebb. Moral education, or the inculcation of ethics has been banned in public schools by a judiciary that believes teaching values inherently favors a particular religious dogma and consequently violates separation of church and state. And, where a respectable group of students are sufficiently moved by the spirit of civic duty to volunteer to work on community projects, far and away the majority prefer the distinctly non–communal activities of watching television or Web–surfing.

Hutchins thought that we were headed for disaster if education alone was entrusted with the enormous job of bettering the society it serves. Theoretically, it can, but only to the extent that the dominant culture permits it to modify the status quo. If this culture, in its philosophy and operating media, opposes independent thinking in its members, education faces an insurmountable barrier. Similarly, if it suppresses individual imagination in its people, it 'overpowers' and suffocates any chance for them to grow intellectually and condemns society to stagnation. Considering what we have covered in this chapter and those preceding it, popular culture appears to have our posterity in a life–threatening chokehold.

In past eras, education served as a beacon to brighter days ahead. A question was posed at the outset of this chapter—do schools and those that work in them still exert the power to return American youth to solid footing? Can the imbalances imposed by popular culture be overcome? I leave it to the reader to make this determination. The injuries sustained by youth, emotionally and cognitively, require critical attention. To date, however, the cures we offer seem like no more than band–aids on a mortally–wounded person.

America's last best hope rested with education. It still does. As a nation, perhaps we may yet overcome the odds stacked against us. Education remains the most powerful weapon in our weakening arsenal. Only it has the potential to transform individual lives, prevailing thinking, and in due time culture itself. Unfortunately, this mission, which it achieved with so much brilliance in the past, now transcends its capabilities. When pitted against popular, it seems culture, education met its match.

8

Dispatches from the Front

I f until now this narrative concentrated on the philosophical, we will now journey into the realm of fact. Just as the Columbine slayings provided a powerful case study of the link between popular culture and disaffected youth. A host of other illustrations, less tragic but no less alarming, exist for our consideration.

Let me start by describing the peculiar and unpredictable world I enter each day when I leave my car in the morning and walk across campus to my office. Perhaps my telling will dispel some misconceptions about universities being cloistered environments that cradle plea-sure–preoccupied students and pompous professors from the real world beyond their elegantly manicured lawns, ivy–blanketed halls, and adolescent idylls. If this tableau describes a select company of expensive private colleges nestled in picturesque New England hamlets, it doesn't do justice to large, public institutions located in urban set-tings, like mine. The university which employs me is grafted into the vibrant intellectual and artistic life of the city surrounding it.

By all measures, our campus is a miniature of this society. As such, the academic community that I am part of faces the same issues and problems as the rest of America. If, as I pointed out earlier and throughout this book, the United States as a whole suffers from a wide-spread social sickness, it follows that learning institutions are not pro-tected by any special immunities. Drug and alcohol abuse, petty crime, identity and financial fraud, racial tension and conflict, behavioral dis-orders, sexual predators and victimization, mental illness, violence at home, dysfunctional relationships and co–dependence—all of these are woven into the tapestry of college life. Numerous students have been and are currently touched by them.

Naturally, an outsider might reply, milder cases of these might arise occasionally, but nothing like what transpires in broader society, of course. As an insider, this is where I beg to differ. The insights my position as dean of students affords me might startle the general public used to seeing universities as cultural repositories where traditional ideas of civility, polished manners and self–disciplining behaviors still reign. If pressed, my observations would also render me a highly disagreeable witness in the court of popular inquiry. The issues covered, feelings admitted to and statements made by students visiting my office can still surprise me after fifteen years in this field. More than that, however, they often leave me uneasy. I'm afraid for the student making the confession. I'm afraid for his unsuspecting peers. Not merely for their physical safety, but for their psychological and social welfare. Colleagues among the professoriate to whom I confide these concerns acknowledge they feel them too. A sense of impending danger gathers, as if that at storm far off on the horizon will suddenly and without warning blow in and descend upon our inconspicuous academic village.

With Columbine receded from the national spotlight, it's simpler to believe that America has recovered its equilibrium, that the problem has disappeared. Making this assumption invites disaster. Just as experts tell us we cannot eliminate crime by building new prisons, nor should we deceive ourselves into thinking that political rhetoric, tighter security or added counseling staff we have introduced into schools have rejuvenated them into wholesome, sane and safe places. If solving the dilemma only turned out to be that simple. Mayhem lurks all around us in the chameleon of popular culture. Any search for solutions must start there.

In the interim, a communique needs to sent to everyone beyond the edge of campus. Without betraying confidences, I hope to give the reader a candid glimpse of what is fermenting behind the building dedications and basketball games at one vast, compartmentalized, yet otherwise unremarkable university. The cases I chose to include in this chapter are genuine. My objective is not to instill fear and leave it at that, for doing so would accomplish nothing. Instead I wish to heighten awareness among a public who otherwise might be lulled into a false sense of security with the memory of Columbine and other youthful acts of infamy slipping into oblivion. Young people are in turmoil. Given the society they live in, we must never think that they are fine. As the experiences I'm about to share with you demonstrate, deep and many are the cracks appearing in the masques adolescents wear. Like a parade of Dorian Grays, their cool outer appearance conceal inner scars and struggles. It falls to us, as interested adults, to do what we can to salve these injuries

In this section, I recount several memorable student interactions that I had while discharging my duties as a dean during a two–month period in early 2000. They should be of special interest to the reader since each affirms the culturally–borne crises raised throughout this narrative. These students, each in their own individual fashion, have been adversely affected by popular culture and the aberrant society it created. One student wrestles with his impulses to do violence. Another has been corrupted by the seedier facets of technology and gotten a whiff of its potential for profit. A third embraces and emulates the diabolical perpetrators of Columbine as his personal heroes and when queried as to this choice, lashes out. Perhaps the worst off of all, is a student who daily endures the bitterness of dysfunctional family life and, due to a disability, has never known the love and support that every adolescent aches for.

The students represented in each profile are authentic. Of necessity, their names, distinguishing characteristics, and some times, gender, were altered to protect their identity. However, the problems they brought to my doorstep are being retold in precise, unedited detail. The only proof of my integrity that exists in documenting these cases would be my professional appointment book for this period. If asked, the testimony of my secretary who maintains a duplicate calendar, escorted the students in to see me and often overheard pieces of these closed–door conversations could confirm my sincerity. That, of course, will hardly be needed. The words of these students say it all.

At intervals, the reader may be tempted to doubt the veracity of these profiles. I label them "profiles" intentionally, for they are vignettes of what I encountered rather than in–depth case studies. Some may simply seem too far–fetched to be believed. To that complaint, I can only respond that things unimaginable and perverse are the calling cards of postmodern society and popular culture. Up to this point, this book has dedicated itself to illustrating that inescapable truth. Before delving into them, however, some prefacing narrative is necessary to properly set the stage.

A Spectre Rises

For many years troubleshooting invariably emerged as the most interesting area of my job. I possessed the power to enforce the rules or, when a lesson of greater value might be learned, bend them in the interests of an individual's growth. Students hanging around campus, hearing that I offered a sympathetic ear, often sought me out for counsel. A portion wanted explanations of university policies and how these applied to a situation that troubled them. Still others met me during fall orientation and later showed up at my door simply because they were feeling lonely and I seemed, as they recalled from an earlier encounter, like 'a guy they could talk to' about personal or academic problems.

With individuals in this latter group, a rapport occasionally developed. These were the students who would show up periodically throughout the year to appraise me of their studies as well as what had been going on in their lives. Our relationships, built on straight talk and trust, developed over months. Watching them mature to make life–impacting choices provided me with a great deal of career satisfaction. In fact, these relationships were the primary reason for staying in this peculiar profession. The 'kids', though some were well out of their teens, made my work enjoyable.

Then something changed. Subtly, without fanfare or reason, the students perturbed by minor matters began to disappear from the scene. It is impossible to be exact because the change was gradual, but I first started to notice it in the second half of the 1990's. An altogether unusual breed of youth arrived on campus with very different expectations.

Sophisticated in a negative sense, they were quick to harangue me or my colleagues about their rights when confronting a failing grade. Verbally, they brandished the threat of litigation like a weapon every time they were reminded of rules or regulations. If they played even an infinitesimal part in creating their current difficulties, they refused to acknowledge any *mea culpa* for it. Unlike previous generations of students, personal accountability was totally foreign to their thinking. Complaints about limits on financial aid (don't dare suggest a bachelor's degree should be done in four years), health care, parking, and dining options flew continually over my desk. After all, they were entitled to them.

There were the others too, who would arrive late for their appointments and collapse into the chair on the other side of my desk. Within a few moments, I could tell they were not quite right and heavily medicated the way their speech trailed off into incoherent muttering. Was this the Ritalin or Prozac generation coming to maturity? Or was it even worse? How they would ever make it through the term, attend class and complete course assignments portended a struggle equal to that of Sisyphus.

If this pitiable collection moved me, another crowd actually frightened me. Though fewer in number, they spoke with thinly concealed wrath. The angry pitch in what they said about their instructors, peers who bothered them, and the world in general left me shuddering. Strive as I might to defuse their fury, I knew that someday one of them would make good on his threats. Another student, professor, or even myself, would be hurt or killed.

I wrote about this worry in a national educational periodical. Apprehensive over the mounting potential for violence on campus, the article was titled "Preparing for the Moment When a Student's Rage Turns to Violence". My intent in penning the essay was to alert unsuspecting members of the university to the growing menace. Below is a passage from that essay:

> "...Whatever the cause of violence, colleges and universities are not prepared for its eruption on their campuses. A *laissez–faire* attitude permeates academic life: no parents, few rules, little monitoring, a great deal of individual freedom.
>
> ...Our vision is skewed toward the utopian. We see campuses as islands largely untouched by the social ills outside...
>
> As a student affairs dean, I often see students who come to lodge complaints about their peers or to reply to charges of misconduct made against them. Most of the cases are misdemeanors–...
>
> However, about 5 percent of the cases I deal with leave me wondering, and a little anxious. A disgruntled student with smoldering eyes tells me there is no way he'll accept the grade he just got, and if the teacher refuses to alter it, the student is 'going to go postal.' Another student, referred to me by a professor for hurling invectives at a peer during class, tells me she's going to "get" her antagonist for stealing her boyfriend and mentions that she has a gun at home.
>
> Ten years ago I would have counseled such students not to use reckless speech, for fear it would have been taken seriously. At the end of the day, however, I would have closed their files and gone home a carefree man, sure that they didn't truly intend to hurt anyone.
>
> Things have changed...What has changed is the degree of anger behind the students' statements. Instead of voicing dissatisfaction over an issue, they are making extreme threats against other human beings. Through my counseling I've watched the hostility intensify over the years. Perhaps part of it comes from a popular culture that

devalues life. Causes are elusive. Yet given recent events, my apprehension seems justified..."

Of course, at the time it was written, this piece was a summary call–to–arms in the fight against campus apathy. A societal evil was encroaching upon our quiet academic village. Little did I realize how close by a time–bomb ticked.

Profile 1–Darrell: Courting Disaster

On a dreary February morning, the tranquility of my office was disturbed by a number of messages from nervous staff and faculty. One of the callers, a tenured professor in the behavioral sciences department, stopped by to personally share her concerns over "Darrell," a student enrolled in her abnormal psychology course. His odd in–class behavior, inappropriate disclosures about his own mental health, and conflicts with fellow students had her worried. This professor informed me that although she was on friendly terms with him, Darrell approached her after class and grumbled threateningly about classmates he said were badgering him. Alarmed by his erratic and malevolent remarks, she decided to notify me. Unknown to her, reports from other employees; in the study skills center and office of Student Life, had been trickling in the same morning. Hoping to nip this volatile situation in bud, I instructed my secretary to track down Darrell through the registration office and arrange a meeting for us as soon as possible.

He arrived on time the following day. I immediately understood why college personnel, especially women, were intimidated by him. Darrell was an African–American student, easily six feet, five inches tall and three hundred pounds. Add to this imposing physique a shaggy goatee, the dull glint of bronze studs gleaming from several orifices, and eyes that shifted rapidly from one object to another, and the tension became palpable. In the ensuing conversation, I soon saw how Darrell's speaking voice, naturally boisterous, rose to match the intensity of his feelings. When I relayed the reason for my summons, he did not seem surprised and admitted that people often misinterpreted his "intense" type of personality.

Without prodding, Darrell volunteered that he was in therapy and taking medication for a condition he did not care to identify. (This kind of disclosure was becoming more common as students receiving treatment felt it excused their eccentricities without assigning any responsibility to them.) He did, however, drop the the name of his therapist in a tacit suggestion that I call her. Darrell felt confident that as long as no one hassled him, and he continued his treatment as planned, everything would "stay cool." "I don't think I would ever really hurt anybody, but I can't promise it." Violent impulses coursed through him every minute of every day, he conceded, but he felt that he could control them pretty well.

Darrell smiled wide to indicate he meant it. Despite his words and my first impressions, there was something boyish, even likable about him once you got past the fearsome exterior. Still, I could not dismiss the fears of so many colleagues. My instincts were that Darrell should be monitored from a discreet, non–invasive distance. Shadowing him would only ratchet up the tension. But he needed to be watched, as inconspicuously as possible. What happened next convinced me this would be a prudent course of action.

He had deposited his oversized backpack at the base of the coat rack in my office when he first entered. As we talked, however, I realized that he was gripping two books tightly in his large fists which had been protruding from it. I inquired what he was reading. Hesitating only a moment, he handed them over. The title embossed on the smaller of the pair read *Hunting Humans*. The larger black book read *The Psycho-pathology of Serial Murder*. I asked Darrell why he was interested in such bizarre literature. Surely he could see how they appeared to confirm everyone's anxieties about him. "What's up with these?" I asked. "Are you interested in this subject?" Waving my comments aside with his hand, he said "Oh, those are for a paper I got to write for my abnormal psych class. They're *interesting*." *Interesting*—that word spoke volumes about his state of mind. Besides, he had gotten them from the university library and if they were there any student had a right to read them, right?. (Checking later, I learned that these were indeed registered volumes in the university's vast collection.) I tactfully recommended suggested that he put these books inside his backpack. It would make his teachers and fellow students a lot less nervous. Darrell shrugged, unmoved, but said he understood and placed them back into the his pack but did not zip it closed.

We conversed a while longer about how his studies were going and the usual stresses he and other students new to college experienced. After about fifteen minutes Darrell stood up and said he had to leave for another class. I advised him to "stay loose", an expression he had repeated several times during our talk and invited him to come and see me if things began to weigh too heavily on him.

Even with fifteen years counseling experience, his was a complex case. I could do one of two things; take him at his word that all was well, or engage in some precautionary follow up with others who knew him better. A subsequent call to his therapist did little to assuage my concerns. Couching her comments in clinical, and therefore, noncommital language, she stated that she did not think Darrell might be a threat to himself or others. Of course, she could not guarantee it. When I mentioned the names of the two books in his possession, the therapist asserted this was simply Darrell 'acting out'. The books were a symbolic warning to others to leave him alone. Her opinion was that if provoked, Darrell was much more inclined to hit a desk, or wall or some inanimate object rather than another human being. Claiming her next patient had arrived, the therapist ended her synopsis there. This conversation did not exactly reassure me.

Because the Federal Rights to Privacy Act (FERPA) as well as counselor–student confidentiality standards prohibited it, I did not have the liberty of divulging the contents of my meeting with Darrell to the staff who first complained about him. Invoking what we deem as 'exigent circumstances' and a legitimate need to know, I discussed this matter with the campus security chief, however, telling him to be on the look-out for any reports mentioning this student. Until the time Darrell broke the law or our student code of conduct, I was powerless to do anything more than watch, wait and hope for the best. Each day he came, went to class, and mingled with other students. He might make it through his academic career without snapping. But what if he didn't? Except for a few students who had seen the flare–ups or gotten to close to the fire burning inside, most would never know the rage simmering just under the surface of the guy sitting next to them in class.

Profile 2–Will: Cybersex entrepreneur

As far back as the summer of 1999, our security chief made me aware of a 'potential sex offender' hiding among the student rank and file. Periodically, bits of information concerning this case filtered up to me. The night custodial crew had discovered, on several occasions, computer–downloaded pornographic pictures on the floor of the same men's room in one of our academic buildings. In other instances, jani-tors actually found these hard–core pictures taped to the walls of a bathroom stall where, based on semen stains on the floor, this person had masturbated while viewing them. Given the audit trail of dates/times when these pictures were printed (visible in the corner of each photo left behind), we hypothesized that the culprit was someone who frequented the computer lab or maybe even worked there.

With some detective work, the pictures were traced to the one com-puter lab with a color laser printer capable of generating high–resolu-tion images like those left behind in the bathroom. Our security chief visited this lab and talked to the manager about the students who worked there. Individually, he questioned them and two of the student assistants thought that it might be a third student employee absent the day of the interviews. Later on, the third student was eventually ques-tioned but admitted to nothing. Ironically, for the next couple of months, the deviant abstained from gratifying himself on campus property. The custodial staff stopped finding obscene images and other unpleasant physical evidence on the floor of the men's room. Apparently, our investigation brushed too close for comfort. The perpetrator had been sufficiently alarmed to stop. Because there were no actual witnesses and the violations were essentially victimless, we closed the case there.

Not long afterward, a request arrived from our ITS (information technology systems) manager for an appointment. When we met, he told me about a problem one of his support technicians stumbled into during a routine updating of software. On refitting several computers in the very same lab as alluded to earlier, this technician uncovered a cache of pornographic images downloaded to their hard drives. Reporting this to the ITS manager, the two of them checked with the lab manager who knew nothing, and then confronted the student employees working in this lab. Surprisingly, one of them acknowledged downloading and storing this material. Since using university information technology for non–academic purposes is strictly prohibited by the student code of conduct, I scheduled an investigative hearing for the following week.

During the interim, several unusual reports trickled in to my office. Apparently related, they originated with two female students who had been accosted a male student with a strange proposition. According to these complainants, they had been solicited by the student to appear in pornographic pictures and videos he was producing for his own Web site. Sex of virtually any variety; alone, with a partner, maybe even a group, whatever they preferred, all were welcome. Any and all of the specialty stuff—leather, S&M, fetishes, was especially hot. As he explained to the girls, his main goal was to capture these interludes on film. By his own account, he and his girlfriend had already starred in several homemade productions and he was looking to widen his repertory. He also planned to utilize on–campus technology, including our closed–circuit television studio, to make these videos. The female students who lodged the complaints gave the name of the student who solicited them. It was the same as the name pencilled in my appointment book. A link existed between the downloading computer lab worker and the aspiring hard–core king.

When we finally met, Will's self–possession surprised me. Nineteen or twenty, he was freckled, articulate, and looked more like a fresh–scrubbed young Republican than an ersatz Larry Flynt. Rather than deny what he had done, he owned up to a commercial interest in scintillating material. Who did it hurt, he asked? So what if people wanted to enjoy this material from the privacy of their own dorm room or apartment? He lucidly (and accurately—I checked later) outlined recent court decisions that struck down restrictions on accessing adult sites on the Internet. Narrowing the scope of his arguments, his own defense rested on the claim that he would build his cyber–empire of skin from a computer platform based at his home where privacy statutes still carried some weight, he exclaimed Therefore, we, the university had no right to interfere. This student did his legal homework in advance of our meeting. I was partly amused but primarily repelled by his reasoning. As for misusing campus resources to launch his sordid sorties, I made it clear that he could not do that. When I informed Will of the rules against sexually harassing fellow students, for that is what his solicitations boiled down to, he pleaded ignorance but added there would not be any such overtures made again. Then, in what appeared to be a premeditated gesture of defiance against college authority, he tendered his resignation as a lab assistant. His sole remaining concern was the punishment I meted out for what he had already done. Obviously, that is a disclosure I'm prevented from making here.

When the smoke cleared some time later, I paid a visit to the campus security office. On a lark, I wanted to see their files on the bathroom offender. Although no charges were ever filed, the names of the computer lab student assistants interviewed by the security chief were noted in the documentation. My hunch had been correct. The name of the third student whom his fellows said might know something glared back at me from the page in my hand—Will.

Recalcitrant to the end, however, I am sure this student pursued his prurient ambitions. In his mind, he was simply giving the students what they wanted and making a tidy profit in the process. Will's case revealed for me how far the deviant dimensions of cyberspace have enveloped youth culture. This student saw no reason why his academic experiences should not be complemented by a business internship in sexual exploitation. Given his utter lack of conscience in seeing the immorality of his actions, it seemed painfully obvious that nothing in his life to that point had taught him otherwise.

<u>Profile 3–Maria: New Face of Indigence</u>

Maria and I bumped into each other, literally, the first week of classes during the fall quarter. I was rushing to a committee meeting, she was hustling to her composition class. Rounding a corner in a crowded hallway, we collided, knocking the books and papers in each other's hands to the floor. Embarrassed she had almost flattened a man who might be one of her professors (seeing my necktie), she sputtered through an awkward apology. I did the same and we both hurried off to our respective destinations.

A few weeks later, in the cafeteria, we met again in standing in a long lunch queue. With the line inching along, she started to talk and our conversation ended up lasting the fifteen minutes we waited to reach the counter. Maria recalled our first inauspicious meeting and said that she appreciated how nice I was to her on that hectic and stressful, for new students anyway, first day of the fall quarter. When I asked her how her classes were going, she replied okay, though they turned out to be a fairly heavy academic load. Perhaps warmed by my interest in her situation, Maria began to talk less shyly about her early experiences here at the university.

She liked one or two of her professors and she guessed the other students were all right, but she really missed Naples, Florida, where her parents lived and she used to sail with them. She thought of it as home. For now, she was living with her brother and his wife. They gave her free room and board while she attended college. In turn she served as their *au pair*. School would be easier, Maria thought out loud, if only she didn't have to spend most of her study time babysitting her niece and nephew. The stress it induced bothered her enough that she had to *increase her medication*. Unprepared for this personal disclosure, I smiled and nodded. Although Maria did not offer specifics about the medication or the condition she had that necessitated it, signs were present in her behavior. I had already noticed her repetition of phrases and forgetting her place in mid–sentence. Nor could she hide a streak of paranoia, often making references to fellow students "being mean" or poking fun at her. By the time our turn to be served came, Maria's discourse and energy trailed off. I wished her luck in her studies and told her to come and see me if she ever needed someone to talk to. A few weeks passed.

A panting student stood outlined in my doorway, trying to catch his breath. Could I come right away? There was this girl you see, who had "lost it bad" and was sobbing uncontrollably in the lobby. He had tried to approach her, but she screamed if he got too close or extended his hand to touch her. Other students were gathering around her watching and it was 'freaking everybody out.' On the way out of my office I instructed my secretary to phone ahead to campus security. They could meet me there and if need be, send for medical assistance. When I reached the lobby a small crowd of students stood listlessly watching a girl hunched over and crying loudly in a chair. Forcing my way through the crowd, I approached her cautiously. Drawing nearer, I recognized the bent figure as Maria.

Sensing someone approach, Maria lifted her head from between her hands and prepared to shriek. I began talking to her in a low voice, reminding her of our friendship and how I only wanted to see what was wrong. She was muttering incoherently to herself and trembling, but she let me sit down next to her. In brief flashes of lucidity, alternating with frightful hallucinations, she told me she couldn't do it anymore. The combined pressures of school work and being forced to babysit every day overwhelmed her. She just wanted to go home, back to Florida. But, Maria divulged, her parents *didn't want her back*. All the cared about was their yacht and cruising the Caribbean. They were tired of taking care of their schizophrenic daughter. All they did was ship her from one older sibling to the other just to get her away from them. She hadn't been allowed to live with them for longer than a month since she graduated from high school, two year earlier.

Maria's confidence struck me hard. From our initial contacts, I surmised she was taking medication for a psychiatric condition. She now confirmed it. But her history of being bandied about from place to place to spare her parents the inconvenience of an emotionally disabled child was new. Hearing it in her anguished tone made me wince. She grabbed my hand and I let her. Apparently rich and self–absorbed, they didn't have time for the arduous responsibility of a needy adolescent. This wasn't the only instance a student in crisis told me such a story, but it was certainly the most moving.

I stayed next to Maria until security arrived whereupon I instructed them to summon an ambulance. I discovered the reason for her hallucinations while waiting with her. Maria admitted to me that she didn't take her medicine that morning. She said the dosage was too strong and it made her groggy all day. I also had her brother phoned at work and, after some grumbling, he agreed to come and meet her for the trip to the hospital. Almost an hour later he arrived. Visibly annoyed, he walked up to Maria, abruptly hoisted her into a standing position despite her tears and protests, and dragged her toward the waiting ambulance. Although it might be unfair to make such an assumption, from his demeanor I couldn't help but think that mercenary motives constituted the reasons he was letting her live with him. He wished to stay on good terms with his wealthy parents. A generous inheritance, perhaps, hung in the balance.

About two weeks later, Maria visited my office. Deflated but coherent, she had been in the hospital for a week and then at her brother's home resting. She said that she would try and finish the term, although she had missed a lot of coursework. After that she couldn't say what would come next. She wanted to go back to Florida. If *they* would let her. After this, I lost track of her. Painful as Maria's case was to witness, I had too many other students caught in similar situations. Apart from holding their hands for moment or offering a shoulder to cry on when they most needed it, I knew the problem was too large for me to make a lasting difference.

Profile 4—Drake: Columbine—Hero Worship

In late January, a loud and agitated student showed up in reception area of my office suite. Overhearing a rather testy exchange with my secretary, I went out to the to investigate the problem. Composing himself a bit, "Drake" told me his name and practically demanded that I see him then and there. Unmoved yet curious, I gestured for him to follow me into my office.

Tall, pale, with a military–style crew cut, Drake's hawkish eyes and sharp tongue contrasted with his slovenly dress. Offering him a seat, I asked him to explain what it was that had him so upset. He explained that he had left behind three notebooks in one of his morning classes. A student in a later class took them down to the college's "lost and found" repository which also happened to be the Security Office. Drake, in the mean time discovering his oversight, returned to his morning class, saw the spiral–bound notebooks were gone and decided to check with lost and found. It was then that his self–described "ordeal" began.

When he went to retrieve his notebooks, three campus security officers were lounging around the office. Drake told them his name and inquired if they had been brought there. Pushing aside some papers on his desk, one of the officers asked if Drake meant these, and pointed at three notebooks Drake recognized as his. This officer said he had read the poetry in one of the books and found it despicable. Another officer asked why he was infatuated with such dark, homicidal topics. Before he could answer, a third officer volunteered that due to perceiving the owner of these notebooks as a potential threat to the campus, they took the liberty of running a criminal background check on him. Stunned by their questions and accusations, Drake relived his anger by pounding on my desk with his fist. The final straw was when one of them asked if he had plans to kill himself. Apparently, one of his poems expounded on this subject, although Drake asserted it was only an 'exercise in artistic expression', not a plan of personal action. Subjected to this humiliation for a few minutes more, his notebooks were returned and he abruptly left. Feeling "violated" now, he was sarcastically referred to the dean of student affairs by the unrepentant law officers should he want to file a grievance.

Having sat quietly through his account of events, I asked him why he thought the security guards read his notebooks, something I knew from experience they almost never did. Drake confessed he had no idea. Hesitating not for a moment, he declared it was true that he was "fascinated with the darker personalities in society". While Drake did not exactly idolize them, he maintained, they were intriguing objects of study. As if to demonstrate, he produced the three notebooks from his pack and placed them on my desk. On the first was 8" x 11" portrait of Marilyn Mason in diabolical concert make–up and costume. Pasted on the exterior of the second, smaller notebook were wallet–size pictures of two boys. On closer inspection, I recognized them as Dylan Klebold and Eric Harris. The third notebook cover was illustrated with bizarre figures and images of weaponry, along with a peppering of words like reckoning and retribution. Putting it down next to the others and glancing over them for a last time, I immediately understood why our security team had acted as they did.

To his dismay, I informed Drake that given these photos and sketches, his notebooks invited scrutiny by any college official who happened to see them. Our first obligation, he must see, was to guarantee the safety of all students, including himself. Ignoring signs or symbols as obvious as these would render us legally and morally derelict. Given events at Columbine, as well as the increased wariness of school administration, ample cause existed for security to assess any potential threat. Finally silent, Drake stared blankly back at me. The next moment, he recovered and spoke. "My rights to privacy have been trampled on! I still feel violated. What are you going to do about it?"

Maybe the tactics our officers took might have been different, I granted. Instead of volunteering personal opinions of his character or interests, the conversation could have proceeded more constructive lines. Seeing a smile creep into Drake's angular face as he assumed he was about to receive an apology, I shifted to the real issue. Essentially, I concluded, both the security officers' concern and conduct had been justified. Any danger thought to be imminent had to be directly explored and decisively discounted. Considering the notebooks' covers, they felt a review of its contents were warranted. These contents reinforced their belief that Drake might harm himself or his peers.

Hearing my conclusions, Drake tore his notebooks off my desk and shoved them savagely into his backpack. "I strongly disagree! My rights have been trashed," he interjected. On his way out, Drake warned that this matter was far from over and that he would be consulting a lawyer for options against the wrong done him.

This was just another day in the front line in my own private war against popular culture. Today it happened to be Drake. Yesterday, it was Will, or Maria or Darrell. When they at last moved on there would be a fresh group of faces and issues to greet me. How could I be so sure? Because there are anonymous hundreds of adolescents wracked with insecurities, fear and loathing. It comes with the postmodern territory and by now all of us are too well briefed on existing realities to feign cluelessness over the injuries done to American youth. Drake is hardly by himself in making Eric Harris, Dylan Klebold or anything associated with them icons for the disaffected crowd. In every suburb of every city in the United States he would find kindred spirits.

Other Glimpses

If I lingered too long on the student profiles above, a multitude of others are ready for the telling. Each of them seem to hit on a different dimension of pop culture and its despoiling of adolescent personalities. Socially, spiritually, and emotionally, students limp along, unaware of the burden they bear. Only the man or woman who remembers how things stood before postmodern culture can understand the seriousness of the handicap they live with. Adolescent views of life are irrevocably skewed toward fantasy. That the universe does not exist solely to gratify their every whim comes as a genuine shock to some. More remote still are their views of acceptable community behavior, much less the timeless truth that actions breed consequences. Persons or policies that get in the way are instantaneously deemed an infringement on individual freedom.

A final demonstration of this arose in the request from a student for funding a new campus club. According to university by–laws, any group wishing to be recognized as a sponsored organization had to collect a certain number of signatures showing sufficient interest and complete an application which included a rationale for how the organization fits into the university's mission. If approved, said group earns official recognition and is eligible for financial support from the student activity fee.

In this case, however, the student wanted to start a Wicca club on campus. In brief, Wicca is the broad name of a society endorsing the beliefs and practices of pagans or witches. Mindful of the appeal of occult–themed television shows and movies (e.g. *Buffy the Vampire Slayer, Charmed*) among youth, I should not have been surprised. Casting spells, reciting incantations, and hunting demons have fired the imagination of many teens.

As a dean, even if I might have a bias against supporting such a club, I am legally bound to obey university policies that bar discriminating against any request for club recognition until an application is filed and legitimate grounds exist for dis/approving its application. In the interim, the Wicca student sought permission to post flyers on campus bulletin boards announcing the formation of this organization. Unfortunately for him, the rules prohibited this—bulletin boards could only carry announcements published by formally recognized student groups. When I told him that under the present circumstances he could not use campus kiosks for posting his flyers, he became livid incensed. The student told me I was denying his rights to freedom of speech. I replied that nothing of the kind had occurred. He was welcome to use the boards once his organization had been recognized but until then, he would have to solicit peer interest by other methods. No, he raged, my decision was arbitrary and unacceptable. He would take me to court over my decision, which, to him, was flagrantly prejudiced against a 'minority position.' Then he stomped out of my office.

Thus far, I haven't heard from him or his attorney. I expect that I still might. Threatening words have become commonplace, legal actions almost as frequent. Anticipating how they might rationalize the university's educational mission with Wicca's *raison d'etre* should prove fascinating. Perhaps they will tie paganism's ancient worship of the earth to the Gaia hypothesis (environmental science) or the tribal religious rites of pre–Christian cultures (anthropology). Equally intriguing is the prospect that in a legal battle, the odds in no way favor me. He might well prevail. After all, freedom of expression has taken on some very unusual interpretations in recent court decisions, one more indication of the excesses of individual rights at the cost of social balance.

Then there are the others. Students caught cheating or plagiarizing face me with looks of astonishment but no regret as I explain that academic dishonesty is a cardinal offense and not tolerated. Or the ones busted smoking marijuana, then protest being singled out for so trivial an offense when peers are getting high on crack or pills. Shortages of parking spaces, classrooms either too cold, hot, or with uncomfortable desks, professors who penalize them for chronic absences—these I group in a dossier stamped "pending grievances–possible litigation." As

I said, mine is a profession both fascinating and, in what I find in many of my students, unexpectedly trying.

Summary

My experiences with young adults have been tremendously instructive on one level, and terribly draining on another. I have learned that despite our being Americans supposedly raised in the same country and not too far apart in years, we are a very different species. At moments, an almost unbridgeable gulf exists between their perceptions and mine. How they see themselves in relation to the world—their desire to take center stage and how people, resources, and protections available in the environment seem to be there exclusively for personal use—is irreconcilable with my mindset. Old–fashioned and outdated, like so many of us thirty and older, I cling to the belief that I have an obligation to those around me, even if it means deferring my wants for the greater good. It is also perfectly clear to me that the world was not created to be my private amusement park, that adults did make a difference in my life, and that nothing is truly due me except that which I have earned through my own hard work. Try such reasoning on the young today and almost half will stare at you in astonished amazement. Three of the four students I described above did precisely that.

Incredulous as it might leave older readers, students believe they have more stress to deal with than previous generations. A national survey conducted by UCLA in 1999 found a record 30.2% of college freshman felt overwhelmed by stress (*Chicago Tribune Internet Edition*, 1/25/00). Competitive admissions, concerns about financial responsibilities, and prioritizing between academics and recreation were cited as sources of stress. As one of the researchers inquired, do students today really have more to worry about, or is merely that they think they do? Subconsciously, perhaps, this stress is the result of being under constant siege by a culture that allows no time to sit back, relax, and breathe.

One thing is certain. "Students are coming to college overwhelmed and more damaged than in the past," agreed an article published in *Change* magazine (Levine & Cureton, 1998, 3). Given current cultural conditions, this is understandable. Fears of being victims of crime, temptations of drug and alcohol abuse, eating disorders, falling into depression and even suicide oppress them. A poll of student affairs deans also showed a marked increase in student isolation. "Requests for single rooms have skyrocketed. The thought of having a roommate is less appealing than it once was." With the evaporation of communal activities and a marked rise anti–social attitudes, students exhibit a preference for private recreation. Television watching has moved from the student lounge to the dorm room. "With student rooms a virtual menagerie of electronic and food preparation equipment, students are living their lives in ways that allow them to avoid venturing out if they so choose." (3–4). College, for decades the parade ground of a youth's social training, has been sterilized of its communality. The authors must have felt the same, titling their essay, "Collegiate Life: An obituary."

It does not take a rocket scientist to explain the same socially–stunted behaviors are surfacing in high school, middle school, and even upper elementary school students. Multiplying incidences of deviant, anti–social, and even criminal conduct among students of assorted ages, like the six–year old in Michigan shooting a classmate because she was mean to him, or the Georgia teens who reenacted the orgies they watched on *The Playboy Channel*, make the point painfully clear. While violence initiated by youth may be the hardest act to stomach, kids have been hurt in other less lethal but equally debilitating ways. Popular culture has done its work well.

Microcosms of society, schools and universities suffer the identical problems As the communities surrounding them. Madness nibbles away at the edge of campus. Once they were untouchable. Now these one–time paragons of social and civic virtue stand directly in harm's way. And those who will be doing the bloodying are already roaming inside the corridors.

9

Postscript: Generations Lost–A Reflection

As I neared the end of this book, during the winter of 2000, news of the death of Charles M. Schulz was released. Schulz was the creator of the 'Peanuts' comic strip whose life in syndication spanned fifty years. When I learned of his passing, I felt a twinge of regret and thought about what the end of this era meant.

Not that I was a dedicated reader of _Peanuts_ these days. Work and family obligations often interfered with indulging in this pleasure. However, I could still vividly recall the _Peanuts_ ensemble from the comics, books, and television specials I loved as a child. Anxious and vulnerable, Charlie Brown, Linus, and the gang were incurably sweet and in spite of numerous insecurities, chock full of hope. Schulz infused them with the range of human weaknesses. Yet in these foibles we recognized our own vulnerability and a vicarious shot at redemption. If at times, these characters seemed a bit too wise and adult–minded for their years, the situations they found themselves immersed in remained purely juvenile. Schulz allowed them to be children. He let them learn from these situations and the consolation they offered each other when these idylls ended. For Schulz, life was like, as we know from Charlie Brown's crucible, that symbolic football being held by someone we think we can trust only to yanked away the moment before we kick it high into a crisp November sky. Childhood served as an apprenticeship for adulthood. The errors made along the way did no permanent harm. Instead, they taught about life. The *Peanuts* ensemble grew from them and so did we.

With Schulz' passing, his view of childhood, trying at times, yet essentially one of incorruptible innocence, perished with him. A journalist aptly observed that Peanuts served as "a mirror for the baby boom generation" (Spiegelman, 2000). As someone riding the cusp of this generation, it resonated with me. Cartoon or not, the world sketched so simply here resembled my own youthful experiences. The only bogeyman we faced then was self-doubt. There was little to fear from the other kids we played with or the adults we knew and trusted.

This brief bout of nostalgia led me to thinking about the differences in the society Schulz's strip represented—America of the 1950's through 80's—versus life today. It made me mourn for all those kids who will never know the unhurried, untainted joys of childhood as we once knew it. The years since wrought massive changes in society. These changes, from almost any angle, have not been in the best interests of youth. Everywhere they turn, a sordid culture forces them to grow up hard, fast and prematurely cynical.

Adolescent boys today will never understand the thrilling, innocent anticipation of that first, wonderful kiss with a girl when for years older friends or siblings have been showing them explicit sexual pictures and movies downloaded from the Internet. Girls won't know the privileged companionship of starting diaries and pouring impassioned hopes and dreams into them only to look back and smile at these growing pains as women because they'll have already communicated these intimate sentiments to virtual friends and strangers in chat rooms during the intervening years. Teens will grow up thinking the clever catchphrases they hear in commercials ("Just do it!") are nuggets of wisdom around which they can build a philosophy of life. Toddlers will rest secure not in the arms of mothers and fathers but day care workers who patch scraped knees, give them milk and cookies, and read them stories before day time naps. Kids probably won't learn 'its not whether you win or lose but how you play the game' because parents and coaches have taken to drilling it into them that all that does matter is winning and being a star in the making. Whether in terms of athletics or peer popularity, a lucky handful visited by early success will prosper while the rest grow up racked by insecurities. Male or female, kids have been deprived of the chance to play unmolested with the sun on their shoulders and a spring breeze rustling through their hair. As the years pass, the premature hardening continues and their cynicism deepens, what does that portend for them as they approach adolescence.

Pop culture stole youth away from those to whom it belongs. Small or big, pre–school or high school, toddler through teen, they have all been victimized.

That the present seems uncertain and the days ahead not necessarily better, troubles me immensely. Devoting an entire book to such a stark vision of contemporary culture did not come easy. I am *not at all* happy about it. However, someone needed to take a realistic and unflinching look at how things stand and the connections between them with the purpose of generating wider concern. Maybe it will even kindle a spark to resist. Normalcy should not seem so elusive, nor so far removed from our reach that we must yearn for it. So why do we? Because as a nation we've realized that if things continue on their current course it may be forever intangible.

Internally most of us know that time stops for no one and as it marches on the variety of worlds we inhabit continue to decay. Society seems to be fragmenting along ethnic, racial, and economic lines. Families are disintegrating as marriages routinely break apart and children shuttle between guardians, homes, and lifestyles. Schools continue to struggle against overwhelming odds in trying to undo the cultural damage already done to students by the time many reach first grade. Ethics, personal responsibility, and tradition—blending to form a moral compass, have been exiled into obscurity. Hastening this downward spiral is a seductive array of media technology. It governs Americans existence and demands their fealty. Embrace it or risk getting left behind. Youth, more or less raised by it, believe this more than adults. Hence they are deeper under its spell. It is here, in such circumstances, that the seeds of our decline have been sown.

Revisiting the thought we began with, I will ask two questions once again. Does popular culture exert a noxious impact on American kids? In its obvious manifestations—films, music, television shows, video games, and the Internet, with their vulgar, abusive and perverse themes—does it detrimentally influence the thinking and behavior of youth? Of course it does. Forget conflicting clinical studies—a few hint at this link while the majority fail to show a legitimate cause–and–effect in the laboratory. Anyone who really believes otherwise does not live in the same reality as the rest of us. The only issue is depth of impact. How profound these influences end up being, when combined with postmodern amorality and crumbling social institutions, depends on the antidote administered by adults. To the extent that parents, teachers, or significant other mature persons exert a supportive presence in a child's or teen's life, they may yet counteract these evils. If, however, as the data suggests, many have stepped away from these roles to pursue their own interests and delusions, popular culture gains an advantage it does not easily relinquish.

In conversations around the office coffee pot or during dinner with friends or family, the question of whether another Columbine, or a tragedy on the same scale, could ever happen again occasionally rears its ugly head. After weighing the balance of information presented in this book, deciding for one's self does not require major mental exertion. All the necessary ingredients for catastrophe still abound. If anything, conditions are probably more conducive now than before since we chose to treat the symptoms instead of the sickness. Convincing ourselves that the danger has passed—school security measures are tighter than ever, after all—our guard is lowered. Concrete steps to prevent school violence have been taken. That is good, but it is only one aspect of an infinitely more complex and multi–faceted problem. Slight progress has been made in dealing with the culture enabling it.

Plots and schemes hatched by kids to maim or kill classmates persist. Newspapers are full of them. The fierce rhetoric spewing from politicians, preachers, and parents about cleaning up pop culture and its trashier domains has abated. Now it's business as usual in Hollywood, New York, cyberspace and wherever else popular culture is manufactured. Silence will reign until the next massacre happens. All but those personally touched by these school slayings have already moved on to new social crusades.

Immediately following Columbine, everyone from the President of the United States to a gawky fifth–grader in Biloxi spoke out against the contaminating influences of popular culture. Record company magnates, television and movie studio heads, and Internet gurus were all on the firing line. An outraged country demanded media accountability. First denying, then minimizing their culpability, this media oligarchy promised a more 'family–friendly' slate of entertainment, recreations, or informational outlets. Eventually placated, a self–appointed watchdog press and pacified public congratulated each other on standing up to this evil empire. Surely, with our concerted effort, better times lay just ahead.

With the restoration of sanity promised, a fundamental lesson of history repeated itself: as time passed, the horrors we experienced that tragic April day were forgotten. Americans returned to their routines while poignant images of the victim's funerals, weeping classmates, and flags flying at half–mast across the nation's schoolyards faded from memory. Except for a couple of aberrations in Oklahoma and Michigan, people assumed the worst was over. As someone whose work every day revolves around students' intimate confessions, I recognize its folly. Just as building more prisons won't solve America's crime problem, nor will installing advanced security systems or calling for kinder and gentler media fare prevent maladjusted behavior among youth.

Those nearest to ground zero obviously know better. A recent survey commissioned by *The Denver Rocky Mountain News* showed attitudes about Columbine and the culture that spawned it are largely unchanged. This poll, conducted just shy of the one–year anniversary of the massacre, collected the opinions of over six hundred Colorado residents. Seven out of ten said "irresponsible parents, a lack of individual responsibility, and a decline in moral values were the main reasons" for the shootings (Lowe, 2000). Of this pool, 84% saw the lack of child–parent quality time as a "major" contributing cause. Another 81% felt teen violence stemmed from parents who didn't teach "moral values" such as the sanctity of human life. Seventy–eight percent identified a denial of responsibility for one's own actions, while 70% blamed the overall unhealthy moral climate of the country. It is interesting how the passage of a year did little to alleviate the anxieties Americans expressed immediately after the killings (see chapter 2 for 1999 survey data). Coloradans, it seems, have not been fooled. They see through the posturing and assurances and realize a sword still hangs over the nation's head. As for the rest of America, all that year did was give the media time to further sensationalize the story. Even officials who participated in actual investigation played their part in this mad circus. For $25, the public is now able to purchase a copy of the Jefferson county sheriff department's crime scene video shot on premises complete with pop music dubbed in to make the experience more entertaining. Absolutely nothing is sacred these days.

As long as we live with this present form of a popular culture full of confusing, contradictory, and insidious messages, prospects for aggressively anti–social outbreaks among adolescents linger the United States. Equally, if not more inhibited, are any chances for youth to benefit from the fruits of education. A buffet of visual, auditory, and motor–skill delights consumes the attentions of adolescents. On the other hand, learning demands a commitment of self and energy youth simply aren't willing to invest. Befriended by media that filled the hours when parents were absent, that answered practical questions about life and morality, and that titillated with one amusement after another, education offers little enticement.

If I achieved my aim, this book has challenged the reader to reflect upon the dismal state of contemporary state of popular culture and the injuries it visits on American youth. Borrowing the terminology of the court room, let us consider the evidence presented. If not beyond a reasonable doubt, the burden of proof in a criminal trial, we have certainly met the criteria used in a civil case. Undoubtedly, a preponderance of evidence has been amassed to convict pop culture of spreading dark, disillusioning and destructive ideas among youth. What we do in following up on this verdict is up to us. All issues have been laid on the table. Now, informed of the breadth and depth of our nemesis, we must begin the search for answers.

To those who criticize this undertaking for not offering solutions, no such promises were ever made. Although Americans, enamored with illusory "self–help" fads, expect quick fixes, they cannot work here. The malady is too deeply rooted in our culture and all its expressions for an instant cure. When it comes to this particular crisis, Stephen Covey's, Deepak Chopra's, or any other pop guru's five–step program to personal bliss or social harmony need not apply. Restoring the balance of things—in families, schools, peer groups, and mass media—will take a monumental long–term effort requiring the support of a wide cross–section of Americans. Sadly, these include the same millions who believe intellectual improvement can be attained through ginseng supplements or pounds can be shed overnight with the hi–fat protein diet. Collective delusion reinforced by media exposures about how to achieve personal happiness and social harmony holds sway. Once recognized as a project of this size and duration—reclaiming our youth and in effect prompting a cultural renaissance—the public at large loses interest.

Is there, however, at least a platform where we can meet and start planning a strategy for eradicating the dangers endemic in contemporary culture, many have asked me after my speaking engagements before them. After years of speeches, discussions with people and a great deal of reflection, I believe there are several areas where we should direct our energies in addressing this crisis.

Parents and the Home

The first efforts must start in the home. When parents resume responsibility for raising their own children as they once did instead of leaving this crucial task to community agencies; schools, day care centers, after–school programs, etc., a crucial first step in countering early external influences will have been taken. In far too many families, mother and father are parents *in absentia*. Kids and teens absorb their values and views from strangers and even worse, the media programs they spend so many hours immersed in. Too often, parents are unavailable to counterbalance these exposures. Quality interaction time between parents and children must be seen as imperative to the latter's well–being and made part of the family's daily regimen. Similarly, structure and constructive discipline along with love need to be included in parental repertoire again. Its absence has actually contributed to the disrespect, disaffection, and disorders exhibited by many adolescents.

Civic Leadership

Congress, the Federal Trade Commission, even the President of the United States are on record speaking out against the poor state of popular culture and specifically, the wretched quality of media programming. Yet all act impotent to change anything. Legislation restricting certain types of entertainment might be unsuccessful—courts continue to liberally interpret "free speech" and probably would again if the entertainment industry challenged laws aimed at regulating content. However, political candidates could certainly promote cleaning up the airwaves/cyberspace central to their platform and in the process put entertainment heads on notice. In time, a critical mass of elected officials could explore political means—bills, federal–agency sanctions, executive orders, to ratchet up pressure. Even if unsuccessful, they would send a message to network/studio chieftains that the public mood is changing. In turn, they could rally public awareness sufficiently to prompt constituent boycotts of industries that persist in churning out violent, sexual, and otherwise anti–social trash marketed to children. Even if legislative avenues to monitor content proved fruitless, more people might be enlightened enough from the effort to voluntarily say no to unsuitable media offering. A vacuum presently exists, and strong leadership dedicated to pursuing this goal could, over time, signal a tuning point in the battle against pop culture.

Education

Primary and secondary education needs to undergo a major paradigm shift in its intents and purposes. Priorities must be refocused on academics, less on peripheral social services. Public schools need to stop relying on technology, i.e., "computers in every classroom", to teach students and get back to basic person–to–person interaction. They also need to insist on vigorous teacher–training programs for new teachers and continuing education for older professionals in the fundamentals (and worry less about today's politically–correct subjects). Thoroughly discussed already, educators must prioritize math and reading proficiency in the curriculum over techno–skill in executing class assignments on the Internet. Financially, the entire public educational infrastructure of the United States should be overhauled, from kindergarten through high school. Effective teaching and lasting learning cannot occur in mentally and physically unsafe spaces. The costs will be enormous, but can we truly think of anything more essential to our country's future than an investment in education?

Limiting Media Exposure

Fabrications, distortions, contradictions and misrepresentation—these cover much of what youth encounter in media interactions. Cynicism, irony, anxiety, and delusions—these can be counted among the seeds sown. Emotional alienation, desensitization, anti–social impulses, and mental/behavioral disorders—these are frequently among the results of the barrage. Why do adults sit idly by and permit it? Simply exercise the choice as a mother, father, teacher, or even older sibling to tune these media out or turn them off. Lead by example. Model alternatives. The availability and accessing of electronic media in adolescent lives needs to sharply reduced or even eliminated from their daily experience. Both practical and theoretical means to curtail the corrosive influences mass media exist. They should be investigated and introduced into at least the places where adults exert control over the environments youth inhabit.

Heightened Reflectiveness Among Youth

Younger Americans must help themselves in resisting the siren song of popular culture. Adults, through teaching and modeling such behaviors, must show them that self–improvement pursuits are far more enjoyable and rewarding than vegetating in front of a television or computer screen. Music lessons, partaking in school or recreational sports leagues, working a part–time job, volunteering at a community service, even reading at the library or home—all of these offer excellent options. In turn, self–esteem among teens will rise and feelings of alienation that accompany 'digital wasting' should decline. Of course, the impulse to defer to the distractions of multiple media too kill boredom in teens will never be reversed until parents introduce them to such alternatives, join with them in these activities, and offer positive, ongoing reinforcement.

These provide a short list of target areas for intervention. This roster is neither detailed or all–inclusive. As we delve deeper into these recommendations, there remains much to be pursued in their implications. Nor do they shrink from taking on those forces menacing American youth, which has always been a problem. Few want to challenge the cultural establishment for fear of being branded as an enemy of these omnipotent powers–that–be. Undeterred, this brief list also provides a framework for my next installment in this narrative series. Knowing where we have come from and are up against, this author has a pretty good idea of how to proceed in mapping out a plan to overcome this potent nemesis.

Of the things we can be sure that will never happen, several stand out. First, the 'culture industries' will not voluntary clean–up their own act. For years, the loudest protests from various parents and educational groups earned little response apart from contemptuous silence. Displaying incredible naivete are political leaders such as the Federal Trade Commission Chair Robert Pitofsky who in a summary statement to a September 13, 2000 report on violence in the media being marketed to children brandished the idea of sanctions and then swiftly retreated. Instead, he called for these entertainment industries to engage in "self–regulatory initiatives". Citing artistic freedom of expression and its protection under that pesky First Amendment, weeding out unfit content is a policing job better left in the hands of those creating the programs. Secondly, we can discount the arguments of those who assert that our problems are based in a troubling but temporary cultural phase. History shows that most civilizations exhibiting the advanced pathologies we are seeing in adults, much less youth as in our case, rarely turn out to be self–healing. While it is true that at times in the past America has experienced mass cultural neuroses, e.g., McCarythyism and its long shadows, never has the delusion been so wide or so ingrained in younger members of society. If youth today never lived a normal life, how can they know what abnormality is? Extending this, if unaware of the condition that affects them, can we really expect that as they grow into adulthood a panacea will arise from them?

However outnumbered, those remain who will, regardless of the odds, try to champion this critical fight. I, for one, am dedicated to this cause and believe there are others who would join me in a small but determined resistance. Otherwise, a quarter or half a century from now, history will judge whether we responded wisely or indifferently. That is, of course, if Americans in the future are even interested to know that for a few moments at the start of the new millennium their ancestors had a chance to rescue a foundering culture and generations of youth in its grip but instead elected to do nothing. There were simply too many distractions to worry about it and not enough time or energy left for us to make the effort.

REFERENCES

Print:

Adorno, T.	(1972) *Dialectic of Enlightenment.* New York. The Seabury Press.
Anderson, C. Dill, K	(2000) Video Games and Aggressive Thoughts, Feelings, and Behavior in the Laboratory and in Life. *The Journal of Personality and Social Pathology.* American Psychological Association. April 2000. V.78. n.4. 772–790.
Aronowitz, S. Giroux, H.	(1991) Postmodern Education: Culture, Politics and *Criticism.* Minneapolis: University of Minnesota Press.
Awkward, M	(1995) *Negotiating Difference: Race, Gender, and the Politics Of Positionality.* Chicago: The University of Chicago Press.
Banks, I.	(1998) Reliance on Technology Threatens the Essence of Teaching. *The Chronicle of Higher Education.* October 18th. v. xlv, n. 8.
Bannet, E.	(1993) *Postcultural Theory: Cultural Theory After the Marxist Paradigm.* New York: Paragon.
Barber, B.	(1992) *An Aristocracy of Everyone: The Politics of Education And the Future of America.* New York: Oxford University Press.
Bargh, J.	(1997) *The Automaticity of Everyday Life.* New York: Erlbaum.
	(1999) The Most Powerful Manipulation Messages Are Hiding in Plain Sight. *The Chronicle of Higher Edcuation.* January 29. B6.
Baudrillard, J.	(1994) *Simulacra and Simulation.* Ann Arbor: The University Of Michigan Press.
Bennett, W.	(1998) *The Death of Outrage: Bill Clinton and the Assault on American Ideals.* New York: Free Press.
Berry, C.	(2000) It's Time We Rejected the Racial Litmus Test. *Newsweek.* February 7th. 13.
Bothun, G.	(1999) Cyberprof: The University in the Next Millenium. *Educom Review.* September/October. 16–17.
Brink, S.	(1998) Doing Ritalin right. *US News & World Report.* November 23. 76–81.

Brott, A.   (1999) *Throwaway Dads: The Myths and Barriers That Keep Men from Becoming Fathers*. Boston: Houghton Miflin.

Cagnetti. L.   (2000) Harry Potter vs. Reality. editorial. *The Cincinnati Enquirer*. January 21st. A20.

Clinton, H.R.   (1996) *It Takes a Village*. New York: Simon & Schuster.

Cook. D.   (1996) *The Culture Industry Revisited: Theodore W. Adorno On Mass Culture*. Lanham (MD): Rowman & Littlefield.

Damon, W.   (1998) The Path to a Civil Society Goes Through the University. *The Chronicle of Higher Education*. October 18. V. xlv, n. 8. B4–5.

Daugherty, P.   (1999) Today's temptations make parents fear kid's secrets. *Cincinnati Enquirer*. June 27, F3.

Decker, S.   (1999) Summer Job 101: Save, don't spend. *USA Today*. June 25. 3B.

DeRoss, A.   (1999) Credit card games getting very pricey. *The UC News Record*. February 10. 4.

Dewey, J.   (1916) *Democracy and Education*. New York: Macmillan.

Dickinson, A.   (1999) Where Were the Parents? *Time*. May 3. 40.

DiFillipo, D.   (1999) Teacher union head runs for Ohio post. *The Cincinnati Enquirer*. December 3. D6.

Doherty, T.   (1999) Hollywood's Gross–Out Comedies: Cultural Crisis or Festive Freedom. *The Chronicle of Higher Education*. October 22. B9–10.

Douglas, L.   (1999) If It Pleases the Class…*The Chronicle of Higher Education*. June
George, A.   4th. A60.

Duin, J.   (1999) Youth Fiction takes a Stark, Eerie Turn: Literature for teens is full of images of rape, demons, torture and more. *The Washington Times*. December 17.

Easterbrook,   (1999) USA Weekend's Third Annual 'America's Poll." *USA Weekend*.
G.   July 4. 6–8.

Editors   (1999) Strange Assignments. *The Middletown Journal*. October 16. A8.

Etzioni, A.   (1983) *An Immodest Agenda: Rebuilding America Before the Twenty–First Century*. New York: McGraw HIll

Evans. H.   (1999) *The American Century*. New York: Alfred Knopf.

Ferguson, A.   (1999) Inside the Crazy Culture of Kids Sports. *Time*. July12. 52–60.

Fidler, R.   (1997) *Mediamorphosis: Understanding New Media*. Thousand Oaks (CA): Sage Publications.

Fisher, B.   (2000) In the News. *UC Currents*. University of Cincinnati faculty newspaper. January 7th. 7.

Fromm, E.	(1955) *The Sane Society*. New York: Holt, Rinehart and Winston.
Gandolfo, A.	(1998) Brave New World? The Challenge of Technology to Time–Honored Pedagogies and Traditional Structures. In Gillespie, K.'s (editor) *The Impact of Technology on Faculty Development, Life, and Work*. New Directions for Teaching And Learning. San Francisco: Jossey–Bass. Number 76. Winter. 23–38.
Gergen, K.	(1991) *The Saturated Self: Dilemmas of Identity in Contemporary Life*. New York: Basic Books.
Gibbs, N. Roche, T.	(1999) The Columbine Tapes. *Time*. 40–57.
Giroux, H.	(1999) *The Mouse That Roared*. Lanham (MD): Rowman & Littlefield Publishing.
Goldstein, J.	(1998) *Why We Watch: The Attractions of Violent Entertainment*. Editor. Oxford (UK): Oxford University Press.
Greenfeld, K.	(1999) A Media Giant. *Time*. September 20. 48–54.
Haber, H.F.	(1994) *Beyond Postmodern Politics*. New York: Routledge.
Hampel, R.	(1998) A generation in crisis? *Daedalus*. Fall. V. 127. N.4. 67.
Harmon, A.	(1999) Web is lonely, researcher's find. *The New York Times*. re–printed in *The Cincinnati Enquirer*. August 30th. A1.
Holmes, A.	(2000) From material to maternal girls. *USA Today*. Friday, March 31. 17A.
Hughes, M.	(2000) Entering the 'Felicity' Zone. *The Cincinnati Enquirer TV Week*. January 23rd. 3.
Hundt. R.	(1999) The Telecom Act, the Internet, and Higher Education. *Educom Review*. November/December issue. 15–18, 48–51.
Hutchins, R.	(1969) *The Learning Society*. New York: Praeger.
Jacobs, J.	(1998) Murderers claim they are also victims. College Press Service feature appearing in *The UC News Record*.(University) of Cincinnati student newspaper. October 28th. 2.
Jones, S.	(1999) Hip–Hop takes the high road. *USA Today*. June 25, 1999. 1E–6E.
Kagan, D. Ozment, S. Turner, F.	(1983) *The Western Heritage*. Second edition. New York: MacMillan Publishing Company.

Keller, J.   (2000) Study finds Internet overuse leads to isolation. from Tribune
                   Media Services and printed with permission in *The UC News Record,*
                   University of Cincinnati student newspaper. February 21. 2.

Kellner, D.   (1989) *Jean Baudrillard: From Marxism to Postmodernism And Beyond.*
                   Stanford (CA): Stanford University Press.

Kenworthy, T.   (1999) Kids ask for parent's time, values. *Washington Post.* re–printed in
                   the *Cincinnati Enquirer.* June 20. A2.

Kiesewetter, J.   (1999) Vids teach kids to kill, weapons expert says. *The Cincinnati
                   Enquirer.* September 14. D1, 8.

                   (2000) Children's programming activist sees light at the end of the tube.
                   The Cincinnati Enquirer. January 13[th.] E1, E7.

Kleiner, C.   (1999) When 'ready to rock' becomes ready to riot. *US News & World
                   Report.* September 6. 59.

Larimer. B.   (1999) Latino America. *Newsweek.* July 12. 48–58.

Lasch, C.   (1984) *The Minimal Self.* New York: Norton.

Leo, J.   (1998) Dumbing down teachers. *US News & World Report.* August 3rd.
                   15.

Levin, G.   (2000) Splitsville for Fox, reality programming. *USA TODAY.* February
                   23. 1D.

Levine, A.   (1998) Collegiate life: An obituary. *Change.* May/June.
Cureton, J   v. 30. Issue 3. 12–17.

Lewis, C.   (1998) Rock–n–roll and Horror Stories: Students, teachers And Popular
                   Culture. *Journal of Adolescent and Adult Literacy.* V. 42. Issue 42. 116–
                   120.

Lokeman, R.C.   (2000) Hollywood's hero: a pedophile. re–printed in *The Cincinnati
                   Enquirer.* April 7th. A12.

Mansfield, S.   (2000) Sarah's Sexy Success. *USA Weekend.* May 26–28th. 9–10.

Manzl, H.   (1990) Feeding on fast food and false values. *The Education Digest.*
                   Condensed from Spring 1989 issue of *Education Forum.* January. v. 55.
                   40–42.

Marquez, C.   (1999) The Columbine Massacre. *Xavier University Magazine.* Winter
                   2000. 17.

Mathis, D.   (1999) Schools Fail at Stopping Violence. *The Cincinnati Enquirer.*
                   December 7. A3.

McCafferty, D.   (1999) He created the Web. Now he's fixing it. Visionary Tim Berners–Lee is making the Web smarter, easier. *USA Weekend*. October 29–31. 4.

McCauley, C.   (1998) When Screen Violence is not Attractive. In Goldstein, J.'s (editor) *Why We Watch: The Attractions of Violent Entertainment*. Oxford (UK): Oxford University Press. 144–162.

McKay, J.   (1987) *A History Of Western Society*. Third edition.
Hill, B.   Boston: Houghton Mifflin Company. Buckler, J.

Medved. M   (1992) *Hollywood vs. America: Popular Culture and the War on Traditional Values*. New York. HarperCollins

Moradi, S.R.   (1997) The Father–Child Connection: A Struggle of Contemporary Man. *Psychiatric Times*. January. v. XIV. Issue 1.

Neal, E.   (1998) Using Technology in Teaching: We Need to Exercise a Healthy Skepticism. *The Chronicle of Higher Education*. June19[th]. V. xlvi. N. 41. B4–B5.

O' Neill, M.J.   (1993) *The Roar of the Crowd: How Television and People Power Are Changing the World*. New York: Times Books.

Oblinger, D.   (1999) Hype, Hyperarchy and Higher Education. *Business Officer*. National Association of College and University Business Officers (NACUBO) publication. October issue. 22–31.

Oldham, P.   (1999) Contending with Distraction. *Education Week*. March 3. v. 18, n. 25. 48.

Pavlik, J.   (1996) *New Media and the Information Superhighway*. Needham Heights (MA): Allyn and Bacon.

Perry, J.   (1999) In Cleveland, it's a back–to–school daze. *US News & World*
McGraw, D   *Report*. September 6th. 34.

Pollack, W.   (1998) *Real Boys: Rescuing our Sons from the Myths of Boyhood*. New York: Random House.

Poster, M.   (1988) Editor. *Jean Baudrillard: Selected Writings*. Stanford (CA): Stanford University Press.

Postman, J.   (1985) *Amusing Ourselves to Death: Public Discourse in the Age Of Show Business*. New York: Penguin Books.

Quinnan, T.   (1999) Preparing for the Moment When a Student's Rage Turns To Violence. *The Chronicle of Higher Education*. August 13th. v. xlv, n. 49. B7.

(1997) *Adult Students "At Risk"*. Westport (CT): Bergin & Garvey.

	(1995) Students run risk with credit card debt. *The Cincinnati Post.* November 20th. 8.
Roach, M.	(2000) Being Bruce Willis. *USA Weekend.* February 11–13. 6–7.
Rosemond, J.	(2000) A generation ago, ADD cured itself. *The Cincinnati Enquirer.* March 3rd. D3.
Salvato, A.	(1995) UC Retreat will reinforce need for class instruction. *The Cincinnati Post.* October 31. 7A.
Schneerson, M.M	(1995) *Toward a Meaningful Life: The Wisdom of Rebbe.* New York: Morrow, Avon.
Skow, J.	(1999) Lost In Cyberspace. *Time.* April 26. 61–62.
Steinberg, J.	(1999) Discord Undermines Efforts to Fix Schools in New York. *The New York Times.* July 27. A1–21.
Sewell, T.	(1999) Souljah addresses student's needs. *The News Record.* University of Cincinnati student newspaper. Monday, November 15. 1–3.
Swerdlow, J. Zwingle, E.	(1999) Global Culture. *National Geographic.* V. 196, n. 2. August. 2–33.
Thomas, E. Wingert. P.	(2000) Bitter Lessons. *Newsweek.* June 19, 2000. 50–52.
Trout, P.	(1998) Incivility in the Classroom Breeds 'Education Lite'. *The Chronicle of Higher Education.* July 24th. V. xliv. N. 46. A40.
Williams, W.	(1999) Student 'rights' gone wrong. Syndicated column appearing in *The Cincinnati Enquirer.* May 2nd. D2.
Yancey, K.B.	(2000) Students springing for upscale vacations. *USA Today* feature reprinted in *The Cincinnati Enquirer.* March 12. 16.
Zillman, D.	(1998) "The Psychology of the Appeal of Portrayals of Violence". in Goldstein, J.'s (editor) *Why We Watch: The Attractions of Violent Entertainment.* Oxford: Oxford University Press. 179–211.

Electronic:

Belec, P.	(1999) Will Roaring 2000's Jazz Up Dow to 41,000? *Yahoo! News.* Saturday, October 9.
Blum, R.	(1999) Lost Children or Lost Parents of Rockdale County. *The Lost Children of Rockdale County.* Commentary. FrontLine Series. Public Broadcasting System. (**www.pbs.org**) 1–3.
Burgheimer, J.	(1995) Surfing with a Keyboard. *SF Teen Cyberzine.* www.well.com/user/citylink/sfteen.htm.
Fry Multimedia	(1999) "360 Degrees" Web Site. **www.frymulti.com/~bfenton/**.

Gillam, C. (2000) Kansas 'Slavemaster' Linked to Five Slain Women *Yahoo! News.* June 6th. 1–2.

Goldberg, C. (1999) Fear and Violence Have Declined Among Teen–Agers, *The New*
Connelly, M. *York Times on the Web.* October 20. 1–5.

Gorman, S. (2000) 'Survivor' Sets Summer TV Ratings Record. *Yahoo! News.* August 24. 1–3.

Holtz, Randy (1999) Shootings Fuel Debate over 'Jock Elitism' at Columbine. *The Denver Rocky Mountain News.* On–line. April 28. 1–3.

KSF (1999) New Study Finds Kids Spend Equivalent of Full Week Using Media. Kaiser Family Foundation. November 17th. **www.kff.org**

Lowe, P. (2000) Poll shows attitudes largely unchanged. *The Denver Rocky Mountain News.* On–line. April 19. 1–2.

Manson, M. (1999) Columbine: Whose Fault is It? *Rolling Stone Magazine Online.* May 28th. **www.rollingstone.com**

Mariott, M. (1999) Blood, Gore, Sex and Now: Race; Are Game Makers Creating Convincing New Characters or 'High–Tech' Blackface? *The New York Times on the Web.* October 21, 1999.

Martinez, A (1999) News Flash: Teen Morality Lives!!!. *LA Youth Notebook.* published by The Los Angeles Times. March/April Issue. 1–2.

McCaffrey, S. (2000) Report: Market boom fueling income gap. *Chicago Tribune Internet Edition.* January 18th.

McCollum, K. (1999) Bill Gates Looks Ahead to the Era of 'Generation I'. *The Chronicle of Higher Education.* Daily news on–line. October 29. 1–2.

MDR (1999) Market Data Retrieval's 1998–1999 Technology Survey Results. **www.schooldata.com**

Mendels, P. (1999) Internet Access Spread to More Classrooms, Survey Finds. *The New York Times on the Web.* December 1st. 1–4.

Miller, S. (2000) AOL to buy Time Warner: Deal worth $184 billion creates media
Friedman, J. behemoth. CBS Marketwatch.com. *Netscape NetCenter.* January 10. 1–4.

NCKOC (1995) National Survey of PreTeens. The National Center for Kids Overcoming Crisis. **www.kidspeace.org**.

NCTV (1999) NCTV–News: Bits and Briefs. National Coalition on Television Violence. **www.nctv.org**.

NY Times	(1999) New York Times/CBS News Poll of Teenager (Complete Results). *The New York Times on the Web.* October 14th. **www.nytimes.com**
PBS	(1998) Affluenza. *PBS online.* Based on broadcast originally televised July 2, 1998. **www.pbs.org**.
	(1999) *Life on the Internet.* Public Broadcasting System Homepage. **www.pbs.org**.
	(1999) The Lost Children of Rockdale County. Based on Public Broadcasting System's *Frontline* Series. October 20th. **www.pbs.org**
Pew R.C.	(1999) Technology Triumphs, Morality Falters. Center for the People and the Press. Pew Research Center. July 3rd. **www.people-press.org**
Satran, D.	(1999) From a Bang to a Whimper–the High–Tech 90's. *Yahoo! News.* November 24.
Speigelman, A.	(2000) Charles Schulz Dies on the Eve of Final 'Peanuts' Strip. *Yahoo! News.* February 14, 2000. 1–3.
Steinberg, J.	(2000) Salary Gap Still Plaguing Teachers. *The New York Times on the Web.* January 13. **www.nytimes.com**
Stern. C.	(2000) Hollywood Rallies Against Clinton Code Plan. *Yahoo! News.* January 30. 1–2.
Sterngold, J	(1999) Los Angeles May Ease up on School Promotion Policy. *New York Times on the Web.* December 2.
TVFA	(1998) Television Statistics and Sources. *TV Free America.* **www.tvfa.org/stats.html**.
USDE	(1999) Educational Excellence for All Children Act of 1999. United States Department of Education. **www.ed.gov**.
	(1999) Highlight from the Baby Boom Echo: No End in Sight. U.S. Department of Education. August 19th. **www.ed.gov**.
Tribune News Svcs.	(2000) College Survey Finds Freshmen Feeling Unprecedented Stress. *Chicago Tribune Internet Edition.* January 24. 1.
Vicini, J.	(1999) U.S. Supreme Court Rejects School Voucher Appeal. *Yahoo News.* December 13.
Whitcomb, Dan	(1999) Massacre Investigators Says Colo. Teens Wanted to Kill 500. *Yahoo News.* April 26.
Zabarenko, D	(1999) World Population Will Top 6 Billion on Oct 12–UN. *Yahoo! News.* September 22.
uncredited	(1999) Internet Business is Growing Wildly. *Yahoo! News.* October 27.

uncredited   (1999) Jobless Rate Dips to Nearly 30–Year Low. *Yahoo! News*. November 5.

uncredited   (1999) U.S. Couples Scale Back Work to Care for Families. *Yahoo! News*. December 3. 1–2.

0-595-21770-2

www.ingramcontent.com/pod-product-compliance
Lightning Source LLC
Chambersburg PA
CBHW061341280526
45784CB00001B/91